George William Cox

The Athenian Empire

George William Cox

The Athenian Empire

ISBN/EAN: 9783743306691

Manufactured in Europe, USA, Canada, Australia, Japa

Cover: Foto ©ninafisch / pixelio.de

Manufactured and distributed by brebook publishing software (www.brebook.com)

George William Cox

The Athenian Empire

CONTENTS.

CHAPTER I.

THE CONFEDERACY OF DELOS AND THE FOUNDATION OF THE ATHENIAN EMPIRE.

		PAGE
	Political education of the Athenian people	1
	The reforms of Kleisthenes	2
	Character of Athenian citizenship	3
	Relations of the Athenians to the Asiatic Greeks	4
	Constitution of the Delian confederacy	4
	Burdens and restraints imposed on the allies of Athens	6
	Growth of democratic feeling in the confederacy	6
	Athens and Sparta two distinct political centres	7
	State of Athens after the Persian invasion	8
479	Rebuilding of the walls of Athens	10
	Fortification of the Peiraieus	11
	Treason of the Spartan Pausanias	11
478	Recall of Pausanias to Sparta	13
477	Death of Pausanias	14
	Bearing of the case of Pausanias on that of Themistokles	14
	Oligarchic opposition to Themistokles	16
471	Ostracism of Themistokles	17
	Sequel of the traditional history of Themistokles	17
	Extent of Persian power on the coasts of Asia Minor	18
477	The assessment of Aristeides	18
	Relations of Themistokles with the Persian king	19

B.C.	
	Fixity of purpose in Themistokles
	Contrast between Pausanias and Themistokles
	Charges of personal corruption brought against Themistokles
	Disputed credibility of the narrative
	Growth of Athenian ambition
	Change in the attitude of Athens towards her allies
466	The double victory of the Eurymedon, and the revolt of Thasos
464	Revolt of the Helots. Alliance between Athens and Argos
	Alliance of Megara with Athens
	Siege of Aigina
	Building of the Long Walls of Athens
455	Culmination of the Athenian empire
452	Fall of Aigina
	Settlement of the Helots and Messenians at Naupaktos
450	Siege of Kition by Kimon
	The Peace of Kallias
	Fall of the land empire of the Athenians
447	Battle of Koroneia
446	Revolt of Euboia and Megara
445	The Thirty Years' Truce

CHAPTER II.

THE BEGINNINGS OF THE STRUGGLE BETWEEN ATHENS AND SPARTA.

	Final developement of the Athenian constitution
	Policy of Perikles
	Reforms of Ephialtes
456	Murder of Ephialtes
	Pan-Hellenic theories of Perikles
	Ostracism of Thoukydides, son of Melesias
	Extension of Athenian settlements
440	The revolt of Samos
	Quarrel between Corinth and Korkyra

B.C.		PAGE
436	Entry of the Corinthians into Epidamnos	41
433	Embassy from Korkyra to Athens, seeking an alliance	41
	Counter-arguments of the Corinthian envoys	42
432	Defensive alliance of Athens with Korkyra	43
	Defeat of the Korkyraians by the Corinthians	43
	Revolt of Potidaia from Athens	44
	Meeting of the Spartan allies	44
	Secret debate of the Spartans	46
	Resolution for war	47
431	Efforts of the Spartans to bring about the expulsion of Perikles	47
	Final demands of the Spartans	48
	Prosecutions of Anaxagoras, Pheidias, and Aspasia	48
	Real position of the Athenians in reference to the cause of the war	49

CHAPTER III.

THE PELOPONNESIAN WAR FROM THE SURPRISE OF PLATAIA TO THE CAPTURE OF SPHAKTERIA.

431	Surprise of Plataia by the Thebans	50
	Treacherous dealing of the Plataians with the Theban prisoners	51
	The families of the Plataians taken to Athens	51
	General excitement of the time	52
	Invasion of Attica by the Spartans	52
	The expulsion of the Aiginetans	53
	Athenian reserve fund	53
	Public funeral at Athens	54
	Funeral oration of Perikles	54
430	The plague at Athens	55
	Ravages of the plague among the Athenians before Potidaia	57
	Irritation of the Athenians against Perikles	57
	Close of the public life of Perikles	58
429	Spartan attack on Plataia	59
	Siege of Plataia	60
	Victory of Phormion in the Corinthian gulf	61

B.C.		PAGE
	Battle of Naupaktos. Second victory of Phormion	62
	Proposed night attack on Peiraicus	63
	Expedition of Sitalkes against Perdikkas	64
428	The revolt of Lesbos	64
	Audience of the Lesbian envoys at Olympia	65
	Investment of Mytilene by Paches	65
427	Surrender of Mytilene	66
	Indignation at Athens against the Mytilenaians	67
	Influence of Kleon	67
	Speech of Diodotos condemning the proposal of Kleon to massacre the Mytilenaians	68
	Withdrawal of the decree for the massacre	69
	Escape of half the citizens besieged in Plataia	70
	The destruction of Plataia	70
	Capture of Minoa by Nikias	72
426	Failure of Demosthenes in Aitolia	73
	Successes of Demosthenes against the Ambrakiots	73
425	Occupation of Pylos by Demosthenes	74
	Failure of Brasidas to dislodge the Athenians	77
	The Spartan hoplites shut up in Sphakteria	78
	Spartan embassy to Athens for peace	79
	Demands of Kleon	79
	The dismissal of the envoys brought about by Kleon	80
	Resumption of the war: difficulties of the Athenians	81
	Engagement of Kleon to effect the capture of the Spartans in Sphakteria	82
	Capture of the hoplites by Demosthenes and Kleon	83

CHAPTER IV.

THE PELOPONNESIAN WAR, FROM THE SURRENDER OF THE SPARTANS IN SPHAKTERIA TO THE MASSACRE OF MELOS.

	Change of public feeling at Athens	84
424	Athenian occupation of Kythera	84
	Alleged massacre of Helots by the Spartans	85
	Designs of Brasidas	86

B.C.		PAGE
	Failure of the plans for surrendering Megara to the Athenians	86
	Schemes of the Athenians for the recovery of their supremacy in Boiotia	87
	Battle of Delion	88
	Storming of the fort at Delion	88
	March of Brasidas through Thessaly	89
	Appearance of Brasidas at Akanthos	90
	Occupation of Amphipolis by Brasidas	91
	Lightness of the imperial yoke of Athens	92
	Punishment of Thucydides	93
423	Truce for one year between Sparta and Athens	94
	Revolt of Skiônê	95
	Recovery of Mendê by the Athenians	96
	Alliance of Perdikkas with the Athenians	97
422	Expedition of Kleon to Makedonia	97
	Battle of Amphipolis. Death of Brasidas and of Kleon	98
	Merits of the policy of Kleon	100
421	The Peace of Nikias	101
	Failure of the Spartans to carry out the terms for the peace	102
	Surrender of the Spartan hoplites taken at Sphakteria	102
420	Formation of a new Argive confederacy	103
	Beginning of the public life of Alkibiades	104
	Deception of the Spartan envoys by Alkibiades	105
	Defensive alliance between Athens, Argos, Elis, and Mantineia	106
419	Interference of Alkibiades in Peloponnesos	106
418	Spartan and Corinthian invasion of Argos	107
	Battle of Mantineia	108
	The establishment of oligarchy at Argos by the Spartans	109
417	Restoration of democracy at Argos	110
	Unsuccessful attempt of the Athenians to recover Amphipolis	110
416	Massacre of Melos	110

CHAPTER V.

THE PELOPONNESIAN WAR. THE SICILIAN EXPEDITION.

B.C.		PAGE
427–4	Earliest interference of the Athenians in Sicily	112
424	Congress at Gela	114
416	Quarrel between Selinous and Egesta	114
415	Embassy to Athens from Egesta	115
	Embassy from Athens to Egesta	115
	Resolution of the Athenians to send a fleet to Sicily	116
	Opposition of Nikias	116
	Reply of Alkibiades	117
	The wishes of Nikias defeated by his own representations of the amount of force needed for the expedition	118
	The mutilation of the Hermai by a band of secret conspirators	120
	Innocence of Alkibiades	120
	Alkibiades charged with profanation	121
	Departure of the fleet for Sicily	122
	Incredulity of the Syracusans	122
	Discouragement of the Athenians on approaching Sicily	123
	Plan of Nikias	123
	Plan of Alkibiades	124
	Plan of Lamachos	124
	Occupation of Katanê by the Athenians	124
	Recall and flight of Alkibiades	125
	Landing of the Athenian army on the shores of the Great Harbour of Syracuse	126
	Presence of Athenian and Syracusan envoys at Kamarina	127
	Inactivity of Nikias	128
	Treason of Alkibiades at Sparta	128
414	Mission of Gylippos to Sicily	129
	Successes of the Athenians before Syracuse	130
	First counter-work of the Syracusans	132
	Death of Lamachos in the attack on the second counter-work of the Syracusans	132

		PAGE
	Entry of the Athenian fleet into the Great Harbour	134
	Further advantages gained by the Athenians	134
	Entry of the Spartan Gylippos into Syracuse	135
	Third Syracusan counter-work	136
	Letter of Nikias to the Athenians	138
113	Occupation of Dekeleia by the Spartans	139
	Naval victory of the Athenians in the harbour of Syracuse, accompanied by the loss of Plemmyrion	140
	Defeat of the Athenian fleet in the Great Harbour	141
	Arrival of Demosthenes with reinforcements from Athens	142
	Night-attack by Demosthenes on the third Syracusan counter-work	142
	Defeat of the Athenians	143
	Resolution of Demosthenes to return to Athens	144
	Opposition of Nikias	144
	Eclipse of the moon	145
	Second defeat of the Athenian fleet in the Great Harbour	145
	Change in the popular feeling at Syracuse	146
	Closing of the mouth of the Great Harbour	147
	Mistake of Demosthenes	147
	Speech of Nikias	148
	Ruin of the Athenian fleet	148
	Stratagem of Hermokrates to delay the retreat of the Athenians	150
	Departure of the Athenians from their camp	150
	Efforts of Nikias to sustain the courage of the Athenians	151
	Surrender of Demosthenes	152
	Surrender of Nikias	152
	Confinement of the prisoners in the stone-quarries of Epipolai	154
	Death of Nikias and Demosthenes	154
	Influence of the catastrophe on the subsequent history of Athens	154

CHAPTER VI.

THE PELOPONNESIAN (OR DEKELEIAN) WAR, FROM THE FAILURE OF THE SICILIAN EXPEDITION TO THE SUPPRESSION OF THE OLIGARCHY OF THE FOUR HUNDRED AT ATHENS.

B.C.		PAGE
413	Effects of the disaster in Sicily on popular feeling at Athens	156
	Effects of the disaster on the enemies and allies of Athens	157
	Persian envoys at Sparta	157
412	Mission of Aristokrates to Chios	158
	Revolt of Chios from Athens	158
	Employment of the Athenian reserve fund	160
	Revolt of Miletos	160
	First treaty of the Spartans with the Persians	160
	Revolution at Samos in favour of Athens	161
	Abortive revolt of the Lesbians	162
	Ravaging of Chios	162
	State of parties in Chios	164
	Arrival of a Syracusan fleet under Hermokrates	164
	Second treaty between Sparta and Persia	165
	Revolt of Rhodes from Athens	166
	Order from Sparta for the assassination of Alkibiades	167
	Counsels of Alkibiades to Tissaphernes	168
	Overtures of Alkibiades to the oligarchs in the army at Samos	168
	Protest of Phrynichos	169
	Counter-plots of Phrynichos and Alkibiades	171
	Progress of the revolution at Athens	172
	Action of the oligarchic clubs at Athens	173
	The rhetor Antiphon	173
	Rupture between the oligarchs and Alkibiades	174
	Third treaty of Tissaphernes with the Spartans	175
411	Revolt of Abydos and Lampsakos from Athens	175
	Revolt of Thasos	176

Contents.

B.C.		PAGE
	Political assassinations at Athens	172
	Reign of Terror	172
	Usurpation of the Four Hundred	178
	Unsuccessful attack on Athens by Agis	179
	Suppression of the oligarchic movement at Samos	179
	Resolution of the citizens at Samos to treat Athens as a revolted city	180
	Election of Alkibiades as general by the army in Samos	181
	Dismissal of the envoys of the Four Hundred from Samos	183
	Fortification of Eetionia by the Four Hundred	183
	Assassination of Phrynichos	184
	Demolition of the fort on Eetionia	185
	Revolt and loss of Euboia	185
	Suppression of the Four Hundred at Athens	186
	Restoration of democracy	187
	Trial and execution of Antiphon	188
	Inactivity of the Spartan fleet at Rhodes	188
	Discontent in the Spartan camp at Miletos	189
	Intrigues of Tissaphernes and Alkibiades	189
	Voyage of Mindaros to the Hellespont	190
	Victory of the Athenians at Kynossêma	191
	Exultation at Athens	191

CHAPTER VII.

THE PELOPONNESIAN (DEKELEIAN OR IONIAN) WAR FROM THE BATTLE OF KYNOSSÊMA TO THE SURRENDER OF ATHENS.

	Declension of the Athenian character	192
	Journey of Tissaphernes to the Hellespont	194
	Victory of Alkibiades over the Spartans in the Bay of Dardanos	194
410	Victory of the Athenians at Kyzikos	194
	Effects of the victory	196
409	Recovery of Pylos and Nisaia from the Athenians	196
408	Reduction of Chalkedon and Byzantion by the Athenians	197

A. H.

B.C.		PAGE
	Arrival of Cyrus on the Egean coast	197
407	Lysandros and the oligarchical clubs	198
	Return of Alkibiades to Athens	198
	Defeat of Antiochos by Lysandros	200
	Alkibiades deprived of his command	200
406	Difficulties of Kallikratidas on succeeding Lysandros	200
	Blockading of Konon at Mytilene	201
	Battle of Argennoussai	202
	Victory of the Athenians, and death of Kallikratidas	202
	Departure of the blockading squadron from Mytilene	203
	Accusation of the Athenian generals by Theramenes and Thrasyboulos	204
	Favourable impression made on the Athenian assembly by the generals	205
	Falsehoods of Theramenes	205
	Conspiracy of Theramenes	206
	Proposition of Kallixenos	207
	Amendment of Euryptolemos	207
	Condemnation and murder of the generals	209
	Return of the Athenian fleet to Samos	209
405	Activity of Lysandros	210
	Arrival of the Athenian fleet at Aigospotamoi	210
	Snaring of the Athenian fleet by the Spartans	212
	Escape of Konon with nine ships	212
	Massacre of the Athenian prisoners by Lysandros	212
	Treachery of some among the Athenian generals	213
	Causes tending to this treachery	214
	Dismay at Athens	215
	Preparations for undergoing a siege	215
	Operations of Lysandros in the East	216
	Blockade of Peiraieus by Lysandros	216
	Fruitless efforts to obtain peace	216
	Mission of Theramenes	217
	Final terms granted by the Spartans	217
	Surrender of Athens	218
	Demolition of the Long Walls	218
	Causes leading to the fall of the Athenian empire	218
	Character of the Athenian empire	219

Contents

CHRONOLOGICAL TABLE	223
INDEX	243

_{*} The references inserted in the text with the letters G. P., belong to the volume on 'The Greeks and the Persians.'

MAPS.

	PAGE
ATHENS AND ITS NEIGHBOURHOOD	6
PLAN OF THE HARBOUR OF NAVARINO, TO ILLUSTRATE THE OPERATIONS OF DEMOSTHENES AT PYLOS	76
ATHENIAN OPERATIONS BEFORE SYRACUSE (PLATE I.)	131
,, ,, ,, (PLATE II.)	133
,, ,, ,, (PLATE III.)	137

THE ATHENIAN EMPIRE.

CHAPTER I

THE CONFEDERACY OF DELOS AND THE FOUNDATION OF THE ATHENIAN EMPIRE.

THE Persian Wars, of which the battles of Plataia and Mykalê practically decided the issue, acquire their supreme importance as a struggle in which the spirit of voluntary obedience to law triumphed over the arbitrary rule of an irresponsible despot. This triumph was won *Political education of the Athenian people.* by the inhabitants of a number of cities, for which independence meant generally little more than suspicion and jealousy of all other cities, breaking out not unfrequently into open war; but it was insured, as Herodotos emphatically asserts, chiefly, if not wholly, by the skill, wisdom, and energy of the Athenians. Circumstances had indeed long been combining to give to Athenian policy a character essentially different from the narrow and shortsighted exclusiveness which ruled absolutely elsewhere. Had it not been for the wider and more generous aims of her great general Themistokles, the enterprise of Xerxes would in the opinion of the historian have assuredly ended in success: and but for the previous political education of the Athenian people the career of Themistokles would have been an impossibility. Not a hundred years had yet passed away from the time when Athens, still a comparatively insignificant city, seemed to lie beyond hope of deliverance under the yoke of the great Eupatrid houses. Shut out from all political power, and placed by the rigid exclusiveness of caste under a ban which made their admission to such power a profanation, the main body of the people, without energy because without a purpose, submitted themselves to each faction as it gained ascendency, or to the despot who availed himself of the rivalry of those factions to compass his own ends. So great was the danger involved in this apathy that Solon denounced the neutrality of citizens in the strife of contending factions as the worst of political crimes: but although his legislation had called into existence a class of peasant land-owners, and by making wealth an indispensable condition for filling the highest offices in the state had dealt a severe blow against the old social system, still his lessons and his warnings seemed for the moment to avail nothing. But when the tyranny of Peisistratos, and perhaps even more that of his sons, had brought home to them the dire mischiefs of irresponsible rule, the people, to whom Solon had at the least given a voice in the election of magistrates and the right of passing judgement upon them at the end of their term of office, threw themselves heart and soul into the designs and plans of Kleisthenes. These plans had for their object nothing less than the complete subversion of the Eupatrid theory which regarded the enfranchisement of persons not belonging to the old religious tribes as an act of defiance against the gods rather than as a mere resistance to oppressive rulers. By suffering these tribes to exist simply as religious societies, while he created a new set

The reform of Kleisthenes.

of tribes taking in the whole free population of Attica or possibly, as it is said, some also who were not free, he introduced a new order of things which was followed immediately by a marvellous wakening of popular energy; and within fifteen years the people, which had submitted passively to the despotism of the Peisistratidai, dared to answer with a flat refusal the order of the Persian satrap Artaphernes who charged them, if they valued their safety, to admit Hippias once more into Athens. (G. P., p. 90.)

But neither the reforms of Kleisthenes nor those of Solon assailed or weakened the conviction that the city was and must be, that which the nation is for us, the ultimate unit of political society. Men on whom the Eupatrids looked down with contempt and disgust had now a share in making the laws which they obeyed; but no approach was made to the wider view which would look upon Spartans, Athenians, Thebans, and Corinthians as members of a single state with common interests and common duties. This mighty change was not to be accomplished for centuries; and, when it should come, it was to be accomplished neither by any Greek city nor by the Hellenic people collectively. Yet for nearly three generations the world was to see a maritime empire which seemed to give promise of effecting this beneficial consummation; and this empire was the direct and immediate result of the Persian Wars. The mere fact that the ruin of the Persian fleet and army brought the Athenians into new relations with the Asiatic Greeks and their former masters quickened at once their sense of duty and their promptitude in action. They were no longer dealing with matters affecting the independence of city communities; and the Spartans, far from being jealous of the influence which the Athenians must acquire, were for the time rather eager that others should undertake a responsibility which in plain terms

Character of Athenian citizenship.

they could scarcely with decency decline. With the consequences of their withdrawal they seem not to have concerned themselves; nor probably had the Athenian leaders any clear foresight of the jealousy and animosity which their maritime ascendency would speedily awaken in Western Hellas. On one point alone Themistokles insisted with unshaken persistency; and this point was the paramount need of putting out the full powers of the Athenian state to secure to itself the dominion of the sea. The results of these efforts he was content to leave to the future; but in the meanwhile the duties which the Athenian generals had to discharge were precisely those which would weaken in them the feelings of city exclusiveness and rouse them insensibly to larger aims and a more generous policy. Having declined peremptorily the Spartan proposal to transfer the Asiatic Ionians to lands west of the Egean sea, they found themselves compelled to protect their ancient colonists against Persian tax-gatherers,—in other words, to set up and to maintain an orderly government with a hostile and watchful power in the rear. They were compelled to lay down rules to be obeyed by each member of the new alliance, to assign to them severally their places and their duties, and to see that none reaped the benefit of the new state of things without performing his own part in upholding it. They had to provide, further, for the administration of justice. Wrongs would be committed not only by the people of one allied city against the inhabitants of another, but by Athenian citizens against their new allies. For all such cases the aggrieved persons must have access to tribunals whose impartiality they should have no reason for calling in question. But, more especially, they must learn for themselves and inforce on others the great lesson that

Relations of the Athenians to the Asiatic Greeks.

Constitution of the Delian confederacy.

the common interests of large numbers of men can never be promoted except by the sacrifice of that independence which, if not curbed, runs into lawlessness, and that the voluntary restraint thus imposed is a real enlargement of freedom. In short, they were putting together the machinery of a great confederacy, consisting of cities some powerful, some insignificant ; and their whole task raised them above the confined atmosphere of men intent on furthering only their own local interests. One of the first consequences of the work thus begun was a course of action which virtually set at nought the doctrine most precious to Greek statesmen generally. When once the new alliance was formed, the adhesion of the several members could no longer be a matter of choice. Whatever benefit might result from the Delian confederacy must from its very nature be shared by every Hellenic city on the western coasts of Asia Minor and more particularly by all the inhabitants of the Egean islands. No satrap must be suffered to vex the continental Greeks with his exactions ; no Persian tribute-ships must be permitted to enter the ports of the allies of Athens. These great ends could be attained only by the common efforts of all the Greeks who lay within the reach of the Persian power ; and although the adhesion of these Greeks was in the first instance voluntary, the step was practically forced upon all. In the eyes of their former masters they had sinned beyond forgiveness ; and the only refuge open to them lay in the protection of that great city without which, according to the emphatic assertion of Herodotos, the yoke of the oppressor would never have been broken.

If, then, any members of this new confederacy should retain and exercise the right of quitting it at their will, a gross injustice would be done, not only to the Athenians but to their nearer neighbours. The burdens needed to carry out the purposes of the new alliance must be borne; the money without which the work could not be done must be forthcoming; and if any repudiated, or even shirked these duties, they would continue to share all the benefits of the confederacy, while they added to the toils and anxieties of those who remained faithful. It was not merely the duty but the interest of Athens to secure these benefits as completely to the meanest as to the most important members of the confederacy; and these members must in their turn be taught that restrictions upon the independent action of individuals are indispensable in the interests of large societies, and that in the Delian alliance the position of the cities was pretty much that of the individual citizens of an autonomous town. This was a great lesson indeed; and unless some opposing force should counteract it, the inevitable result would in the end be the growth of a real Hellenic nation. Unfortunately this opposing force, at no time lacking, was soon to be brought into violent action. While the Athenians were resolved to insist at all costs on the obedience of their allies to the rules which they cheerfully obeyed themselves, it was no part of their plan to interfere with the internal arrangements of the confederate cities; nor in fact can such interference be at any time laid to their charge. But Aristeides, like the Athenian statesmen of earlier generations, had felt instinctively that the growth of maritime enterprise must foster ideas fatal to the exclusive theories of the Eupatrid nobility; and by these the 'sea-faring mob' of the Peiraieus was regarded as the seedbed of democracy. The Athenian seamen, now brought into daily contact with the citizens enrolled in the new confederation, formed a natural intimacy with those whose political faith most nearly resembled their

Burdens and restraints imposed on the allies of Athens.

Growth of democratic feeling in the confederacy.

own,—in other words, with the democratic party, or, as the oligarchs would term them, the democratic faction or rabble in each city. The speedy result was the strengthening of democratic feeling to a degree which awakened the liveliest alarm in all cities where an oligarchy still retained power ; and a new motive for secession was thus added to the more natural motives which gradually cooled the zeal of some who had been most earnest in the early days of the alliance. In these cities the oligarchs looked necessarily to Sparta, the supposed stronghold of Eupatrid intolerance ; and Spartan dulness in discerning the shadows of coming events was more than compensated by the clearsightedness of the Corinthians, who had now learnt the lesson preached to them in vain by the exiled tyrant Hippias. (G. P., p. 93.)

There was, in truth, a general gravitation in the Greek cities to two distinct centres ; the democratic citizens looking to Athens, the rest regarding themselves as the natural allies, if not the subjects, of Sparta. The fuel was thus prepared which might at any time be kindled into a fatal conflagration ; and from the first it was certain that the conflict of these opposing principles must come and would probably be not long delayed. Fifty years, it is true, passed away after the overthrow of the Persians at Plataia and Mykalê, before the antagonism between Sparta and Athens was brought to a head ; and nearly thirty years more were needed for the demolition of the great fabric of Athenian empire. But practically this whole period of nearly three generations was spent in the efforts of oligarchical statesmen to upset and destroy a system which, as they felt, must be fatal to the autonomy of each separate Hellenic city. It cannot be said that their instinct deceived them. The only question is whether the empire of Athens was, or was not,

Athens and Sparta two distinct political centres.

more to the benefit of her allies than the supremacy of Sparta, and whether t might or might not in the end have welded the city communities of Greece into a nation. There are at least indications that such a result would have been achieved but for the sleepless animosity of the Corinthians and the more stolid hatred of the Spartans.

At the outset there was little indeed to rouse the jealousy either of Sparta or of Corinth. Athens was little better than a heap of ashes. Its temples were burnt, its fields ravaged, its farm buildings taken down or demolished. A disaster affecting still more gravely the prosperity of the country was the departure of the Metoikoi, or resident foreigners, who would not be persuaded to bring back their capital and their skilled workmanship to a land which could offer them no security either of person or of property. Without their wealth it was impossible that the country could retrieve its losses, or that Athens should become supreme on the sea as Themistokles had determined that she should be. He saw therefore that nothing less than the adequate fortification of Athens could induce them to return; and he saw not less clearly that the true interests of the people would best be promoted by transferring the city from Athens to Peiraieus, leaving the Akropolis to serve as the homes of the ancient gods, whose temples should be there maintained in fitting splendour. But neither now nor yet a little later when he proposed the fortification of the Peiraieus could he venture in plain terms to propose the abandonment of the old city with all its time-honoured associations; and for the moment a serious difficulty seemed likely to hinder even the lesser enterprise of restoring the walls of Athens. Following the old type of Aryan civilisation, the city of Sparta consisted of four unwalled hamlets: and with honest stupidity or with excellent craft the Spartans now

State of Athens after the Persian invasion.

ATHENS AND ITS NEIGHBOURHOOD

began to speak of walls as rather a luxury for robbers than a necessity for honest freemen. The fortifications of Thebes had done nothing but strengthen the hands of Xerxes or Mardonios; and the Corinthian isthmus could be made to serve as a screen for the defence of the whole peninsula and therefore of all who might there seek a refuge. If such arguments were to be accepted, it was clear that the policy of all the extra-Peloponnesian cities was to be directed by the chances of a Persian invasion of the Peloponnesos itself; nor was Themistokles a man to hesitate in condemning the unwarrantable tyranny which would inforce such a notion, or in ridiculing the stupidity which seemed to believe that the conditions of war must remain for ever unchanged. But at the moment he was compelled to be wary and measured in speech; and when the Spartans requested that the Athenians, instead of rebuilding their own walls, should join with them in dismantling the walls of all other cities to the north of the isthmus, he contented himself with taking no notice of the proposal, at the same time urging the Athenians to send him as ambassador to Sparta, but not to dispatch his colleagues until the walls had reached a height which would enable them to bid defiance to attack. In obedience to his earnest pleading the work was carried on with the speed almost of magic, while Themistokles at Sparta expressed himself at a loss to understand why his colleagues failed to put in their appearance. When at length the irritation of the Spartans seemed to threaten serious consequences, Themistokles, again professing his ignorance, urged them to send envoys to Athens and satisfy themselves as to the facts; but he had taken care to insure their detention, and he had no sooner heard that they were in safe keeping, than, throwing off the mask, he told them all that had been done, insisting that Athens had a full

Rebuilding of the walls of Athens.

right to be girt about with walls, unless this right was to be denied to every city in the Peloponnesos. Anything like freedom of speech, he argued, would be impossible, if any one city stood on a vantage ground with respect to the rest; and the allies of Athens must extend to her that freedom of action which, if thwarted by Athens, they would assuredly claim for themselves.

But Themistokles felt that his work was still only half done, or rather that the most essential part of it was not even begun, so long as Athens was left without the direct protection of her navy. There was something almost absurd in claiming a maritime supremacy for a city the inhabitants of which had been compelled twice within the same year to leave their homes and seek a refuge elsewhere. The dominion of the sea would render any such disasters impossible; but if the old city could not, as he would have wished, be abandoned, the harbours on which it must depend for its future prosperity must be placed beyond reach of attack. According to his plan the harbours of Peiraieus and Mounychia (the open waters of Phaleron he regarded as unsuitable for his purpose) were to be surrounded by a wall so strong and high that even in time of war old men and children should suffice to guard it. It was raised only to half the height which he had designed for it; but even thus his end was effectually attained. *Fortification of the Peiraieus*

Everything was thus tending to place Athens amongst the foremost of Hellenic cities; and for the time everything seemed to disconcert the devices of her enemies. The Spartans were not easily stirred to active enterprise; and in their own generals they found the most effectual hindrances to any schemes of Pan-hellenic supremacy, if we are to suppose that any such schemes had been formed. At Plataia Pausanias, if we may believe the story, had expressed his amazement *Treason of the Spartan Pausanias.*

at the folly of the luxurious tyrant who cared to conquer a barren land and a hardy people (G. P., p. 196). But even while he spoke, he was, it would seem, dazzled by Persian wealth, and enamoured of Persian pleasures. In any case, the fact of his treason is as little open to question as the traditional details of its execution are worthy of credit. There is no doubt that on the fall of Byzantion he sent to the Persian king the prisoners taken in the city, spreading the report that they had escaped. He forwarded at the same time, we are told, by the hand of the Eretrian Gongylos a letter in which he informed Xerxes that he wished to marry his daughter and to make him lord of all Hellas, adding that with the king's aid he felt sure of success. The spirit of Cyrus or Dareios would have been roused to rage at the presumption of the petty chief who aspired to an alliance with the royal house of Persia on the score not of what he had done, but of what he hoped to be able to do by and by. The letter was certainly brief enough to come even from a Spartan; but it may certainly be set aside as spurious. Conspirators do not usually keep about their persons dangerous papers, when these papers are moreover quite unnecessary; and least of all would a Spartan conspirator be tempted to do so. If again we cannot suppose that Pausanias would keep copies of his own letters to the Great King, it is altogether less likely that he would preserve the letters from the king which, if discovered, must bring about his condemnation. The text of Thucydides contains, it has been said, copies of some of the letters addressed by Pausanias to Xerxes before the final missive which his Argilian slave, suspecting mischief to himself, placed in the hands of the Ephors. This letter contained the charge that the bearer should be put to death. The letters carried by the previous bearers had contained, we are told, the same injunction. How then were the contents of those letters made known? They could be recovered only from the archives of Sousa; and to the unlikelihood that such letters would be preserved at all must be added the far greater unlikelihood that they would ever be given up to the king's professed enemies. But further there is no reason to suppose that Pausanias was himself able to write; and we may well ask where he could find a scribe so trusty as to be made acquainted not merely with his treacherous schemes but with the injunction that the bearers of his letters should be put to death. In short, these letters, as we possess them, are forged; and the fact of their forgery has a most important bearing on the alleged conduct of a more illustrious man than Pausanias. But keeping ourselves for the present to the case of the Spartan general, we can scarcely help thinking that the gratitude of Xerxes was easily earned if the deliverance of a few captives from Byzantion could wipe out the memory of the carnage at Plataia. However this may have been, reports reached Sparta that Pausanias, clothed in Persian garb, was aping the privacy of Oriental despots, and that when he came forth from his palace it was to make a royal progress through Thrace, surrounded by Median and Egyptian body-guards. Recalled to Sparta, and deprived of his command, he made his way again to Byzantion, and established himself in a forti- *Recall of Pausanias to Sparta.* fied position from which he was forcibly dislodged by the Athenians. But the Spartans, hearing that the victor of Plataia was busy hatching his treasons at Kolonai, sent a messenger bidding him to obey their summons on pain of being declared the enemy of the people in case of refusal. Whatever trust he may have placed in the kindly feelings of the Ephors, he had more confidence in the power of money, while he found even a better stronghold in Spartan law, which would trust nothing less than the actual confession of the prisoner. The facts thus far ascertained furnished nothing more than presumption against him; and even when his Argilian slave brought to the Ephors the letter which made death his recompense for the delivery of it, they could only advise him to take refuge in the Temenos (or sacred ground) of Poseidon at Cape Tainaron, in the hope that Pausanias, following his servant thither, might, in the hearing of some of the Ephors hidden between the double walls of the hut, say something to criminate himself. Their hope was not disappointed. Pausanias soon came to ask the Argilian why he had taken sanctuary. The slave retorted by asking what he had done to deserve the treachery which for his faithful service designed to reward him with death. Pledging himself solemnly that no harm should happen to him, if he would but depart at once on his errand to the Persian king, Pausanias made an admission of his guilt which satisfied the Ephors hidden behind the partition wall; but getting a hint of what was to happen, Pausanias in his turn took sanctuary at the shrine of Athênê of the Brazen House (Chalkioikos), where, the roof being stripped off and the doors walled up, he was left to die of hunger. It cannot be said that he had more than a just recompense for treason of the blackest sort; but the religious feeling of the time was shocked by the violence which left a criminal to starve in a sanctuary, and a curse was supposed to cleave to all who had taken part in it.

Death of Pausanias.

The fate of Pausanias was more or less closely connected with that of Themistokles. It is perhaps enough to say that of his supposed complicity in the schemes of the Spartan general there is no evidence whatever; nor after the death of Pausanias were any documents discovered which established the guilt of the great

Bearing of the case of Pausanias on that of Themistokles.

Athenian statesman. But the very splendour of his services had arrayed against him forces which could scarcely fail sooner or later to bear him down. The enthusiastic admiration of the Spartans had given place to feelings of dislike or even hatred after the diplomacy which had outwitted them during the rebuilding of the walls of Athens; and the influence of Sparta was at all times paramount with that faction or party of Athenian citizens who even without external pressure would be sure to regard Themistokles with extreme suspicion and dislike. No one man had ever done so much to strengthen the democratic element in the state; in other words, none had been more successful in lowering the ascendency of the Eupatrid oligarchs. The animosity of these men, once roused, was sleepless and pertinacious. They could afford to work slowly, so long as they knew that they were working surely. They could first get rid of the obnoxious citizen, and then string together narratives of his alleged misdeeds which, as time went on, would sufficiently blacken his memory; and although in the historian Thucydides, from whom comes practically our whole knowledge of the later career of Themistokles, we have a writer of unswerving honesty and of almost unwearying care in the sifting of evidence, we have in him also a man whose sympathies lay wholly with the aristocratic or oligarchic party. If, again, it cannot be said that Thucydides is strictly a contemporary historian when he writes about a man who died perhaps during the year which witnessed his own birth, it must further be remembered that the keenness of his scrutiny was directed to the examination rather of oral traditions than of written documents. In the case of the latter he was too much disposed to think that they must be what they professed to be; and we have already been obliged to dismiss as spurious some letters from Pausanias to the Persian king which he readily accepted as genuine. It is not to Thucydides therefore that we could look for a summing-up from the point of view of democratic Athenian citizens; and it is therefore no slight thing if his narrative furnishes strong presumption that the stories circulated about Themistokles were one-sided and exaggerated, and in no small part groundless.

It cannot, however, be denied that in Aristeides the victor of Salamis had a rival formidable not only from Oligarchic opposition to Themistokles. the uprightness of his personal character but from his wisdom in reading the signs of the times and his promptness in acting in accordance with them. Before the invasion of Xerxes Aristeides had thrown the weight of his influence against that developement of the Athenian navy which seemed to him likely to secure undue preponderance to the democratic element in the state. But the conduct of the people, when the storm burst upon them, convinced him that the lowest class of citizens who by the constitution of Kleisthenes were left ineligible to the Archonship were not less deserving than the rest of filling the higher offices in the city; and he had the good sense to propose the abolition of a restriction which the excluded class would probably not long tolerate. If, as seems not unlikely, he was prepared for the further change which should determine the election of the archons by lot, this readiness in adapting himself to the times could not fail to extend his popularity and thus to throw a larger measure of power into the hands of the oligarchic party in their struggle with Themistokles. This illustrious man was now accused of complicity in the schemes of Pausanias by some citizens who were bribed by the Spartans to bring the charge. But the time for their triumph had not yet come, and for the present Themistokles not only escaped but was more popular than ever. Diodoros, it is true, speaks of his countrymen as forgetting his services and desiring his humiliation partly through fear, partly through envy. But these feelings, it is obvious, could be entertained towards him only by those who took pride in their Eupatrid descent; and, in corroboration of this belief, Diodoros asserts distinctly that by the main body of the people he was still and always regarded with a singular love and affection. Nor is this fact in the least discredited by his ostracism, which only proves that his absence from Athens appeared to one-fourth of the citizens a measure desirable in the interests of the city. Leaving Athens, he betook himself to Argos; but here the Spartans would not suffer him to remain undisturbed. By their means he was again charged with sharing in the treason of Pausanias, and hearing that orders had been issued for his arrest, he fled to Korkyra, and thence passed over into the territory of the Molossian chief Admetos. In after years the story ran that, making his way after many difficulties and dangers to Ephesos and journeying on thence into the interior, he sent to Artaxerxes, who had become king after the murder of his father Xerxes, a letter thus worded, 'I, Themistokles, have come to thee,—the man who has done most harm to thy house while I was compelled to resist thy father, but who also did him most good by withholding the Greeks from destroying the bridge over the Hellespont while he was journeying from Attica to Asia; and now I am here, able to do thee much good, but persecuted by the Greeks on the score of my good-will to thee. But I wish to tarry a year and then to talk with thee about mine errand.' The young king, we are told in this version of the tale, at once granted his request; and when at length, having thoroughly learnt the Persian language, Themistokles went up to Sousa, he acquired over Artaxerxes a pro-

Ostracism of Themistokles 471 B.C.

Sequel of the traditional history of Themistokles.

digious influence resting on the promise that he would make the Persian ruler monarch of all Hellas. Returning to Asia Minor, he spent the rest of his life in great magnificence, having the three cities Magnesia, Myous, and Lampsakos to supply him with bread, wine, and vegetables, but doing nothing to fulfil his promise, until at length he died by a voluntary death to escape from an impossible task.

The story refutes itself by asserting that nearly twenty or perhaps more than twenty years after the formation of the Delian confederacy, two cities lying almost under the shadow of Mount Mykalê, and a third on the shores of the Hellespont at the very gate of the Propontis, could be made by a Persian king to furnish a revenue for his favourites. If he could bestow these towns as appanages, he might put any others along the Egean coasts to the same use; and thus the work of the Greeks in destroying the fleets and the armies of Xerxes would have gone for nothing. If the resources of these towns were at the disposal of Artaxerxes, there was no reason why his tribute-gatherers should not be seen in every Ionian city, and therefore no reason why his armies should not take ample vengeance for the revolt which followed the fight at Mykalê. In short, if this story is to be believed, the account given of the assessment of Aristeides must be summarily rejected. Fully fifteen years earlier the confederate leaders had been called upon to determine the proportions in which the allies should contribute men, ships, and money for the common cause. The sum total of this assessment on the allies amounted to 460 talents. The items are not given: but it seems to have been based on the amount of tribute which the cities on the eastern shores of the Egean had paid to the Persian king; and thus as the tribute for the Nomos or district, which

Extent of Persian power on the coasts of Asia Minor.

The assessment of Aristeides, 477 B.C.

included the Ionians, Magnesians, Aiolians, Lykians, and some others, amounted to 400 talents in silver, the remainder would represent the contributions of the islanders. Yet here we have the inhabitants of certain towns, assessed as members of the Delian confederation, still at the beck and call of the Persian despot; and we are left to wonder what the allies had done during the long period of some twenty years towards breaking the yoke which Cyrus had placed on the necks of the Hellenic subjects of Kroisos. Long ago, when Pausanias was hatching his treasons, Spartan authority was able to reach him at Kolônai in the Troad, and he felt himself constrained to obey the messenger who bade him follow on pain of being declared the enemy of the people if he should refuse. But now spending years of luxurious ease at Magnesia, Themistokles could bid defiance to his countrymen, whose order for his arrest had, as we have seen, driven him away from Argos.

Thus at the outset we find ourselves dealing with a story open to the gravest suspicion; and this suspicion must be increased when we learn that, in another version, the Persian king, far from regarding Themistokles as a benefactor to the royal house, had put a price of 200 talents upon his head, and that Themistokles was accordingly unable to reach Sousa except in the disguise of a stranger designed for the king's harem. Other tales were told which represented Mandanê, the sister of Xerxes, as demanding him for the indulgence of the savage vengeance of Eastern peoples, and which spoke of Themistokles as escaping only through his singular ease in the use of the Persian language.

Relations of Themistokles with the Persian king.

Nor is it enough to note merely that the vast wealth which Themistokles is said to have carried away with him into exile renders superfluous the bribes for which he pledged his services to the Persian despot. No judgement passed on his supposed conduct during his later years can have a claim on our consideration, unless it surveys his whole career. The faculties which concentrate all the powers of a man on one especial purpose are just those which leave the least chance of a radical change in more advanced life; and for this fixity of purpose no man has ever been more remarkable than Themistokles. So mighty had been the impulse which he imparted to Athenian enterprise, so completely had it strengthened the Athenian character, that his great rival, as we have seen, gave his aid in the working of that maritime policy the introduction of which he had opposed. In this business of his life he had displayed a rapidity of perception which gave to his maturest judgements the appearance of intuition, a fertility of resource and a readiness in action which were more than equal to every emergency. He had kept those about him in some degree true to the common cause, when a blind and stupid terror seemed to make all possibility of union hopeless. Yet of this man the traditional history would have us believe, not that he yielded to some mean temptation—not that he began his career in poverty and ended it in wealth; but that from the beginning he distinctly contemplated the prospect of destroying the house which he was building up, and of seeking a home in the palace of the king on whose power and hopes he was first to inflict a deadly blow. We are told that at the very time when by an unparalleled energy of character and fixity of purpose he was driving the allies into a battle which they dreaded, he was sending to the Persian king a message which might stand him in good stead when he should himself come as a suppliant to the court of Sousa; and that he deceived his enemy to his ruin in order to win his favour in the time of

Fixity of purpose in Themistokles.

trouble which he knew to be coming. We are yet further asked to believe that in the Persian palace he actually found the refuge which he contemplated—that his claim to favour was admitted without question—that he pledged himself to inslave his country, and for twelve or fourteen years received the revenues of large towns to enable him to fulfil his word; and yet that during this whole time he made not a single effort to fulfil even a part of his promise to the Persian king.

When we look closer into the case, we find that the Spartans merely spoke of the proofs which had satisfied them of the complicity of Themistokles in the treason of Pausanias. We are not told that they exhibited these proofs to the Athenians, or that they could be exhibited; and if the genuineness of the letter intrusted to the Argilian slave be granted, this only proves the spuriousness of the previous letters in which Pausanias expressed his desire to marry the daughter of Xerxes (p. 12), and shows still more clearly that the letter of Themistokles (p. 17) placed in the hands of Thucydides is a forgery. In short, there is nothing in the case of Pausanias which will help us to any conclusion in that of Themistokles. The work of the former was ended on the field of Plataia. The mind of Themistokles after the victory of Salamis was turned to the harder task of building up the Athenian confederacy and of imparting something like a fixed principle of union to a mass of atoms which were at any time ready to fly asunder. For Pausanias withdrawal from command meant a return to the life of a mere citizen in a place where he felt that he ought to be king, and to a rigid and monotonous routine which to him had manifestly become intolerably irksome. Conscious of possessing not merely the esteem but the love of the main body of his countrymen, Themistokles had in Athens everything

Contrast between Pausanias and Themistokles.

that could make life worth living for—the sense that a great future lay before the state which he had saved from ruin, and that the coming Empire of Athens was in great part his own work. Nor must we forget for a moment that this work needed the fullest concentration of mind and will. It was one which had to be carried on in the face of overpowering difficulties and which a divided heart and wavering purpose could never have accomplished.

Nor do the charges of bribery brought against him furnish much presumption of his guilt. Beyond the sums *Charges of personal corruption brought against Themistokles* which he is said to have bestowed on the Spartan and Corinthian leaders, we are not told that he made any use of the money given to him by the Euboians (G. P. p. 164), although we might well suppose that a bribe would have turned the scale in more than one emergency. In these instances the corruption lay with the recipients of the bribe, not with Themistokles, who never swerved in his purpose: and the other charges brought against him of extorting money for his private use from the Egean islanders (G. P. p. 182) may be fairly set aside as unproven, if not as false. With his messages to Xerxes before and after the battle of Salamis we may deal not less summarily. If the first was sent, (G. P. p. 172), it was superfluous except as a device for hastening on a battle which Xerxes had no intention of declining, or perhaps even of delaying. The second (G. P. p. 179) would have been regarded by the despot as a stupid and malicious trick, while, if we look upon it as a device for securing himself a home when he should have turned traitor, it compels us to believe that a man engaged in saving his country from dangers seemingly overwhelming, and struggling with the jealousy, the selfishness, or the disaffection of his colleagues, was actuated at one and the same moment by two entirely distinct and conflicting motives. Bent on setting his country free, he was on this hypothesis not less bent on securing a place of retreat among the very enemies whom he was driving out. The idea is ludicrous. Such a condition of mind could, assuredly, have produced nothing but distraction of purpose and weakness in action; a turmoil of contrary desires with which the calm judgement and profound energy of the man stand out in incomprehensible contrast. Of the treachery thus imputed to him we may perhaps form some notion if we should suppose that before the fight of Trafalgar Nelson had already done his best to secure the goodwill of the tyrant Bonaparte whose fleets he was advancing to encounter.

In short, wherever we turn, we are met by inconsistent or contradictory statements, by shadowy inferences or unwarranted assumptions. We may take the two letters in which Pausanias and Themistokles respectively make their overtures to the great king. *Disputed credibility of the narrative.* The former may have been too presuming and boastful to be altogether agreeable to an eastern monarch; but it was at least free from the falsehoods which formed the substance of the letter of Themistokles (p. 17). The plea that the instinct of self-preservation alone had led him to resist and repel the invasion of Xerxes must to his son Artaxerxes, who could not be altogether ignorant of the phenomena of Medism, have appeared not less ridiculous than false. The boast that as soon as he could safely do so he had compensated his injuries with greater benefits must have seemed an extravagant and wanton lie. More than any other man he had toiled to destroy the Persian fleets and armies, and even to ruin the Persian empire by raising up against it the most formidable confederacy which it had ever encountered. For any good service done by him to the Persians we shall assuredly look in vain. It is useless to go further. It is just possible, although most unlikely, that some sort of agreement may have been made by him with Artaxerxes; but the terms of it we shall never discover. It is enough to know that no definite results followed, and we may therefore safely infer that it pledged him to no direct enterprise against the freedom of Athens or of Hellas. The story of his suicide was disbelieved by Thucydides; by Diodoros it was regarded as a crowning stratagem to prevent all further attempts on the part of the Persians against Greece. That Themistokles, had he chosen, might have inflicted great damage on the growing empire of Athens, we cannot for a moment doubt; that not a single injurious act can be alleged against him proves, not that he cheated the king by a train of gratuitous falsehoods extended over a long series of years, but that Artaxerxes imposed no such obligations as the price of his hospitality. We are thus brought to the conclusion that from first to last Themistokles well deserved the warm affection which his countrymen generally felt for him during his life, and with which they honoured his memory after his death; that his ostracism was due to the exertions of the oligarchic party, stimulated by the menaces or the bribes of the Spartans; that the order for his arrest which made him fly from Argos was in like manner the result of Spartan intrigues acting on the animosity felt towards him by his personal enemies; that in his absence these enemies strung together those slanders which would be most readily propagated by the oligarchic factions in every city; and that these reports in the course of thirty or forty years were worked into the shape of the traditional narrative preserved to us by Thucydides. We may well feel a legitimate satisfaction in this result of an inquiry which acquits the greatest of Athenian statesmen not merely of treason but of any attempt to injure his country, and exhibits the Athenian empire as a fabric raised by men whose moral consistency may command our respect while their political sagacity must win our admiration.

If, then, there is no evidence that Themistokles desired and deliberately pledged himself to undo the work of his life, we may well suppose that he regarded the rapid growth of Athenian power with mingled exultation and pride. Anger and resentment he may or must have felt; but these feelings would have for their object only that party among his countrymen whose enmity persistently followed him, not the main body of the people by whom he knew himself to be beloved. The obstacles to be surmounted, even when the Persian fleet had been ruined at Mykalê, were formidable indeed. The story which represents Artaxerxes as giving three Hellenic cities to Themistokles may be absurd, because it attributes to him the absolute ownership of a vast territory in which, at best, he could have possessed only a few military strongholds. Probably by that time he retained not a single post in that long and beautiful strip of land which had formed the brightest jewel in the crown of the Lydian kings. But fifteen or twenty years earlier it was found to be a hard, in some instances an impossible, task to dislodge the Persian garrisons from the cities which they occupied; and Doriskos, where Xerxes had reviewed his mighty force, was still in the hands of a Persian Governor when Herodotos was composing the later books of his history. The carrying on of the struggle must, in short, involve a serious strain for those who might persevere in it, and Sparta felt neither bound nor inclined to incur it. The Asiatic Greeks on their side were not slow to perceive the real state of Spartan feelings; and when the Spartan commissioners, headed by Dorkis, came to supersede Pausanias, they were met by a passive resistance which made them still more anxious to be rid of a costly and unprofitable

Growth of Athenian ambition.

duty. With Athens the case was in every way different. In reliance on her earnestness and her power to help them, the Asiatic Hellenes were again in revolt against the Persian king; nor could she fail to see that interest and duty alike called her to place herself at the head of the cities which were willing to submit to her guidance while they rejected the supremacy of Sparta. The whole history of the war had made it clear that her power, as Themistokles had insisted, was based upon her fleet, and that this power was capable of indefinite expansion. The security of Attica, which was bringing back to the city the wealthy and skilled population of alien residents, could be maintained only by her command of the sea; and this command secured further the benefits arising from the whole commerce of the Egean, together with the trade, chiefly in corn, which streamed from the Black Sea through the gates of the Hellespont. So wonderful was the progress made, and so great was the ambition roused by this success, that Athenian statesmen began to dream of a land empire for their city not less brilliant than their supremacy by sea; but Themistokles assuredly never supposed that within a few years the power of Athens would extend from the harbours of Megara to the pass of Thermopylai, and if he could have foreseen it he would have deprecated these conquests as mischievous, if not fatal, to her real interests. The fact that Delos was chosen as the centre of the new confederacy is sufficient proof that no such schemes were at the time entertained by others.

The events which led to these results were shaped by circumstances which could not have been anticipated;

Change in the attitude of Athens towards her allies.

but of the course of these events we have unfortunately a singularly bare and meagre record. It is not that the history of this important time has been lost, but that it never was written. From Thucydides we learn that the confederacy of Delos was at first an association of independent states whose representatives met in the Synod on terms of perfect equality, but that ten years later a change became manifest in the attitude of Athens towards her allies; that at first all contributed ships and men for the common service, whether with or without further contributions in money; and that the change in the relative positions of Athens and her allies was brought about wholly by the acts of the latter. It was absolutely necessary in the presence of a common danger, that these should faithfully keep to their engagements; it was not less necessary that Athens should compel them to the performance of their duty in case of slackness or of failure. But with the Ionians it was the old story. The Athenians were for them hard taskmasters only because they hated the very idea of long-continued strenuous exertion. But they were dealing now with men who were not to be treated like the Phokaian Dionysios in the days of Aristagoras (G. P. p. 104); and as in some shape or other they must bear their full measure of the general burden, the thought struck them that their end might be gained if they paid more money and furnished fewer ships and men, or none. Their proposal was accepted, and its immediate result was to inhance enormously the power of Athens, while in case of revolt they became practically helpless against a thoroughly disciplined and resolute enemy. To this end they were rapidly hastening, and the measure in which they were freed from the fear of Persian exactions marked the degree of their impatience under a confederation of which they felt themselves to be no longer voluntary members.

With this change of feeling the Delian Synod was doomed. Its members could no longer meet as equals; its deliberations became a mere waste of time; and Delos was obviously no longer a fit place for the common treasury. Hence the Synod ceased to meet, and the funds were transferred to Athens. The days of the Athenian Hegemonia, or leadership, were now ended; the empire of Athens had begun, and neither in laying its foundations nor in raising the fabric can the Athenians be charged with any lack of promptitude. The victory of Kimon destroyed, it is said, on one and the same day at the mouth of the Eurymedon, in Pamphylia, the Phenician fleet of 200 ships and the land forces with which it was destined to co-operate. Not many months later a quarrel with the Thasians about their mines and trade on their Thrakian settlements ended in open war. Not content with blockading Thasos, the Athenians sent 10,000 men as settlers to the spot called the Nine Roads, the site of the future Amphipolis; but these, advancing rashly into the inner country, were cut to pieces by the Edonians, to whom the Milesian Aristagoras had fallen a victim (G. P. p. 103). Undismayed by this disaster, the Athenians still blockaded the Thasian port. The siege had lasted two years, when the Thasians resolved to ask aid from Sparta. They saw that the quarrel between themselves and the Athenians was one which must be decided in a struggle between the two foremost cities of Hellas; and the readiness with which the Spartans entered into a secret engagement to invade Attica proves that, apart from the specific causes of offence, the mere greatness of Athens was a wrong which they could not forgive, and that they had advanced not a step beyond the narrow exclusiveness of the old Aryan civilisation. To this fear and consequent hatred of Athens, and to this alone, we must trace the outbreak of the Peloponnesian war. But for the present their power to aid the Thasians was not

The double victory of the Eurymedon, and the revolt of Thasos.

466 B.C.

465 B.C.

463 B.C.

equal to their will; and the Thasians, subdued at last, were compelled to pull down their walls, to give up their ships and their Thrakian settlements, and to make up the contributions which they would have paid if they had not revolted.

The inability of the Spartans to invade Attica arose from a revolt of the Helots, who construed an earthquake which followed the death of Pausanias as a sign calling upon them to rise against their masters. The insurgents were shut up in the old Messenian stronghold of Ithômê; and the Spartans, always at a loss in siege operations, besought the help of the Athenians, against whom they had made a secret pact with the Thasians. This petition was warmly seconded by Kimon, the winner of the double victory at the Eurymedon, who prayed his countrymen not to suffer Hellas to be lamed of one leg, or Athens to draw the cart without her yoke-fellow. Kimon himself, sent with an Athenian army, failed to carry Ithômê by assault, and was dismissed by the Spartans on the plea that they had no further need of his services. Conscious of their own premeditated treachery, they imputed the same double-dealing to the Athenians; but they miscalculated the effect of this insult. The indignant Demos at once proposed an alliance to the Argives, who eagerly welcomed it as a means of recovering their old supremacy in the Peloponnesos. Megara at the same time, tired out with Corinthian incroachments on her boundaries, flung herself into the arms of Athens, which thus became possessed of the two Megarian ports, Nisaia, on the Saronic gulf, and Pegai on that of Corinth, while her possession of the passes of Geraneia rendered Spartan invasions of Attica practically impossible. Still further to strengthen their hold on

Megara, the Athenians joined the city by long walls to its southern port of Nisaia, and within the fortress thus made they placed a permanent garrison.

This enrolment of Megara in the new league, to which the Thessalians were also admitted, roused the fiercest wrath of the Corinthians, and of their allies of Epidauros and Aigina. A defeat of the Corinthians made the Aiginetans resolve on measuring their full strength with the men who had robbed them of their ancient maritime supremacy. They went into battle relying on the tactics which had proved successful against the Persians at Salamis and Mykalê; they came out of it ruined as a maritime power, and dreading Athenian strategy as much as they dreaded the fleets of Xerxes two and twenty years before. The island was strictly blockaded, and the Spartans had thus another opportunity for striking a blow at Athens, while her forces were busied elsewhere; but the Helots were not yet subdued, and they were obliged to refuse help not only to the Aiginetans, but also to a Persian envoy who prayed them to invade Attica in order to draw off a large Athenian force which had been sent to aid the Egyptians in their revolt against Artaxerxes. In truth, the history of this time, with its rush of events and its startling changes, exhibits on the Athenian side a picture of astonishing and almost preternatural energy. One army was besieging Aigina, another was in Egypt; and yet this was the time chosen by Perikles for carrying out at home the plan which, on a small scale, had been adopted at Megara. To join Athens with Peiraieus on the one side, and Phalêron on the other, one wall was needed of about four and a half, and another of about four English miles in length. Such an enterprise could not fail to exasperate the fears and jealousy of the Spartans, and to alarm the conservative statesmen of Athens,

Siege of Aigina.

Building of the Long Walls of Athens.

who were especially anxious to keep on good terms with Sparta. But it was a necessary result of the policy of Themistokles: and it became evident to the Spartans that, if the growth of Athens was to be arrested, it could be done only by setting up a counterpoise to her influence in northern Hellas. Hence, in order to check Athens, they swallowed down their horror of organized federations, and set to work to restore the supremacy of the Boiotian city which had been most disgracefully zealous in the cause of Xerxes. The Spartan force sent across the Corinthian gulf defeated the Athenians at Tanagra, within sight of the Euripos, and returned home through the passes of Geraneia. Two months later the Athenian Myronides marched into Boiotia, and by his splendid victory in the vineyards of Oinophyta raised the empire of Athens to the greatest height which it ever reached. The Boiotians and Phokians became the subject allies of the Athenians, the natural consequence being that in each city the Demos rose to power and drove out the oligarchic party. This great success, which made Athens supreme from the harbours of Megara to the passes of Thermopylai, was followed by the humbling of Aigina. The walls of this ill-fated city were razed, and her fleet was taken away, while a tribute was imposed on her for the maintenance of the Athenian confederacy.

Culmination of the Athenian Empire.

The fall of Aigina, 455 B.C.

But the enterprises undertaken by the Athenians at this time were by no means attended with uniform success. The fact to be chiefly noted is the energy which remained undiminished even by serious reverses. Of these reverses the most terrible was the disaster which deprived them of the whole fleet sent to help the Egyptians in their revolt against the Persians; but even this great cata-

Settlement of the Helots and Messenians at Naupaktos.

strophe was, in some measure, compensated by the event
which enabled them to place at the entrance of
the Corinthian gulf a population bitterly hostile to the Spartans. After a gallant resistance of nine
years, the Helots in Ithômê were obliged to surrender on
condition of departing forthwith from the Peloponnesos.
The Athenians offered them a refuge in Naupaktos, and in the expelled Messenians they
found always the most trusty and devoted allies. Three
years later, the Spartans, by making a truce for five years,
enabled the Athenians to turn their whole mind to operations against the Persian king. The carrying out of
this was the great work of Kimon's life. At home his
influence was waning before the ascendency of Perikles;
at the head of a fleet he might not only strike fresh
terror into an enemy often already defeated, but enrich
both his country and himself. We may be
sure, therefore, that he went on a welcome
errand, when with 200 ships he sailed for
Kypros (Cyprus); but we have from Thucydides only a
few sentences, which tell us that, while he was blockading
Kition, Kimon died, and that the Athenians, compelled
to abandon the siege from lack of food, won a victory,
both by sea and land, over the Phenicians and Kilikians. Later historians tell us that the Persian king,
dismayed at the long run of ill-luck which attended
his arms, sent to Athens ambassadors charged with proposals for peace, and that the Athenians, in
their turn, sent Kallias to Sousa, and through
him concluded the treaty which bears his name. By this
convention the Persian king, it is said, bound himself to
send no ships of war beyond the eastern promontory of
Lykia, and to respect the Thrakian Bosporos as the entrance to Hellenic waters. The reality of this treaty has
been called into question by the fact that it is unnoticed

455 B.C.

452 B.C.

Siege of
Kition by
Kimon.
450 B.C.

The Peace
of Kallias.

by Thucydides, although by the orators of a later generation it was regarded as among the most splendid of Athenian achievements. The explanation of this seeming inconsistency may perhaps be found in the fact that the convention wrought no change, and simply gave a formal sanction to arrangements which under existing circumstances seemed advantageous to both parties. To the Athenians living at the time the treaty was, in itself, of so slight importance as to be scarcely deserving of notice: to those of later generations it became the evidence of political conditions which had become things of the past, and to which they looked back with a jealous and sensitive pride.

Athens had thus reached the zenith of her greatness, not by an unbroken series of victories, but by the persistent resolution which will draw from success the utmost possible encouragement, while it refuses to bend even beneath great disasters. *Fall of the Land-empire of the Athenians.* On a foundation of shifting and uncertain materials she had raised the fabric of a great empire, and she had done this by compelling the several members of her confederation to work together for a common end,—in other words, to sacrifice their independence, so far as the sacrifice might be needed; and refusal on their part had been followed by prompt and summary chastisement. She was, indeed, offending throughout, and offending fatally, the profoundest instinct of the Hellenic mind,— that instinct which had been impressed on it in the very infancy of Aryan civilisation. Whatever might be the theories of her philosophers or the language of her statesmen, Athens was doing violence to the sentiment which regarded the city as the ultimate unit of society; and of this feeling Sparta availed herself in order to break up the league which threatened to make her insignificant by land as it had practically deprived her of all power by sea. The temper of Sparta was, indeed, sufficiently shown in her readiness to restore to her ancient dignity the city which had been most zealous in the cause of Xerxes; the designs of Athens were manifested by the substitution of democracy for oligarchy in the cities subjected to her rule. These changes, it is obvious, could not be accomplished without the expulsion of the Eupatrid citizens who might refuse to accept the new state of things; and, as few of them were prepared to accept it, a formidable body of exiles furious in their hatred of Athens was scattered through Hellas, and was busily occupied nearer home in schemes for upsetting the new constitution. Nine years after the battle of Oinophyta the storm burst on the shores of the Lake Kopaïs. A battle fought at Koroneia ended in a ruinous defeat for the Athenians, those who survived the battle being, for the most part, taken prisoners. Roman feeling would probably have left these unhappy men to their fate, as it refused to ransom the prisoners taken by Hannibal at Cannæ. The Athenians were more humane, or could less afford thus to drain their strength; and to recover these prisoners they made no less a sacrifice than the evacuation of Boiotia, the immediate consequence being the return of all the exiles to the several cities, and the restoration of the ancient oligarchies.

<small>Battle of Koroneia. B.C. 447.</small>

Of this change the revolt of Euboia was the natural fruit; but scarcely had Perikles landed with an Athenian army on the island, when the more terrible tidings reached them that the Megarians, renouncing their alliance, had massacred the Athenian garrison within the Long Walls, and that a Spartan army was ravaging the fertile lands of Eleusis and Thrious on Attic territory. Unappalled by these dangers, Perikles returned hastily from Euboia, and after the

<small>Revolt of Euboia and Megara. B.C. 446.</small>

departure of the Peloponnesians (brought about, as some said, by bribes) went back to the island, which he subdued thoroughly. The Athenian spirit, it was clear, was as vigorous as ever; but it was also certain that the idea of an Athenian empire by land must be classed in the ranks of dreams which are never to be realised. Her hold on the Peloponnesos was to all intents already gone, although she still held the two ports of Megara; and hence, like the alleged treaty of Kallias, the truce for thirty years, which followed the re-conquest of Euboia, gave only a formal sanction to certain accomplished facts. As things had now gone, the Athenians gave up little when they surrendered Troizen and Achaia, together with the Megarian harbours. But it was easier to evacuate Megara than to forgive the Megarians, to whom ten years of friendship had given the power of inflicting a deadly blow on the imperial city with which of their own free will they had allied themselves. During all that time Athens had done them no wrong, and had conferred on them many benefits. No changes in Megara are known to us which might account for this sudden desertion. For some unexplained reason they abandoned the alliance which they had so eagerly embraced, and they roused in the Athenian mind a feeling of hatred which exacted a stern vengeance in after years.

The thirty years truce. B.C. 445.

CHAPTER II.

THE BEGINNINGS OF THE STRUGGLE BETWEEN ATHENS AND SPARTA.

First developement of the Athenian Constitution. At Athens, since the expulsion of the Peisistratidai, each step of the developement of the constitution had been followed by an increase of energy and more united action on the part of the people. Any serious check to this general harmony would have made the oligarchic party predominant; and their policy, studying the interests rather of Sparta than of Athens, would have rendered impossible that series of enterprises which brought upon her a coalition of the oligarchical states of Hellas. But although the philo-Lakonian party was strong, the party of progress was stronger still, and at the head of it stood Perikles and Ephialtes. Of the former of these two men it may be enough to say that with the wisdom and foresight of Themistokles he combined an integrity of character altogether beyond that of his great master. Moving amongst venal men Perikles escaped even the imputation of corruption. Seeing clearly from the first that Themistokles had turned the energy of his countrymen in the right direction, he set himself to the task of carrying out his policy with unswerving zeal. Like Themistokles he saw that Athens must keep hold of the sea, and the Long Walls (p. 30) which he built made her practically a maritime city. Like him, also, he could see when the bounds had been reached beyond which Athenian empire ought not to pass; and he inforced on himself, and urged with all the strength of his eloquence

Policy of Perikles.

on others, the principle that only at the peril of her existence could Athens commit herself to a career of distant conquests. With an earnestness equal to that of Perikles, Ephialtes joined a keener sense of political wrongs, and a more vehement impatience of political abuses. All classes of citizens were now eligible for the Archonship; but eligibility seldom, if ever, led to the election of a poor man. The public officers, although accountable to the people at the end of their term of office, exercised in the meantime a jurisdiction without appeal; and the virtually irresponsible court of Areiopagos, consisting only of life-members, possessed not merely a religious jurisdiction in cases of homicide, but a censorial authority over all the citizens, while it superseded the Probouleutic Senate (G. P. p. 88) by its privilege of preserving order in the debates of the Ekklesia or great public assembly. This privilege involved substantially the power of choosing the subjects for debate, as inconvenient questions might for the most part be ruled to be out of order. To Ephialtes first, and to Perikles afterwards, it became clear that attempts to redress individual cases of abuse arising from this state of things were a mere waste of time. The public officers must be deprived of their discretionary judicial powers; the Areiopagos, retaining its functions only in cases of homicide, must lose its censorial privileges and its authority in the Ekklesia, while the people themselves must become the final judges in all criminal as well as civil cases. To carry out the whole of this scheme they had a machinery ready to hand. The Heliaia in its Dikasteries or Jury-Courts had partially exercised this jurisdiction already; nor was anything further needed than to make these Dikasteries permanent courts, the members of which should receive a regular pay for all days spent in such service.

Reforms of Ephialtes.

It was natural that the excitement produced by these plans of reform should make it necessary to resort to the remedy of ostracism. The measure was eagerly welcomed by the Conservative party, who thought that the vote must fall upon Ephialtes or Perikles. In fact, it fell on the oligarchic Kimon, and the proposed political changes were accomplished. The formidable jurisdiction of the Archons was cut down to the power of inflicting a small fine, and they became simply officers for managing the preliminary business of cases to be brought before the Jury Courts. The Areiopagos became an assembly of average Athenian citizens who had been chosen Archons by lot. In short, the old times were gone; and the rage of the oligarchic faction could be appeased only with blood. Ephialtes was assassinated, but the despicable deed served only to strengthen the hands of Perikles.

Murder of Ephialtes. B.C. 456. (?)

Under the guidance of this great statesman Athens reached her utmost glory; but although he could hold together a large empire and inforce that unity of action which was needed for its maintenance, it cannot be said that his mind grasped the idea of anything like national union in the sense which those words bear for us. The judgement of the allies was not to be asked in any course of action on which Athens had resolved, and any unwillingness to take part in such action was treated as rebellion. Perikles had, indeed, his Pan-hellenic theories; but these theories were to be carried out rather by magnifying Athens than by treating the allies as if they also were Athenians. Athens with him was to be the 'School of Hellas,' by uniting within her walls all that was greatest in science, all that was most brilliant in culture, all that was most magnificent in art. This great task involved vast expenditure; and here he found himself opposed by

Pan-Hellenic theories of Perikles.

Thoukydides, the son of Melesias, who, taking the place of Kimon, held that the revenues of Athens should still be used in distant enterprises against the Persian king. Again it became necessary to take the vote of ostracism. The decision went against Thoukydides, and the public works proposed by Perikles were all carried out. To prevent an enemy from occupying the large extent of ground inclosed between the two long walls already built, a third wall was carried from the city parallel to the western wall, at a distance of 550 feet, to the harbour of Mounychia. But the costliest works of Perikles were confined within a much narrower circuit. A new theatre was built for the exhibition of plays during the Panathenaic festival: huge gates, called Propylaia, guarded the entrance to the summit of the rock on which art of every kind achieved its highest triumphs, while high above all towered the magnificent fabric of the Parthenon, the home of the virgin goddess, whose form, standing in front of the temple, might be seen by the mariner as he doubled the cape of Sounion. *Ostracism of Thoukydides, son of Melesias. B.C. 443.*

The great aim of Perikles was to strengthen the power of Athens over the whole area of her confederacy. The establishment of settlers (Klerouchoi), who retained their rights as Athenian citizens, had answered so well, that he resolved to extend it. The islands of Lemnos, Imbros, and Skyros were thus occupied; and Perikles himself led a body of such settlers as far as Sinôpê which became a member of the Athenian alliance. At the mouth of the Strymon, where the previous effort (p. 28) had led to dire disaster, Hagnon succeeded in founding the colony of Amphipolis; but two years before the settlement of this city Athens had to face the revolt of another ally. Urged on by resentment against the demos which *Extension of Athenian settlements. B.C. 437.*

at Samos, as elsewhere, made common cause with the Athenian people, the Samian oligarchs revolted, and induced the Byzantines to join them. Nine months later, the Samians were compelled to raze their walls, give up their ships, and pay the costs of the war; but in the meantime, they, like the Thasians (p. 28), had appealed for aid to Sparta, and the Spartans, no longer pressed by the Helot war, summoned a congress of their allies to consider the matter. For the truce (p. 35), which had still twenty years to run, they cared nothing; but they encountered an unexpected opposition from the Corinthians, who, in the synod convoked in favour of Hippias had protested against all interference with the internal affairs of an autonomous city (G. P. p. 93). In the same spirit they now insisted on the right of every independent state to deal as it pleased with its free or its subject allies; and the Spartans were compelled to give way.

The revolt of Samos. B.C. 440.

The relations of the Corinthians with their own colony of Korkyra were destined soon to change their opinion about the principle which they had thus laid down. The tradition which asserted that the first sea-fight among Greeks was a battle between the Corinthians and the Korkyraians forecasts exactly the relations of these two great maritime states. The fierce hatred which divided them may have sprung from jealousies of trade; but it certainly cannot be traced to any deep political convictions. The city of Epidamnos on the opposite coast had been colonised from Korkyra; but these settlers from a democratic community seem to have become oligarchs in their new abode. The strife of faction in the new colony was followed by expulsions of partisans on the losing side; and these exiles, allying themselves with their savage neighbours, did so much mischief that the demos of Epi-

Quarrel between Corinth and Korkyra.

damnos appealed to Korkyra, and when their prayer was there rejected, to Corinth. A Corinthian army accordingly entered Epidamnos, and the Korkyraians, sailing thither in great wrath, demanded their instant departure. Their demand being refused, the Korkyraians prepared to blockade the town, and the Corinthians retorted by making ready a large fleet for active operations. To avert the storm gathering over their heads, the Korkyraians now sent envoys to Corinth, expressing their willingness to submit matters to arbitration. To the reply of the Corinthians that the proposal could not even be considered unless the siege of Epidamnos were first raised, they answered that it should be raised if the Corinthians would themselves quit the place, or that, failing this, they would leave matters as they were on both sides, a truce being entered into until the arbiters should decide whether Epidamnos should belong to Corinth or to Korkyra. However unprincipled the conduct of the Korkyraians may have been, they had now, technically at least, put themselves in the right; and the Corinthians were wholly without excuse in the declaration of war by which they had replied to these proposals. The immediate result of the contest was the surrender of Epidamnos to the Korkyraians, and two years passed without any decisive operations; the Corinthians in the meanwhile getting together a fleet so powerful that the Korkyraians saw no way of escape except through an alliance with the Athenians.

Entry of the Corinthians into Epidamnos. B.C. 436.

B.C. 435-3.

When the envoys appeared at Athens, they confined their arguments, perhaps rightly, to the principles of commercial exchange. They needed help, and they insisted on their ability to make an adequate return for it. To gratitude on the part of the Athenians they made no claim.

Embassy from Korkyra to Athens seeking an alliance. B.C. 433.

They had kept away from the fight at Salamis, and since that time they had carefully avoided all alliances. The result of this policy, they admitted, was not pleasant. They had called down on themselves the full power of enemies with whom they were quite unable to cope single-handed. To the Athenians they offered an alliance which might be of the greatest use in the struggle which was manifestly coming between the two great states of the Hellenic world; and the terms of the Thirty Years Truce allowed the Athenians and Spartans severally to admit into their confederacy cities which up to that time had not belonged to either.

To a great extent the speech of the Korkyraian envoys placed the Corinthian ambassadors at a disadvantage.

Counter-arguments of the Corinthian envoys. By rejecting arbitration under conditions which were undoubtedly fair, the Corinthians had put themselves in the wrong; and to get rid of this difficulty they could only resort to hair-splitting. The arbitration, they urged, was proposed too late: it should have been offered before the Korkyraian blockade of Epidamnos was begun. This plea might have been reasonable if arbitration were a means for preventing the commission of wrongs, rather than of redressing them when committed. With more of truth they dwelt on the selfish isolation of the Korkyraians who, having kept aloof thus far, now wished to obtain the alliance of Athens only because they needed help; and with even more force they reminded the Athenians of the service which they had done them in the recent Synod by refusing to interfere between an imperial city and her free and subject allies, demanding that this principle should be observed by the Athenians in their turn.

The fear of suffering a navy as powerful as that of Korkyra, and second only to their own, to be absorbed by a hostile confederacy, constrained the Athenians somewhat against their will, to enter into a defensive alliance with the Korkyraians; and the son of Kimon was dispatched in command of ten ships only, with strict injunctions to remain neutral unless the Corinthians should attempt to land on Korkyra or on any Korkyraian settlements.

<small>Defensive alliance of Athens with Korkyra.</small>

The conflict which took place not long after in the strait between Korkyra and the mainland exhibited a scene of confusion which the Athenian seamen probably regarded with infinite contempt. The discovery that the ship itself should be the most effective of all weapons in crippling the enemy had so revolutionised their naval system that they had come to dread a combat within a narrow space, as much as they had shrunk at Salamis from fighting in open waters. Their object had then been to come to close quarters with the enemy in order to bring into action the hoplites and bowmen who crowded the decks of the triremes; and to this fashion the Korkyraians still adhered. With the Athenians the warship discharged practically the functions of the modern ram, but with a delicacy and rapidity of manœuvre scarcely attainable with the more bulky vessels of our own day. By skilful feints of attack they sought to distract or weary their enemy, and then the beak of the trireme was dashed with a fearful impact against his ship and as suddenly withdrawn. Hence they must have surveyed with some wonderment the confused throng of a battle resembling not a little a fight on land. But the left wing of the Korkyraians, chasing the ships opposed to them to their camp on shore, left their right wing to be borne down by numbers so overwhelming that, to save them from destruction, the Athenians joined in the fray. But further conflict was arrested by the approach of an Athenian squadron, on sight of which the Corinthians suddenly fell back. On the following

<small>B.C. 432.</small>

<small>Defeat of the Korkyraians by the Corinthians.</small>

day, instead of renewing the fight, they sent to ask if the Athenians wished to hinder their movements; and on receiving the answer that they were free to go wherever they pleased, so long as they left Korkyra and her settlements unmolested, they hastened on their way homewards.

They went back with feelings of animosity to the Athenians, which only grew more intense with time.

Revolt of Potidaia from Athens. 432 B.C.

Their efforts were bent on bringing about the revolt of their own colony of Potidaia, which was now a tributary ally of Athens; and this result was achieved when the Potidaians received from Sparta a positive promise that any attack made on their city should be followed by an immediate invasion of Attica. Thus for the third time (pp. 28, 40) Sparta either pledged herself to break the truce with Athens, or showed her readiness to do so. The revolt of the Potidaians was shared by the Chalkidians and Bottiaians; and the incautiousness of the Athenians, who for a time transferred the war into Makedonia, allowed the Corinthians to throw into Potidaia reinforcements which enabled it

B.C. 432-0.

to withstand a siege of two years. Before its fall, the fatal war had been begun which was to end in the ruin of Athens herself.

In truth, men's minds were becoming exasperated on both sides. Smarting under the chastisement inflicted by the Athenians on enemies who had once been friends, the Megarians complained loudly of their exclusion from the Athenian ports as a direct breach of the truce. But in this matter Athens, although she might perhaps have shown more forbearance, had done nothing which she had not a full right to do; and the Megarians, by making Athens mistress of the highway into the Peloponnesos and then suddenly breaking compact with her, had inflicted on her a most serious mischief. Nor can it with justice be said that

Meeting of the Spartan allies.

Athens had done actual wrong to the Spartan confederacy in any of the other matters laid to her charge. The quarrel between Korkyra and Corinth was a quarrel between two single cities, one of which happened to belong to the Spartan league; and both by the terms of the truce and by the international morality of the time Athens had the right of making a defensive alliance with any state not included in that confederacy. That this view was for a long time the Spartan view, may be inferred from the stress which the Corinthians laid on the indifference with which their wrongs had been treated by the Spartans. On the other hand, by bringing about the revolt of Potidaia, the Corinthians had interfered between Athens and a city which had been included in the Athenian alliance, while they had also striven to detach from her the other allied cities on the northern shores of the Egean. In other words, they had made a deliberate effort to break up the Athenian empire; and thus in the council summoned by the Spartans for the purpose of ascertaining the grievances of their allies, they could only slur over their own injustice, and misrepresent the conduct of the Athenians. This they did by affirming that the Athenians had seized Korkyra for the sake of its fleet, and were holding it by force, while they had blockaded Potidaia as being a most useful station for their dealings with the Thrace-ward settlements. The statement clearly implied that in both cases the action came from the Athenians, and that Potidaia in particular had done nothing to provoke the blockade. The rest of their speech resolves itself into a series of contrasts between Athenian energy, versatility, and foresight on the one hand, and Spartan dilatoriness, obstinacy, and stupid self-complacence on the other. Whatever might be the truth of the picture thus drawn, this speech, so far as the existing truce was concerned, was invective, not argument. Hence the Athenian envoys, who, happening to be present on some other errand, obtained leave to speak, addressed themselves to the task, not of rebutting the charges of the Corinthians, but of explaining the real motives of Athenian policy. They reminded the Spartans that they had deliberately declined to carry on the work which the Athenians had felt bound to take up; that great schemes, begun in pure self-defence, cannot always be laid aside when their immediate purpose has been attained; and that although her allies must feel the pressure of a common burden, yet the solid benefits secured to them far outweighed this annoyance. It was of course true that the allies had been constrained to sacrifice in some measure their independence; but unless they did so, the confederation could not be maintained at all, and Athens could not afford to let it be broken up, if only because she knew that, if she did, the cities now in alliance with her would all gravitate to Sparta, and make her absolutely despot of Hellas. The subjects of Athens might chafe at the slight constraint now imposed on them; but the yoke was light indeed in comparison of that which they had borne as subjects of the Persian king, or of that which would be laid upon them, if Sparta should succeed in ruining her rival. They would then feel how vast was the difference between the system which allowed to all the allies whether against each other, or against their rulers an appeal to a common law, and a system which, like that of Sparta, placed every city under the iron rule of an autocratic oligarchy.

In the secret debate which followed this council, the wise and sober warnings by which the Spartan king, Archidamos, sought to dissuade them from coming to any hasty decision, were neutralised by the insolent audacity of the ephor

Secret debate of the Spartans.

Sthenelaïdas, who did his best to hound on his countrymen to take a leap in the dark. It was for wrongdoers, he said, to consider beforehand the effect of the crimes which they intended to commit; it was for the Spartans to decree without further thought a war in which the gods would defend the right. This doughty speech carried the assembly with him, and a formal synod of allies was accordingly informed that in the opinion of Sparta Athens had broken the truce, and was asked to decide whether this offence furnished a sufficient case for war. The historian Thucydides takes no notice of any speech except that of the Corinthians, and this may fairly be described as full of falsehoods. In short, now that personal hatred had led them to abandon that principle of non-interference on which they had so long insisted, they felt that it would be foolish to stick at anything, and that it would be well to talk of the sacred mission which bound the Spartans to liberate Hellas from an all-embracing despotism. By such pleadings the fears of the allies were excited to the necessary point; and the decision of war was accepted by a large majority. *Resolution for war.*

But the Spartans and their allies were not prepared to begin the struggle at once; and in the meantime it was worth while to make every effort to get Perikles expelled from Athens. He belonged to the family of the Alkmaionidai, to which the curse of Kylon (G. P. p. 89), as the Spartans chose to say, still clave: but to their request that the Athenians should, as they phrased it, drive out this curse, the reply was that the Spartans must first get rid of the curse which rested on them for the matter of Pausanias (p. 14). A second embassy insisted that the Athenians should raise the siege of Potidaia, and withdraw the decree excluding the Megarians from their ports. A third embassy de- *Efforts of the Spartans to bring about the expulsion of Perikles. 431 B.C.*

manded briefly the autonomy of all Hellenes now included in the Athenian confederacy. By the advice of Perikles an answer was given to the demands of Sparta as moderate as it was dignified. By Hellenic law the Athenians had as much right to exclude the Megarians from their ports as the Spartans had to intrust to the ephors the power of driving all strangers from Sparta without assigning any reason for their decrees. If the Spartans would give up these Xenelasiai or expulsions of strangers, the decree against the Megarians should be withdrawn. The allies of Athens should also be left wholly free or autonomous, if they were in this condition when the Thirty Years Truce was made, and also if the Spartans would leave to their own allies generally the power of settling their internal affairs to their own liking. Lastly Athens was as ready now as she had ever been to refer the whole dispute to the judgement of arbiters approved by both the cities.

Final demands of the Spartans.

In the conduct of Perikles at this decisive crisis it is difficult to determine whether we should more admire the determined energy with which he braced himself to meet a conflict which must be terrible in its course even if it should be happy in its issue, or the generous and unselfish patriotism which could stir him to efforts thus sustained, in spite of personal wrongs not easily to be forgotten. If his own integrity was unassailable, he might be struck through his friends. The philosopher Anaxagoras was accordingly driven into exile; the illustrious sculptor Pheidias was thrown into prison, where he died before his trial could come on; and although Aspasia, the mother of his son Perikles, was acquitted on the charge of aiding Anaxagoras in undermining the faith of the people, the prosecution caused him extreme anguish.

Prosecutions of Anaxagoras, Pheidias, and Aspasia.

To the city, which in spite of the blows thus dealt

against him by his political antagonists, Perikles served with such single-minded generosity, the shuffling and disingenuous conduct of her adversaries cannot possibly be imputed. At no time had she entertained any desire of reducing Sparta or her confederate cities to the condition of her own subject allies. It was little more than a happy accident which made her for a short time supreme from the Corinthian isthmus to the Gates of Thessaly; and when with the battle of Koroneia (p. 34) this supremacy passed away, she confined herself resolutely to the task of maintaining her empire by sea. This empire in no way endangered the position of Sparta; nor could it be said that it had either directly or indirectly done her any harm. The real breach of the peace had come not from Athens but from Corinth; and the revolt of Potidaia, stirred up by the Corinthians, was a formal violation of the Thirty Years Truce. The Athenians might therefore enter on the war with a good conscience; and some years later the Spartans admitted that in the controversy which preceded the outbreak of the strife Athens was in no way to blame. Her strict moderation was shown by the steadiness with which to the last she refrained from doing anything which might be construed as an act of war. During the nine or ten months which passed after the formal congress at Sparta and the actual outbreak of the war, Athens might have anticipated matters with her unprepared enemies, and crushed them when they were comparatively powerless. She could not do this without making herself as unjust as they were; and this she would not do. Sparta had promised repeatedly (pp. 28, 40, 44) to aid the enemies of Athens if she could; and one of those promises she made while Athenian citizens were helping her against the revolted Helots. Athens had been guilty of no such double-dealing with Sparta, and

Real position of the Athenians in reference to the cause of the war.

she refused to avail herself of the opportunity of striking her down, when she could have done so without danger or even risk to herself.

CHAPTER III.

THE PELOPONNESIAN WAR FROM THE SURPRISE OF PLATAIA TO THE CAPTURE OF SPHAKTERIA.

Surprise of Plataia by the Thebans. B.C. 431. FOR nearly eighty years Plataia had been in the closest friendship with Athens; but the little city was only eight miles distant from Thebes, the stronghold of that reckless oligarchy which after the fall of Mardonios had refused with desperate deliberation to abandon the cause of despotism. Nor even in Plataia was the party extinct which desired to escape from all connexion with Athens; and this party concerted with the Thebans an arrangement for surprising the town during a time of festival. The citizens were asleep, when the traitors admitted their Theban friends within the gates, and a herald invited the Plataians to return to the Boiotian confederacy. Thinking that opposition would be useless, the Plataians at first accepted the terms offered to them; but discovering the scanty numbers of the assailants, the Plataian demos set to work to barricade the streets and then by piercing the internal walls of their houses to provide the means of combined action without rousing the suspicion of the Thebans. In that blackest darkness which immediately precedes the dawn they burst upon the Thebans, who resisted stoutly, until showers of stones hurled on them from the roofs by screaming women and howling slaves filled them with dismay, and their want of acquaintance with the town left them like a flock of routed sheep. A few only escaped through an unguarded gate; but the greater part, hurrying into a building which formed part of the city wall, found themselves in a prison where they had looked for an open passage, and were compelled to surrender unconditionally. The reinforcement which was to have supported them had been detained partly by the darkness and still more by the swollen stream of the Asopos. Their first impulse, when on reaching Plataia they found that their scheme had miscarried, was to seize every Plataian found without the walls; but a herald warned them that, if they did any harm to person or property within Plataian territory, the prisoners in the city should be instantly slain, adding that, in spite of their shameful breach of the truce, their departure should be followed by the restoration of their countrymen.

On the strength of this promise, ratified, as they declared, by a solemn oath, the Thebans returned home. The Plataian version of the story was that they made no positive pact, but merely said that the prisoners should not be killed, until negotiations for a settlement of matters should have failed. Even thus the Plataians stand convicted out of their own mouth. *[Treacherous dealing of the Plataians with the Theban prisoners.]* They entered into no negotiations, but slew all their prisoners as soon as the Theban reinforcement had departed, and thus opened the floodgates for that exasperated warfare which was to leave Hellas little rest, so long as (it might almost be said) it was to have any history at all.

On receiving tidings of the success of the Plataians the Athenians instantly sent a herald to warn them against hurting their prisoners until the matter should have been well considered. In the eyes of Perikles these prisoners furnished a hold on Thebes and through Thebes on Sparta which was worth their weight in gold: but the Athenian messen- *[The families of the Plataians taken to Athens.]*

gers reached the city only to find that the Plataians had thrown away a splendid opportunity for the sake of satisfying a savage rage. It is gratifying to find that Athens was not yet thus blinded to self-interest as well as to justice. The mischief could not, however, be undone; and the Athenians, taking away all who were unfit for military service, left the town provisioned simply as a fortified post.

Both sides now prepared vigorously for the conflict, and for both it was a time of fierce excitement; nor did the Spartans shrink from inviting the aid even of the Persian king against their Hellenic kinsfolk. The Corinthians had shown that they were acting from an unreasoning fury; and at Athens a large population had grown up which knew nothing of warfare carried on at their own doors. The stern reality was pressed upon them, when the order was issued that the dwellers in the country must break up their pleasant homes. The city of Athens and the town of Peiraieus with the space within the Long Walls were crowded with the immigrants; and when the Acharnians in this wretched confinement saw their luxuriant fields ravaged by the Peloponnesian army under Archidamos, they were with the utmost difficulty restrained from sallying forth to take immediate vengeance. Their corn was being reaped by the hands of other men; yet Perikles, although he knew the fierceness of the resentment which his policy excited, would not swerve from the course which he had marked out for himself. But when at length the Spartans were moving to the coast land of Oropos, an Athenian fleet of 100 ships, sailing from Peiraieus, was joined by fifty Korkyraian vessels off the Peloponnesian coast. Landing on the southwesternmost promontory of Messene, the Athenians had almost succeeded in carrying Methônê

General excitement of the time.

Invasion of Attica by the Spartans.

by assault, when Brasidas, the son of Tellis, who held a Spartan outpost in the neighbourhood, dashed through the Athenian force, and threw himself into the city. The promptitude now displayed by this young officer was an earnest of military exploits such as no other Spartan general ever equalled.

But the Athenians were bent on doing sterner work before the summer should draw to its close. Aigina had long been called the eyesore of Peiraieus; and so long as its old inhabitants were suffered to dwell in it, it would remain an eyesore still. *The expulsion of the Aiginetans.* The decree was passed for their expulsion; and the Aiginetans were cast out upon the Peloponnesian coast to find such refuge as the Spartans might give them in gratitude for their help during the Helot war. This refuge some of them found in Thyrea; and thus it came to pass that the Spartans had a bitterly hostile population on the mouth of the Corinthian gulf, and the Athenians a population not less resentful on the march-lands of Lakonia and Argolis. On its return homeward the Athenian fleet effected a junction with the land army in the Megarian territory, which was now ravaged by 10,000 Athenian and 3,000 Metoikian hoplites.

It was obvious that a struggle had begun which might bring either side to desperate straits before it came to an end. Hence the Athenians determined not merely to take all possible precautions for the protection of Attica, but to set aside a reserve *Athenian reserve fund.* fund not to be touched before they found themselves face to face with a supreme necessity. A thousand talents were placed in the Akropolis under a solemn sentence that any citizen, asking a vote to dispose of this money for any other purpose than that of resisting an attack on the Peiraieus itself, should be punished with instant death. The decree was a mere form, and was known to be nothing more. If anyone should wish to divert the fund to other uses, he had nothing to do but to propose a repeal of the existing Psephisma or decree, and then bring forward his motion. In the meantime, the anathema expressed the sense of the people that the money was not to be used except in the last resort; and thus the act was one not of barbarism but of the clearest foresight and of the most judicious adjustment of means to ends.

The year closed at Athens with the public interment of those who had fallen in the service of their country.

Public funeral at Athens. The citizen chosen to deliver the funeral oration was Perikles, and he determined to address the people as if they were fresh from battles as momentous as those of Plataia, Salamis, or Mykalê. It was of the first importance that at the beginning of the contest the Athenians should know what they were fighting for; and, in fact, during the year now coming to an end the people had made greater efforts than even those which had marked the struggle with Persia.

Funeral oration of Perikles. If ever there was a time when the Athenians needed to be reminded of the self-devotion of their forefathers, that time was the present: and accordingly Perikles passed in rapid review the course by which the Athenians had created their empire and the results which had been thus far achieved. Within the space of fifty years Athens had pushed back the power of Persia beyond the limits of Asiatic Hellas, had raised up against the barbarian the barrier of her maritime empire, and had developed at home a genius in art, in science, and in government such as the world had never seen. Fifty years later, the fruits of this developement were almost as splendid as ever; but the old spirit of indomitable perseverance was gone. In the age of Perikles alone could the union of the two be found; and thus his funeral oration becomes an invaluable picture of a state of things realised only for a few years, yet exhibiting in some respects a higher standard than that which we have reached at the present day. The contrast was necessarily pointed at Sparta, and the picture which it presented was that of a state which trusted rather to the spirit and patriotism of her citizens than to a rigid and unbending discipline. In the assurance that when the time for effort and sacrifice should come they would be found fully equal to the needs of the moment, Athens could afford to dispense with the network of rules and the inquisitorial system which tormented the Spartan from his cradle to his grave. As to the measure of self-sacrifice, Athenians, falling on the battle-field, gave up infinitely more than the Spartans. The latter scarcely knew the feeling of home: the home of the former was associated with all that could fill his life with beauty and delight and inspire him with the most earnest patriotism. He had received the highest political and judicial education, and he found himself the member of an imperial society whose greatness took away from its subjects all the bitterness of servitude. Well therefore might Perikles rise to a strain of enthusiasm when, after his sketch of their political and social life, he addressed himself to those who were mourning for brothers and kinsfolk fallen in battle. These had shown themselves worthy of the men who had raised the fabric of Athenian empire, and had left to their survivors the task of following their example, or, if age had ended their active life, a memory full of quiet and lasting consolation.

With this picture of sober resolution, arising from the consciousness of a substantially righteous cause, the history of the first year in this momentous struggle comes to an end. The narrative of the second year opens with a startling contrast. The

The plague at Athens.

invading army of the Spartans had not been many days in the land, when they learnt that their enemies were being smitten by a power more terrible than their own. For some time a strange disease had been stalking westwards from its starting point in Nubia or Ethiopia. It had worked its way through Egypt and Libya; it had ranged over a great part of the Persian empire; and now, just as the summer heats were coming on, it burst with sudden and awful fury on the Peiraieus. The crowded state of the city and of the space between the Long Walls added to the virulence of the poison; and the fearful rapidity of the disease taught the sufferers to accept as their death warrant the first sensations of sickness. The scenes which followed, no Hellenic city had ever witnessed before. The evil indeed was almost too great for human endurance; and a people to whom at other times seemliness in all social and religious offices was the first concern, now cared nothing for decencies of ritual, and flung their dead, as they passed along, on funeral pyres raised for others. In the midst of all this suffering there were not wanting, as there never are wanting, some who carried out with a literal zeal the precept which bade them eat and drink, because on the morrow they should die. But of these frightful horrors there was at least one alleviation. Those who had recovered from the plague were safe from a second attack; and far from abandoning themselves to an inert selfishness, they exhibited a noble rivalry in kindly offices, and unwearied in their tender care for those who were less happy than themselves, showed that consciousness of good attained may be a more powerful stimulus to well-doing than the desire of conquering a crushing evil.

For forty days Archidamos ravaged the lands of Attica; but before he left it the Athenian fleet, in spite

B.C. 430.

of the misery going on within the city, was retaliating along the Peloponnesian coast. The plague followed the crews on board their ships; but the losses thus caused were as nothing in comparison of those which ensued when, later on in the summer, the ships were sent to aid in the reduction of Potidaia. *Ravages of the plague among the Athenians before Potidaia.* The infection brought by the new troops spread with such terrific speed amongst the Athenians who had preceded them in besieging the place, that in less than six weeks 1,500 died out of 4,000 hoplites. At Athens the malady seems to have crushed utterly the energy of the people. While envoys were sent to Sparta to sue for peace, the people with vehement outcries laid all their sufferings at the door of Perikles. *Irritation of the Athenians against Perikles.* Summoning the assembly by the authority which he possessed as general, this great man met the people with a more direct rebuke of their faint-heartedness and a more distinct assertion of his own services than any to which he had in more prosperous times resorted. For the present disasters, he told them, he could take no blame to himself, unless they were ready to give him credit for every piece of unexpected good luck which might befall them during the war. Sudden calamities, he allowed, must shake the strongest mind, and a painful effort is needed to restore the balance. For Athenians such an effort was not merely their duty, but it would assuredly bring with it its own reward. There was, in truth, no excuse for their losing heart. Far from having any fears for the result, they were fully justified in facing their foes with a lofty sense of superiority, while there was only one danger which they could not afford to encounter,—the danger involved in the abandonment of their imperial power over their allies.

The reasonings of the great statesman led the people

at once to resolve that they would make no more proposals to the Spartans, and that the war should be carried on with vigour. The plague had now laid its hand heavily on his house. His sister, and his two sons, Xanthippos and Paralos, were dead; and his grief when he had to place the funeral wreath on the head of his younger son showed that at length the iron had entered into his soul. There remained still the son of Aspasia, who bore his own name; and the people allowed him to inroll this surviving child, although his mother was an alien, amongst the number of Athenian citizens. But although he lived for two years and a half after the surprise of Plataia, we hear no more from this time of the man who, more than any other, saw what the capabilities of his own countrymen were, and seized the best means of bringing out their good qualities. No Athenian, according to the testimony even of his enemies, ever carried such weight in the councils of his countrymen, and none ever eschewed more the arts by which demagogues are supposed to seek popularity. The picture drawn by Thucydides exhibits him as a leader who has no reason to fear, and nothing to hide from, his countrymen, and whose policy was throughout justified by results. The key note of that policy was the indispensable need of sweeping away all private interests, if these should clash with the interests of Athens in this great struggle. The resources of the state were not to be wasted or risked in enterprises which at best could tend only to the benefit of individuals, while enterprises to which the state was committed were not to be starved or mismanaged in order to further the purposes of factious politicians. Nothing can be more severely emphatic than the sentences in which Thucydides insists that on these two rocks the Athenians made shipwreck. Perikles worked for the welfare of Athens and

Close of the public life of Perikles.

for that alone : they who came after him were bent first on securing each the foremost place for himself ; and, as we shall see, the inevitable consequences followed. Their powers, and the resources of the city were not concentrated on the great tasks which without such concentration could never be accomplished. If we may say that the true greatness of Athens began with Themistokles, we must also allow that with Perikles it closed. Henceforth her course was downward. The social and political conditions which made Athens what she was in the days of Perikles were such as must arise when the theory of the independent Polis or City, educating all her citizens to the utmost, was carried to its logical results, aided by the genius of a people keenly sensitive to all impressions of art and science, of poetry, music, painting, and rhetoric. But they were conditions which could not be combined again in the same harmony. Hence the age of Perikles stands pre-eminent as the most brilliant phase in the history of mankind, and the genius of this splendid age is embodied in Perikles himself.

Two invasions of Attica had now failed to produce the results aimed at by Sparta and Corinth. At the beginning of the third year of the war, the invading force was sent to Plataia, the territory of which had been declared (G.P., p. 196) sacred ground. *Spartan attack on Plataia. B.C. 429.* The Spartans had nothing to gain from the enterprise ; and it is surprising that the Thebans, who acted simply from inveterate hatred of the Plataians, should be able thus to divert the Peloponnesian army to an unprofitable, as well as costly task. For the Plataians, unjustifiable though the conduct of the Spartans certainly was, it was unfortunate that they should be obliged to appeal to the Athenians before they gave an answer to the Spartan demands. These were that the Plataians should either join them in breaking down the tyranny of

Athens, or remain neutral, if they could not duly appreciate the blessings of oligarchic liberty. But the Plataians felt that as neutrality meant the reception of both sides as friends, the gates of their city would be thus opened to their worst enemies. To the fears thus expressed Archidamos, the Spartan king, replied by pledging himself and his allies to restore to them at the end of the war, without loss, all their property in lands, houses, or fruit trees, if in the meantime the Plataians would leave them in trust to the Spartans, and seek a refuge elsewhere. Under the circumstances it would assuredly have been wise to close with this proposal, but their wives and children were in Athens, and without the consent of the Athenians they could give no answer. Their envoys sent to Athens brought back the simple message that the Athenians had never yet betrayed Plataia, and would never abandon her to her enemies. These words insured the ruin of the Plataiains, while they pledged the Athenians to a course of action which was either impossible or too costly. In fact, no attempt was made to relieve the town, and the chief hope of the little band of men shut up within its walls lay in the proverbial stupidity of the Spartans in siege operations.

The history of the siege shows how little numbers availed in a blockade under the rude conditions of ancient warfare. The mound which the Spartans sought to raise between wooden walls carried out at right angles from the wall of the city was rendered useless first by the raising of the city wall to a greater height in front of the mound, and then by excavations at the base. By way of further precaution the Plataians, starting from two points on either side of the portion of wall assailed by the Spartans, raised a crescent-shaped wall to the height of the old city wall, so that when the enemy should have carried the outer wall, they would find

Siege of Plataia.

precisely the same task before them in a more cramped and exposed position. The Spartans succeeded no better with their battering engines, which were turned aside by means of nooses, or decapitated by heavy beams let down by chains fastened to two horizontal poles stretched out from the wall. An attempt to set fire to the city having also failed, Archidamos gave orders, it is said, for the complete circumvallation of the town, and on the completion of this work led away the main body of the besiegers.

Some disasters which at this time befell the Athenian arms in Chalkidikê were more than compensated by the brilliant successes of Phormion, in whom his countrymen found the most able of all their naval commanders. At the invitation of the Ambrakiots and other clans, the Spartan admiral Knemos crossed the Corinthian gulf with a force which was to aid them in reducing the Akarnanian town of Stratos, and in wresting Akarnania itself from the Athenian confederacy. The Chaonians, and other wild tribes who took part in the expedition, went first, thinking of nothing but a headlong rush which should carry the place by storm. To the Stratians their disorderly haste suggested the idea of ambuscades to take their assailants in flank, while their main body should sally from the city gates. The plan was completely successful; and Knemos was compelled to fall back on the Anapos, a stream flowing into the Achelôos about ten miles below Stratos. The reinforcements which should have reached them had fallen into the hands of Phormion. No sooner had the Corinthian ships moved from the Achaian Patrai than they saw the Athenian squadron bearing down upon them from Chalkis on the opposite coast. The day was drawing to an end, and the Corinthians pretended to take their station for the night on the Achaian shore, their in-

Victory of Phormion in the Corinthian gulf.

tention being to steal across under cover of darkness. Phormion kept the sea all night, and at daybreak his triremes confronted the Corinthian ships, which were then creeping across the gulf. These ships were awkwardly built and poorly equipped; and when they formed themselves into a circle with their prows outward, leaving just space enough for five of the best vessels reserved within the circle to dart upon the enemy, Phormion saw that the issue of the day was in his own hands. Soon after sunrise the breeze blows strongly from the gulf, making it impossible for ships to maintain the steady position which even in still water is full of difficulty for unskilful seamen. Phormion therefore sailed round their fleet with his ships in single line, gradually contracting his circle; and when the breeze came down upon them, the Corinthian ships, confined within a space narrowing from moment to moment, were thrown into the wildest confusion. In the midst of this tumult, Phormion gave the order to attack. What followed was not battle, but rout. Twelve Peloponnesian ships were taken with most of their crews; those which were not taken or sunk escaped to the Eleian docks at Kyllênê, where they were joined by Knemos on his return from Akarnania.

Indignant at an event which they could ascribe only to cowardice or sluggishness, the Spartans sent Brasidas with two other commissioners, as bearers of peremptory orders to Knemos to bring on a second engagement. Phormion, on his side, had sent to Athens earnest entreaties for reinforcements; but Perikles was now dying, and the Athenians seemed to think that they were doing right in sending the ships first on an unimportant errand to Krete. Phormion was thus left with his twenty triremes, while seventy-five Peloponnesian triremes watched him from the opposite Achaian shore. For six or seven days not a

Battle of Naupaktos. Second victory of Phormion.

movement was made on either side. The Spartans feared an engagement on the open sea; Phormion was not less afraid of being drawn within the strait gate of the gulf. But the fear of Athenian reinforcements at length led the Spartans to resolve on action; and when their fleet began at daybreak to move in lines four deep from Panormos to the northern coast of the gulf, Phormion supposed that they were bearing on Naupaktos, and felt that he dared not allow so large a force to approach it. But he had no sooner fairly entered the gulf than the Peloponnesian fleet faced about. Nothing but their swiftness could now save the Athenian ships. Eleven escaped by the speed of their movements even from this supreme peril. The rest were taken, those of the crews who could not swim being slain. The Spartans now moved as if their work was done; but the rearmost of the Athenian triremes, finding itself chased by a single Leukadian vessel far in advance of the rest of the Peloponnesian fleet, swept swiftly round a merchantman which chanced to be lying at its moorings, and dashed into the broadside of its pursuer. The Leukadian ship was disabled at once; but the exploit so impressed the crews of the vessels which were coming up behind, that they ceased from rowing, while some found themselves among the shoals. Seizing the favourable moment, the ten Athenian triremes, which had taken up a defensive position near Naupaktos, flew to the attack. The conflict was soon over. The Spartan ships fled for Panormos, six being taken by the Athenians, who also recovered all their own triremes but one.

The great plan of the Spartans, which was to drive the Athenians from the Corinthian gulf, had thus completely failed; but Brasidas thought that a blow might be struck against Athens itself by a sudden attack on Peiraieus. The seamen

Proposed night attack on Peiraieus.

were embarked at the Megarian port of Nisaia; but either the weather or their fears led them to substitute the easier task of a raid on Salamis. The assault was made known at Athens by means of fire signals, and excited extreme alarm. Hurrying down in full force to Peiraieus the Athenians hastened to Salamis only to find that the enemy had departed already, taking with them the three guardships stationed off the promontory of Boudoron for the purpose of barring access to the harbour of Megara.

The Athenians were not more successful in a larger enterprise which was destined to bring upon the Makedonian king Perdikkas and the Chalkidian towns the vast power of the Thrakian chief Sitalkes. But armies of mountaineers are not easily gathered or held together. The Athenian ships which were to co-operate with them were behind their time; and Seuthes, the nephew of Sitalkes, having received the promise of Stratonikê, the sister of Perdikkas, in marriage, urged with determined earnestness the necessity for retreat. Thus in thirty days from the time when the army set out, the order was given for return, and the great host melted away.

Expedition of Sitalkes against Perdikkas.

The fourth year of the war brought with it for the Athenians not only another Spartan invasion, but a crisis so sudden and so serious that, for a time, their power of action was almost paralysed. All Lesbos was in revolt, with the exception of the single town of Methymna. Besides Chios this island was the only one which now retained the privileges of free members of the Delian confederacy; but the Lesbian oligarchs valued still more highly the old system of isolation, which the Athenians seemed destined everywhere to break up. Even before the beginning of the war, the oligarchs of Mytilene, like the men of Thasos (p. 28), Samos (p. 40), and Potidaia (p. 44), had besought the aid

The revolt of Lesbos. B.C. 428.

of Sparta in their meditated revolt; and they now again sent thither ambassadors charged with an appeal still more earnest and pressing. These envoys were admitted to plead their cause before the Hellenes assembled to celebrate the great Olympian festival. If the report of their speech by Thucydides may be trusted, they stand practically self-condemned. The most zealous advocate of the imperial city could scarcely have framed an harangue more completely justifying her policy, or exhibiting in a clearer light the general moderation and equity of her rule. For themselves, these Lesbians have no grievance whatever to urge. They even admit that they had been treated with marked distinction. All that they could say for themselves was, first, that the idea of revolt had been forced on them by the slavery to which other members of the Delian confederation had been reduced; and secondly that they had been compelled to carry out their plan prematurely. Of the real relations of Athens with her free and her subject allies they said not a word. On the independence of these allies in the management of their internal affairs they kept careful silence; but the checks put on quarrels and wars between two or more allied cities were resented as involving loss of freedom. With even greater unfairness they charged the Athenians with deliberately abandoning all operations against the Persian king, and confining themselves to the subjugation of their allies. They might with equal reason have charged them with Medism during the invasion of Xerxes.

Audience of the Lesbian envoys at Olympia.

The Lesbian envoys further urged on the Spartans the need of invading Attica a second time, on the ground that the Athenians, exhausted by the plague, had, further, spent all their reserve funds. This last statement was true. Of the 6,000 talents stored in the treasury at the beginning of

Investment of Mytilene by Paches.

the war 1,000 only remained,—that sum, namely, of which under pain of death, no one was to propose to make use except for the defence of the city itself from invading armies or fleets. But the Athenians were resolved to show that, in spite of the plague and of poverty, they were still able to hold their ground and to deal hard blows on their enemies. A thousand hoplites were sent to Lesbos under Paches, who completely invested the city of Mytilene; but the rocky bed of a winter torrent so far broke the work of circumvallation that a Lakedaimonian named Salaithos managed to scramble up it into the town.

The surrender of Mytilene. B.C. 427. The Spartan invasion of the fifth year of the war was even more merciless than those which had preceded it. It was also prolonged in the hopes that tidings of success might be brought from Lesbos: but none such came. Alkidas, who had been sent out with a Spartan fleet, failed to make his appearance; and Salaithos, despairing of his arrival, armed the Demos as hoplites, in order that they might sally out from the city against the besiegers. The step was fatal. The commons, instead of obeying the orders issued to them, insisted on an immediate distribution of corn to alleviate the famine which already pressed hard upon them, or threatened in default of this to throw open the gates to the Athenians. Thus pushed, the oligarchs at once made a convention with Paches, who pledged himself to inflict no punishment on any Lesbian until the Athenian people had given their judgement in the matter. Soon afterwards, Alkidas, learning what had taken place, resolved on returning home. On his way he signalized himself by a savage massacre of the prisoners whom he had seized in the merchant vessels which, under the impression that any fleet in Egean waters must be Athenian, had approached his ships without suspicion. Having vainly pursued him as far as Patmos, Paches returned to Lesbos, after disgracing himself at Notion by an act of treachery worthy of Alkidas himself. In Lesbos he now reduced the towns of Pyrrha and Eresos, and having obtained possession of the Lakedaimonian Salaithos, sent him to Athens with a thousand Mytilenaian prisoners. Salaithos could scarcely expect mercy; and although he promised, probably with little likelihood, to draw off the besiegers from Plataia if his life were spared, he was instantly slain.

No event had yet happened so seriously endangering the empire of Athens as the revolt of Lesbos. At no time, therefore, had the feeling of resentment and the desire for vengeance run so high. Moved by this mastering passion, the Athenians were in no mood for drawing distinc- *Indignation at Athens against the Mytilenaians.*
tions between the guilty and the innocent, and accordingly they welcomed the proposal of murdering the whole adult male population of Mytilene, probably 6,000 men, in addition to the 1,000 prisoners already at Athens. Of the orators who spoke most vehemently in favour of this proposition, the most violent, if we may believe Thucydides, was Kleon. Although this man is here mentioned by the historian for the first time, he had long since gained some notoriety by his opposition to Perikles. In the broad and coarse pictures of the comic poet Aristophanes, he is the unprincipled schemer who *Influence of Kleon.*
wins influence by cajoling the people with the most fulsome flattery. No picture could be more untrue. If we may trust the narrative of an enemy, adulation of the Demos was the last sin which could be laid to his charge. It would be more true to say that he acquired power by blustering rhetoric, by boundless impudence, and by administering the harshest rebukes to the people, so long as there was some popular feeling to which these rebukes in the end appealed. His rudeness and gross-

ness were thus forgiven by the aristocratic party to whom the policy of Perikles was distasteful; in other words he had in his favour a powerful sentiment in their dislike of the great statesman who had dealt the last sweeping blow against their ancient privileges. In the case of the Mytilenaians he had on his side a feeling still more powerful, and probably a large majority came to the debate vehemently eager to take the vengeance to which Kleon gave the name of justice. So vast, however, was the massacre proposed, that the feeling of anger was speedily followed by a feeling of amazement at the ocean of blood which was to be shed in order to appease it; and a resolution was carried to reconsider the question. On the following morning Kleon stood up again to administer a stern rebuke to the Demos and to urge the paramount duty of giving full play to the instinct of resentment. That against the Lesbians he had a terrible indictment, it is impossible to deny; but, if the report of Thucydides may be trusted, he uttered a direct falsehood when he asserted that the oligarchs and the Demos had been guilty of the same crime and therefore deserved the same punishment. The plea was palpably untrue. The Demos was not armed until the oligarchs felt that thus only could they escape imminent ruin; and no sooner had they grasped their weapons than they used the power thus gained in the interests of Athens. This distinction forms the keynote of the speech by which Diodotos sought to bring the people to a better mind. In all the states of her alliance Athens had now beyond doubt a body of stanch friends; and even in Lesbos they had been overborne only by the violence of the oligarchic faction. By following the advice of Kleon, they would declare that no heed would be taken of shades of guilt or of distinctions between guilt and innocence; and thus

Speech of Diodotos, condemning the proposal of Kleon to massacre the Mytilenaians.

friends and foes alike would be goaded to desperate resistance, while money spent in blockades would leave the Athenians in possession only of heaps of ruins when the siege was ended. The question to be decided turned, he insisted, not on the wickedness of the rebels but on the measures needed for the welfare of Athens. It was absurd to form expectations of future gain on the mere severity of punishment. The black codes which punished all offences with death had not been specially successful in lessening the number and atrocity of offences. Unless they were prepared to encounter everywhere a monotony of hatred and disgust, they would adopt his amendment, that the prisoners then at Athens should be put on trial, and that the lives of the Mytilenaians in Lesbos should be spared.

This amendment was carried by a small majority: but the trireme which had been dispatched with the decree for ordering the massacre had had a start of nearly twenty-four hours, and there seemed to be little chance that the more merciful decision could take effect. *Withdrawal of the decree for the massacre.* Stocking the second ship with an ample supply of wine and barleymeal, the Lesbian envoys promised the crew rich rewards if they reached the island in time. Their energy may have been still further quickened by the desire of saving Athens from a great crime and a great disgrace. They reached Lesbos, not indeed before the first trireme, but before Paches had begun the execution of the decree which he had already published. Here ended the repentance and the mercy of the Athenians. The thousand Mytilenaians at Athens were put to death; the walls of Mytilene were pulled down; its fleet was forfeited; an annual tribute was imposed upon the city; and Athenian Klerouchoi (p. 39) were settled upon its territory.

The subjugation of Lesbos preceded only by a few

days or weeks the destruction of Plataia. As the siege wore on and the hope of aid from Athens became more and more faint, the Plataians resolved to make an attempt to force their way through the lines of the besiegers. Nearly half, however, drew back when the hour for action came: but the result proved the wisdom of the 220 men who still persevered. With wonderful patience they had made all possible preparations for ascending and descending the walls in possession of the besiegers; and with wonderful skill and good fortune they availed themselves of a dark and stormy night to carry out their enterprise. When at length, after surmounting a thousand dangers, they found themselves in an open country, the flashing of torches showed that the patrols of the enemy were hurrying up the heights of Kithairon in the hopes of overtaking the fugitives. The Plataians, thinking that they would scarcely be suspected of running towards the lion's den, marched straight for nearly a mile on the road to Thebes, and hastening thence from scenes associated with the heroic devotion of earlier days, took the mountain road which led through Erythrai to Athens.

Escape of half the citizens besieged in Plataia.

For some months longer the Plataians left in the city held out against an enemy more terrible than man; but although famine was fast doing its work, the Spartan leader had a special reason for arresting it before its close. If the Plataians could be brought to a voluntary surrender, there would be no need, in the event of either truce or peace, to give up the place along with others which had been forcibly occupied. The Plataians were invited, therefore, to submit themselves freely to the judgement of the Spartans, who would punish only the guilty. They were in no condition to refuse these terms; but they could at once see what was to come when, on the arrival of the special

The destruction of Plataia.

commissioners from Sparta, they were called upon to answer simply the one question, whether during the present war they had done any good to the Spartans and their allies. The very form of the question showed that no reference would be suffered to their previous history; but only by such reference was it possible to exhibit in its true light the injustice of their present treatment. They were to be sacrificed, in spite of all that they might urge, to the vindictiveness of the Thebans; and these took care to paint in glaring colours the crime of which the Plataians had been guilty after the surprise of their city. They had promised to keep their prisoners unharmed until they had tried the effect of negotiation: they made no attempt to try it, but straightway slew all the men, in breach of a solemn promise. The retort brings us back to the monster evil of this horrible war—the exasperated and vindictive spirit which forgot prudence, reason, and policy in the blind longing for revenge. It matters not whether we take the Theban version of the story or that of the Plataians. These by their own mouth stand on this point self-condemned (p. 51). If one crime was to serve as the justification for another, the Thebans had full warrant for demanding the death of the Plataians. But there was no need to urge a request with which the Spartans had made up their minds to comply. The prisoners were again called upon to answer, one by one, the question to which their speech had evaded a distinct reply: and as each man answered necessarily in the negative, he was taken away and killed. So were slain 200 Plataians and 25 Athenians who had been shut up in the town; and so fell the city of Plataia, in the 93rd year of its alliance with Athens, to rise once more, and to be once more destroyed. The town was razed to its foundations, and its territory, declared to be public land, was let out to Boiotian graziers. The play was played out, as the Thebans would have it. The facts can scarcely be described in any other terms, for, awful though the drama may be, the existence or the ruin of Plataia could have no serious issue or meaning in reference to the war.

The summer of the fifth year of the struggle between Athens and Sparta was marked by the capture of Minoa, an islet used by the Megarians as a post to defend their harbour of Nisaia. The general in command of the victorious force was Nikias, a man who is said to have filled the office of *strategos* even as a colleague of Perikles, but who is first noticed at this time by Thucydides. From this moment he becomes one of the most prominent actors on the stage of Athenian politics, until his career closes under conditions thoroughly abhorrent to a nature singularly unenterprising and cautious. Deficient in military genius, possessed of not much power as an orator, caring more for the policy of his party than for the wider interests of his country, this strictly conservative and oligarchic statesman gained an ascendency at Athens not much less than that of Perikles, and in part for the same reason. In all that related to money Nikias, like Perikles, was incorruptible; and this fact, joined with the decency of his life, secured for him an influence with the people which, from every other point of view, was quite undeserved. Personally, indeed, he had much to recommend him to the affections of his countrymen. Endowed with ample wealth, he made use of his riches, not for indulgence in luxury and pleasure, but chiefly for the magnificent discharge of the liturgies, or public offices, imposed on the wealthiest citizens. The munificence with which at such times he exceeded the obligations of the law answered a double purpose. It soothed a sensitive conscience as a religious offering to the gods; and it procured for him a

Margin: Capture of Minoa by Nikias. B.C. 427.

general respect which the purity of his life heightened into admiration. In no way tainted with the philosophical tastes of Perikles, Nikias spent his leisure time in listening to the discourses of prophets whom he kept in his pay, while both his temper and the need of attending to his property made him either unambitious of public offices or even averse to filling them. Here, again, a carefulness, which took the form of modesty, increased the eagerness of the people to place him in positions which he wished rather to avoid, and to comply even with unreasonable demands which he made in the hope of avoiding them.

The sixth year of the war was comparatively barren in events affecting immediately the Athenian empire. An unsuccessful attempt of Nikias to bring Melos and Thera, the two southernmost of the great central group of Egean islands, into the Athenian confederacy, was matched by an attempt, not much more successful, on the part of the Spartans, to found a military colony at Herakleia, in Trachis, not far from the mountain passes associated with the exploits of Leonidas. A more serious scheme was that by which Demosthenes, the commander of an Athenian squadron off Leukas, dreamt of restoring the supremacy of Athens in Boiotia by an attempt made, not from Attica, but from the passes of the Aitolian mountains. The enterprise ended in terrible failure, and Demosthenes, not daring to face the people, remained in the neighbourhood of Naupaktos. His help was soon needed by the Akarnanians, whom he had offended by insisting on his march through Aitolia, when they wished him to engage in the siege of Leukas. They were now, at the beginning of winter, assailed by the Ambrakiots, who seized Olpai. By the aid of Demosthenes, they won a battle in which

Failure of Demosthenes in Aitolia. B.C. 426.

Successes of Demosthenes against the Ambrakiots.

the Spartan commander, Eurylochos, was slain, while the Ambrakiots were compelled to make a disorderly retreat to Olpai. Another body of Ambrakiots, constituting, in fact, the main force of their state, was cut to pieces at Idomenê chiefly by means of the Messenians in the service of Demosthenes; and Ambrakia now lay at the mercy of the Akarnanians, who might have carried the town on the first assault. To this step they were strongly urged by Demosthenes; but having gained their immediate end, they reverted to their old grudge and refused to follow his counsel. This campaign, marked by fearful carnage, had done little for Athens but much for Demosthenes. Without calling on the state to aid him, he had won a victory which ensured to him the condonation of his previous mistakes. The Athenians had gained nothing beyond a pledge on the part of the Ambrakiots that they would take no part in any operation directed against Athens; and even this gain was balanced by the engagement which bound the Akarnanians to abstain from all movements against the Peloponnesians.

Occupation of Pylos by Demosthenes. B.C. 425. Seventh year of the war.

The seventh year of the war began with the usual invasion of Athens by the Peloponnesians, which during the previous year had been prevented by a rapid succession of earthquakes. But before they had been a fortnight in the country Agis, the Spartan king, son of the old Archidamos, received tidings which caused him to hurry homewards with all speed. The Messenians of Naupaktos, who had suggested to Demosthenes his unfortunate Aitolian expedition, now urged upon him the vast advantages which would accrue to Athens from the occupation of a strong military post on Spartan territory; and the reputation which he had gained by his victories at Olpai and Idomenê procured for him the consent of the people for employing in any operations along the

Peloponnesian coasts the fleet of forty ships which they were sending to Korkyra and Sicily. But the generals with whom he sailed were less disposed to listen to him when he suggested that Pylos would serve well for the object which he had in view. Although, however, they insisted upon sailing on, a storm brought them back to Pylos, and there Demosthenes again vainly urged his scheme upon them; nor had he more success at first with the subordinate officers or with the men. The storm, however, lasted on for days, and the men began of their own accord to fortify the place by way of passing the time. They had no iron tools for shaping stone, and they had brought with them no vessels for carrying mortar. The blocks were, therefore, laid together, so far as was possible, without mortar; and in parts where cement was indispensable, they carried the mortar on their backs with their hands folded over the burden. They soon took a serious interest in the work which they had begun almost in sport. Six days sufficed to complete the wall on the exposed land side, and Demosthenes was left with five ships to hold the place. The spot thus chosen is described by Thucydides as a rocky promontory, separated from the island of Sphakteria by a passage wide enough to admit two triremes abreast. This island stretched from north-west to south-east, a passage capable of admitting eight or nine war-ships abreast dividing it from the mainland. Within this breakwater lay the spacious harbour of Pylos. Either time has altered considerably the configuration of the ground, or the historian was not accurately informed as to measurements; but there can be little doubt, or none, that the bay of Pylos is the present bay of Navarino, and that the spot which witnessed the success of Demosthenes has witnessed also the destruction of the Turkish fleet by Sir Edward Codrington and his French and Russian colleagues.

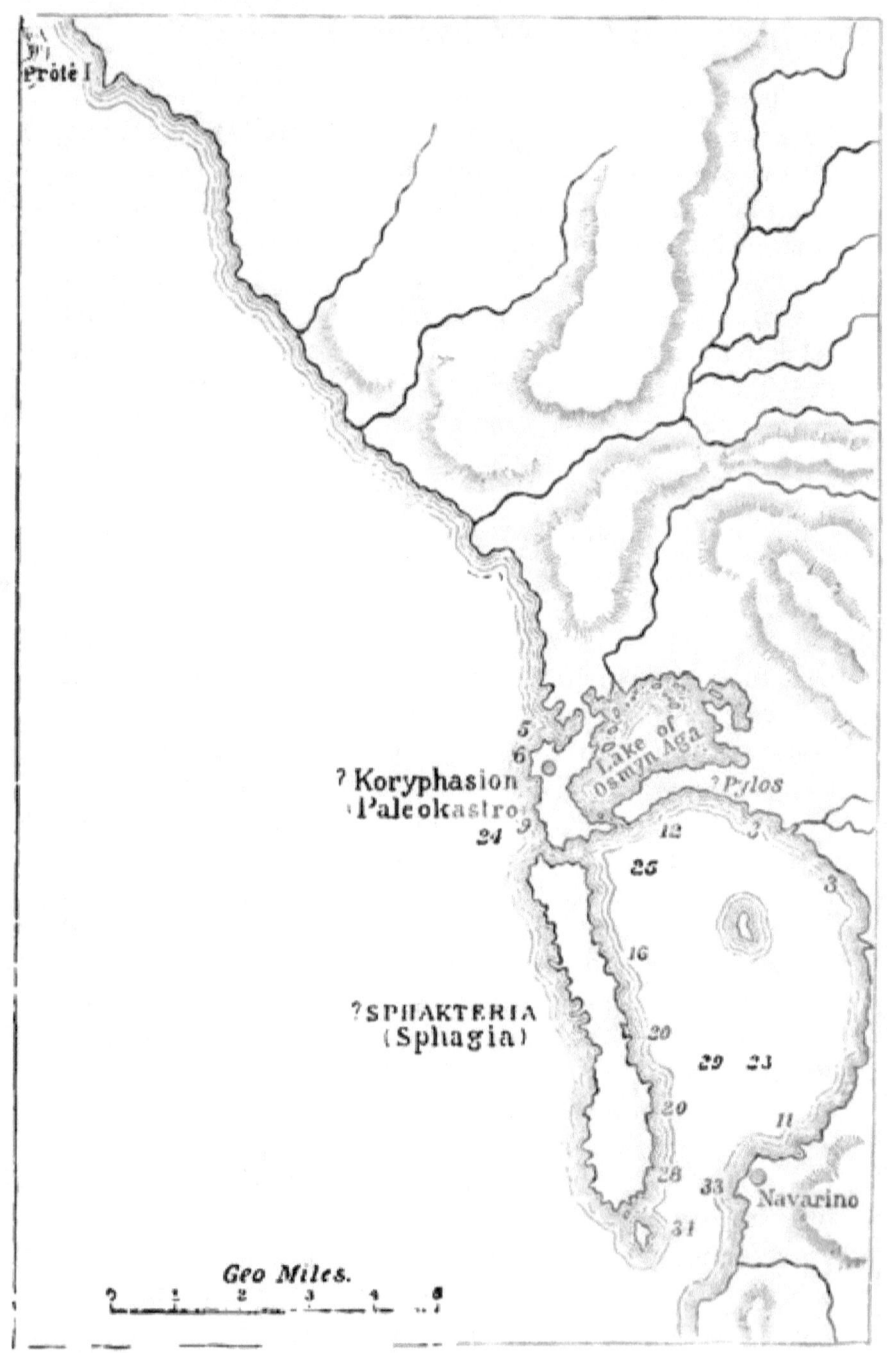

PLAN OF THE HARBOUR OF NAVARINO, TO ILLUSTRATE THE OPERATIONS OF DEMOSTHENES AT PYLOS.

The tidings that the Athenians were masters of Pylos had brought Agis and his men away from Attica. The plan of the Spartans was to strain every nerve to crush the Athenians by a simultaneous attack by land and sea before they could receive any reinforcements; and for this purpose a body of hoplites, under the command of Epitadas, was placed on the islet of Sphakteria. On his side Demosthenes had done all that an able and brave leader could do. Having sent two ships to summon with all speed to his help the Athenian squadron at Zakynthos, he drew up his remaining triremes on the shore under the walls of his fort, and hedged them in with a stout stockade. The greater part of his force he reserved for the defence of the landward wall, while with sixty hoplites and a few archers he himself went down to the beach. The day went precisely as he had anticipated. Peloponnesian besiegers were never much to be feared, and we are only told that they did nothing. The attack by sea was made by detachments of four or five ships at a time; but the Athenians were ready to encounter them at the narrow openings by which alone they could approach the fort, and they had a powerful ally in the rocks and reefs which gird in this dangerous promontory. The captains of the ships shrank naturally from risking the destruction of their vessels. Furious at the sight, Brasidas asked them whether for the sake of saving some timber they meant to allow the enemy to establish himself in their country; and insisting that his own ship should be driven straight upon the beach, he took his stand on the gangway, ready to spring on land. But in this position he was exposed to showers of darts and arrows; and as he fell back fainting with his left arm hanging over the side of the vessel, his shield slipped off into the water. Dashed up presently by the waves on the beach, it was seized

Failure of Brasidas to dislodge the Athenians.

by the Athenians, who with it crowned the trophy reared after the battle. Evening closed on the strange victory of Athenians on the Peloponnesian coast over Peloponnesians who sought in vain to effect a landing from their own ships on their own shores. For two days more the Spartans vainly strove to obtain a footing on the beach; on the third the Athenian fleet arrived from Zakynthos. For that night the Athenian commanders were compelled to fall back on the island of Prôtê. On the fourth day they advanced with the intention of forcing their way in, unless the enemy should come out to meet them on the open sea. With a strange infatuation the Spartans awaited their attack within the harbour; and the Athenians sweeping in at both entrances dashed down upon their ships, disabling many and taking five.

The Spartan hoplites shut up in Sphakteria. The Spartans saw with dismay and grief that their hoplites were now cut off in the island; and something must at once be done, if these men, many of whom belonged to the first families of Sparta, were to be saved from starvation or from the risk of being captured by an overwhelming force. Hurrying at once to Pylos, the ephors arranged a truce, pending the return of envoys from Athens with the decision of the people whether for peace or for the continuance of the war. The terms were that the whole Lakedaimonian fleet should be handed over to the Athenians, to be given up again at the end of the truce, and no attack was to be made on their fortifications, the Spartans being allowed on these conditions to send in a fixed daily allowance of food and wine to the hoplites cut off in Sphakteria. The infraction of any one clause of the agreement was to nullify the whole.

Not many days had passed since the Athenians had witnessed the premature retreat of Agis with the Spartan army; but they little thought that the next scene in the drama would be the sight of Spartan envoys suing for peace with a tone of moderation in little harmony with their general character. The blockade of their hoplites in Sphakteria had opened their eyes to many duties of which they had thus far been strangely forgetful. They had learnt the value of forbearance and kindliness and the folly and wickedness of carrying a quarrel too far. The Hellenic world, they added, was sorely in need of rest, and the boon would be not the less welcome because they knew not now who had begun the quarrel, and had but a vague notion as to what they were fighting for. The Spartans were no doubt perfectly sincere for the time in their professions of kindly feeling towards the Athenians, and they never spoke more to the purpose than when they said that the time for ending the war had come. It was true that when Athens was down under the scourge of the plague, they had treated with contempt the Athenian proposals for peace; but of the more moderate citizens many were content to overlook this inconsistency in their desire to further the interests not of Athens only but of all Hellas. Unfortunately among these moderate men not one was to be found who could venture to force these interests on the attention of the people. Perikles was dead, and Kleon was living with a spirit unchanged from the day when he hounded on his countrymen to slaughter the friendly Demos as well as the rebellious oligarchy of Mytilene. Insisting that the Athenians should demand nothing less than the surrender of the hoplites in Sphakteria with their arms, he added that, when these men had been brought to Athens, the Spartans might make a further truce on condition of giving back to the Athenians Nisaia and Pegai (p. 29), Troizen and Achaia (p. 35). In making this demand it would be hard to say that Kleon was either wrong or un-

Spartan embassy to Athens for peace.

Demands of Kleon.

just. With regard to Megara, the justification was two-fold. The Megarians, having voluntarily sought their friendship (pp. 29, 34), had requited the good services of the Athenians with an ingratitude which might rather be called treachery; and further, as Megara could never stand alone, the state which held it in subjection and alliance would hold the key of the isthmus. It was not therefore to be expected that the Athenians would allow the Spartans to retain the privilege of throwing their armies into Attica at their will.

So far Kleon was thoroughly justified; nor would he have been in the least abandoning his position had he assented to the request which the Spartan envoys now made, that commissioners should be appointed to discuss terms with them and submit the result to the people. But with amazing folly he burst out into loud denunciations of Spartan doubledealing. He had suspected from the first that they had come with no good intent: he was sure now that they wished only to cheat the people, before whom he bade them say out plainly whatever they had to say. The envoys were taken by surprise. They were wholly without experience in addressing large popular assemblies: nor had any citizen of the moderate or conservative party, from Nikias downwards, the courage to demand that the request of the envoys should be submitted to the decision of the people. The Athenians chose to follow Kleon; and Kleon in bringing about the contemptuous dismissal of the envoys was emphatically in the wrong.

The dismissal of the envoys brought about by Kleon.

The return of the envoys to Pylos brought the truce to an end; but alleging some infraction of the covenant, the Athenians refused to surrender the Peloponnesian fleet. The extreme importance of preventing the escape of the hoplites in Sphakteria, suggested probably this most dishonest measure, which made it impossible for the Spartans to relieve Epitadas and his men unless they could first recover some portion at least of their fleet after storming the fortifications of Demosthenes. But in spite of the vast advantages which they thus gained, it seemed as though the Athenians would find that they had undertaken a task beyond their powers. Their slender garrison was besieged by an army which hemmed them in by land, and their whole supply of drinking water came from one solitary spring on the summit of the little peninsula. On the other hand, the hoplites in Sphakteria had not only an excellent spring in the centre of the island, but received large supplies of food and wine brought to them by Helots urged on to the task by the promise of freedom, or by freemen stimulated by assurances of rich reward. The next tidings which came to Athens told the people that at the beginning of the winter season the triremes must be all withdrawn, and that on their departure the imprisoned hoplites would at once make their escape. According to the Athenian fashion of shifting all responsibility upon advisers, popular indignation ran high against Kleon. The leather-seller (for such was his occupation) was indeed sorely perplexed, while his opponents, moved by mere selfishness, were in the same measure delighted. On the spur of the moment he charged the messengers from Pylos with falsehood; but when he was chosen to go as a commissioner to ascertain the state of things at the spot, he felt that he would have to retract his words, if they should be right, or be convicted of a lie, if he should misrepresent matters. But he was none the less justified in telling the Athenians that, if they believed the messengers, it was their business to send forthwith adequate reinforcements to Pylos, and that if the generals then present were men, they would

Resumption of the war. Difficulties of the Athenians.

go at once, as he should go if he were in their place. The reference to himself was at the worst only an indiscretion: but Nikias, instead of admitting that Kleon had simply pointed out to him his clear duty, answered that, if the task seemed to him so easy he had better undertake it himself. Seeing that Nikias was in earnest, Kleon more than atoned for his fault by candidly confessing his incompetence for military command. With incredible meanness, if not with deliberate treachery, Nikias stuck to his proposal; and the eagerness of the people to ratify the compact was increased by the wish of Kleon to evade it. As for Nikias, it is enough to say that, regarding the matter as a fair trap for catching a political opponent, he could calmly propose to risk the destruction of an Athenian army by despatching on an arduous, if not an impossible, errand, a man whom he believed to be wholly incompetent. When at length Kleon said that he would go, he added that he should set out with the assurance of bringing back within twenty days, as prisoners, the Spartan hoplites then in Sphakteria. Thucydides speaks of this promise as a sign of madness: yet Kleon had only asserted that Athens was able to do what Nikias pronounced to be impossible, and he had further taken care that his colleague should be the general who had achieved a harder task among the Akarnanian and Amphilochian mountains. He could scarcely have shown sounder sense or greater modesty; yet Thucydides tells us that his speech was received by the Athenians with laughter, and that soberminded men were well pleased at an arrangement which would insure one of two good things—either the defeat of Kleon, or a victory over the Spartans, which might open a way for peace, the former being what they rather desired. In the judgement of Englishmen, these sober-

Engagement of Kleon to effect the capture of the Spartans in Sphakteria.

minded men would be mere traitors; but it is not easy to avoid the conclusion that the laughter came, not from the people generally, but only from the members of the oligarchic clubs, and from those who were afraid of offending them.

Having reached Pylos, Kleon at once proposed to the Spartans to surrender the hoplites, who should be well treated until terms of peace should be arranged. But the Spartans would not hear of it, and Demosthenes, with Kleon's full consent, made ready for the attack. In fact, Kleon behaved throughout as the mere lieutenant of the general in whom he rightly placed implicit trust. *Capture of the hoplites by Demosthenes and Kleon.* The great aim of Demosthenes was to do the work by means of the light-armed troops: an encounter of hoplites would lead probably to the slaughter of many of the enemy whom it was of great consequence to take alive. From the first the Spartans had no chance. All attempts on their part to reach the compact mass of Athenian hoplites were foiled by showers of weapons from the light-armed troops on either side. At length they began to fall back slowly to the guard post at the north-western end of the island where the ground is highest: but this step of itself insured their doom. They had abandoned the only spring in the islet, and in a few hours more or less thirst would do its work; but Demosthenes was specially intent on saving their lives, and a Messenian guide undertook to lead a large force by a secret path which should bring them to a higher position in the rear of the enemy. As soon as the Spartans were thus surrounded, Demosthenes sent a herald to demand their unconditional surrender. The circumstances admitted of no debate, and the dropping of their shields showed that they accepted the inevitable terms. Of the 420 hoplites who had been cooped up in the island, 292 lived to be taken prisoners, and of these not less than 120 were genuine Spartiatai of the noblest lineage. The work was done. Within twenty days from the time of his departure Kleon redeemed what Thucydides calls his mad pledge, by bringing to the Peiraieus the costliest freight which had ever been landed on its shores.

CHAPTER IV.

THE PELOPONNESIAN WAR, FROM THE SURRENDER OF THE SPARTANS IN SPHAKTERIA TO THE MASSACRE OF MELOS.

THE success of Demosthenes and Kleon changed the public feeling of Athens from a desire for peace to a re-solution of carrying on the war with energy. Nearly three hundred Spartan hoplites were prisoners at Athens, ready to be brought out and slain if a Peloponnesian army should dare to cross the borders of Attica. The Spartans were, in proportion, lowered in their own self-esteem and in the eyes of the Greek tribes generally. Their humiliation was shown in more than one embassy for peace; but there was no Perikles now living to warn the Athenians against press-ing good fortune too far. They had put one thorn in the side of their enemies by the oc-cupation of Pylos; in the following, or eighth, year of the war, they thrust in another by the seizure of Kythera, the island off the south-eastern promontory of Lakonia, which had been for the Spartans a port for mer-chant vessels from Egypt and Libya, and a station from which they could with ease keep off all privateers from their coasts. The enterprise was concerted with a friendly body among the people who wished to be rid of the

Change of public feeling at Athens.

Athenian occupation of Kythera. B.C. 424.

oligarchic rule of Sparta; and when Nikias and his colleagues arrived with 2,000 hoplites and some horsemen, the resistance was more nominal than real. From Kythera, Athenian ships made descents on many places along the Lakonian shores, and their troops, landing at Thyrea, where the expelled Aiginetans (p. 31) had found a refuge, carried the place by storm. The Aiginetans taken within it were carried to Athens, and there put to death. Thus was swept away the remnant of that people who had shared with the Athenians the glory of Salamis; and a catastrophe as horrible as that of Plataia attested the strength of the fatal disease which rendered impossible the growth of an Hellenic nation.

Among those who risked their lives to convey food to the hoplites shut up in Sphakteria were the Helots, to whom they promised freedom as a reward. Other Helots, probably those who were not manumitted, deserted, it seems, to the Messenians at Pylos, or made their escape to Kythera. *Alleged massacre of Helots by the Spartans.* Fearing the extent to which these desertions might be carried, the Spartans, it is said, proclaimed that all who regarded their exploits on behalf of Sparta as giving them a title to freedom, should come forward and claim it, under the assurance that if their claim should be sound, the boon would be granted. Two thousand, we are told, were selected as worthy of liberty, and with garlands on their heads went round to the temples of the gods. A few days later, of these 2,000 men not one was to be seen, and none was ever seen again. In the opinion of the historian Thucydides the Spartans were suffering under a paroxysm of selfish fear, which had its natural fruit in cowardly and atrocious cruelty. The contrast of their own feeble policy with the energy of the Athenians made them sink lower in their own esteem; and their expectations for the future were not of victory but of disaster. Whether such a state as Sparta was worth the saving, is another question; but there is little doubt that it must have fallen had it not been for the singularly un-Spartan genius of Brasidas. This eminent man saw that only a diversion of the Athenian forces to a distant scene would loosen the iron grasp in which they now held the Peloponnesos; and such a diversion was rendered possible by invitations which came at this time from the Chalkidic towns (G.P. p. 30), as well as from the faithless Makedonian chief Perdikkas. These invitations were accompanied by offers to maintain any Spartan force which might be sent to aid the towns in their design of revolt against Athens. The Spartans eagerly intrusted the task to Brasidas, and still more eagerly seized the opportunity of getting rid of another large body of Helots. Seven hundred were armed as hoplites; and the mere fact that after the slaughter of the 2,000 these did not take dire vengeance after they crossed the Lakonian border, or at the least desert to the Athenians rather than face them in battle, might lead us to think that the story of that horrible massacre was only a dream.

Designs of Brasidas.

Before Brasidas could get together his Peloponnesian allies for their northern march, his presence was wanted nearer home. The minority which, even when Megara had revolted from the great city, had felt that union with Athens was better than independence under an oligarchy, now concerted, with the Athenian generals Hippokrates and Demosthenes, a plan for the surrender of the city. This plan was betrayed, and the Athenians, bringing tools and workmen from Athens, had all but succeeded in walling in the port of Nisaia (p. 29), when Brasidas presented himself at the gates of Megara and demanded admittance; but both the parties within the city were now on their guard, and resolved to admit no

Failure of the plans for surrendering Megara to the Athenians.

one, until one or other side should have gained a decisive victory. Rightly divining the reason of his exclusion, Brasidas advanced towards the sea, and offered battle; but the Athenian generals doubted whether they could run the risk of a defeat, which would be most severely felt, in order to encounter a force levied from many Peloponnesian cities, which would lose at the worst only a small fraction of their troops. They had, moreover, already gained Nisaia, and cut off the connexion of Megara with its long walls. They abandoned, therefore, all further attempts on Megara itself, and its gates were at once opened to admit the army of Brasidas. Before the end of the year the Megarians obtained possession of their long walls, and levelled them with the ground.

The enterprise of Brasidas should have awakened the Athenians forthwith to a sense of the paramount need of baffling it at all costs. His success would undo all the results gained by the occupation of Pylos and the seizure of Kythera. But far from fixing their whole mind on this task, they were dreaming of restoring their supremacy in Boiotia, which they had lost by the battle of Koroneia; and they were full of hope on finding that in many of the Boiotian cities there were not a few who would gladly free themselves from the heavy yoke of the Eupatrid houses. By the help of these natural allies of Athens, it was arranged that Demosthenes should sail from Naupaktos to Siphai at the eastern end of the Corinthian gulf. Thus gaining a footing in the south, they would in the north have a like advantage by being admitted into Chaironeia, while in the east they would have even a stronger base of operations by fortifying the sacred ground of the Delion, or temple of Phoibos Apollon. The success of this plan depended on the exactness of its execution; and unhappily the Athenian

Schemes of the Athenians for the recovery of their supremacy in Boiotia.

commanders were not punctual. Arriving at Siphai, Demosthenes found that the plot had been betrayed, and that both Siphai and Chaironeia were held by the Boiotians in full force. In spite of this discovery, 20,000 men set out from Athens to fortify the Delion. In five days Hippokrates had practically done the work; but these five days were fatal to his enterprise. Hurrying towards Delion, the Boiotian troops found that the main body of the enemy had crossed the border; but the scruples which they felt about attacking them on Attic soil were speedily removed by the Boiotarch Pagondas, who told them that the Athenians were their enemies wherever they might be, and professed his inability to understand the subtle distinctions which forbade them to encounter an enemy on his own ground. It was late in the day: but they resolved to fight at once. The Theban hoplites were drawn up twenty five men deep; the Athenian front had a depth of only eight men. The contrast points to a growing consciousness that with opposing forces consisting of men equal in strength, bravery, and discipline, weight must determine the event. The battle which followed was fiercely contested; but a body of Thebans, whom Pagondas had sent round a hill, appeared suddenly before the Athenians, and threw them into a confusion which soon became irretrievable. Nearly 1,000 Athenian hoplites, with their general, Hippokrates, lay dead on the field, which the Thebans carefully guarded, while they made ready for the assault of Delion on the following day.

Battle of Delion.

After the battle an Athenian herald, coming to demand the bodies of the dead for burial, was met by a Boiotian herald, who, going back with him to Delion, charged the Athenians with profaning a sacred site, and added that the dead should not be restored to them until they had evacuated

Storming of the fort at Delion.

the Temenos, or close of the god. The obvious rejoinder, that Hellenic law allowed no conditions to be interposed for the burial of the dead, must have been followed by the surrender of the bodies; but the Athenians chose rather to say that as they had occupied the ground, the shrine built on it was Attic property, and therefore could not be profaned by them, and that, being thus in their own territory, the Athenians could not be asked to abandon it. To this absurd plea the Boiotians might have retorted that the conquest of a whole country carrying with it the temples raised within its borders was a very different thing from the occupation of a single sanctuary as a base of operations against the territory to which it belonged. But the temptation to repay the Athenians in their own coin was too strong to be resisted, and the Boiotians replied that if the Athenians were in their own land, they could take what they wanted without asking leave of anyone. Even here the Athenians might have insisted that Attica did not extend beyond their intrenchments, and therefore that the dead must be yielded up unconditionally. But this reply was not made, and the Boiotians proceeded at once to attack the Athenian fortifications. These, built chiefly of wood, were set on fire by means of a large beam which, being hollowed out, served as a tube through which a current of air was forced from bellows at one end to a cauldron containing charcoal and sulphur, fastened by strong iron chains at the other end. The garrison fled, and the fort was taken; and when the Athenian herald again appeared, the bodies of the dead were surrendered without further demur. So ended a scheme which, so long as Brasidas was at large, ought never to have been taken in hand. By thus wasting their energies they enabled that vigilant leader to reach Thessaly, and, in spite of the leaning of the main

March of Brasidas through Thessaly.

body of the people to the Athenian side, to carry his army through it into Makedonia; nor until he had achieved this task were they awakened to a sense of their danger. Even then they merely declared war against Perdikkas— a superfluous manifesto against a chief who passed his life in betraying or deserting all his allies in turn. Nothing can show more clearly the fatal loss sustained by Athens in the death of Perikles than the weakness now displayed in their measures for maintaining that which they knew to be the very foundation of their empire. We may well doubt whether Perikles would have approved either of the attempts made by Demosthenes to re-establish the supremacy of Athens in Boiotia: that he would have staked the whole power of the state in encountering and crushing Brasidas is not to be doubted at all.

The grapes were all but ready for the gathering, and the produce of the year was therefore at his mercy, when Brasidas appeared before the gates of Akanthos, at the base of the great peninsula of Aktê, or Athos. He had looked for the eager welcome promised to him by the Chalkidian oligarchs: he was surprised to find that the gates were guarded, and that he could do no more than pray for permission to plead his cause before the Akanthians in person. With this request the demos, whose whole substance was in his hands, reluctantly complied. His business was to convince them that they could secure their own welfare only by revolting from Athens; and he proceeded to address them after the following fashion. Assuring them that Sparta was honestly anxious to confine itself to the one task of putting down an iniquitous tyranny, he told them that he had come to set them free, and was amazed at not finding himself welcomed with open arms. He could not allow them to slight the proffered boon. Their refusal would tempt the other allies of Athens to think

Appearance of Brasidas at Akanthos.

that the freedom which he promised was visionary, or that his power to secure it was not equal to his will. But when he sought to win their confidence by assuring them that he had bound the Ephors by solemn oaths that they should allow all the cities which might join him to remain absolutely autonomous, it may not have struck him that the need of imposing such oaths might leave on others the impression that the Spartan magistrates were not much to be trusted without them. He had, however, two further arguments in store—the one addressed to that centrifugal instinct which pre-eminently marked the Hellenic race in general, the other to their purses. He assured them that when he spoke to them of freedom, his words were to be taken in their literal meaning, and not as denoting merely liberation from the yoke of Athens. They were to be left absolutely to themselves, and they were free now to decide whether they would or would not join Sparta. But if they should say him nay, their ripe grapes would be trampled under foot and their vineyards ravaged. This special pleading carried so much weight, that a majority of the citizens, voting secretly, decided on revolt from Athens. The farce of free debate and free voting was ended, and Stageiros soon followed the example of Akanthos in revolting from Athens.

A few weeks later Brasidas appeared before the walls of Amphipolis (p. 39), a post as easily defensible by the Athenians as it was important. On no object could time, care, and money have been better bestowed than on the safe keeping of this key to two vast regions: by a mournful infatuation it was allowed to fall without a struggle into the hands of Brasidas. On a stormy and snowy night the inhabitants learnt that his army was under their walls, and that their lands, and all who happened to be without the city, were at his mercy. In spite of this, the citizens not only insisted

Occupation of Amphipolis by Brasidas.

that the gates should be kept shut, but that the Athenian general Eukles should send a request for immediate aid to his colleague Thucydides, the historian, who was then with his fleet off the island of Thasos, about half a day's sail from Amphipolis. Hurrying thither with all speed, he found that Brasidas had been before him. Feeling the importance of securing Amphipolis at all cost, the Spartan leader offered the full rights of citizenship to all who might choose to remain; to those who preferred to depart he allowed five days for the removal of their property. The terms were accepted, and in another twenty-four hours the Spartans would have been masters of Eion also; but in the evening of the same day the seven ships of Thucydides entered the mouth of the Strymon, and this fresh humiliation was avoided. The care with which he points out the greatness of the danger from which his arrival saved the city, betrays the anxiety of a man who wishes to place himself right with those whose severer judgement he has good cause to fear.

We can scarcely lay too much stress on the fact that in both these towns of Akanthos and Amphipolis the majority of the people is disinclined to alliance with Sparta, and that in neither case is free debate or free voting allowed. No more conclusive evidence could be desired in favour of the imperial city than that which is furnished by the whole history of the campaign. If, in spite of the reiterated promises of Brasidas that there should be no interference whatever with their management of their internal affairs, their opposition was with difficulty overcome, the conclusion follows that, apart from the passion for inter-political independence, the subject-allies of Athens had no special grievance calling for redress. Had they been oppressed by a tribute beyond their means to pay; had they been preyed on by collectors who drew from them sums beyond the defined assessment; had the means of

Lightness of the imperial yoke of Athens.

redress for injuries committed been denied to them or rendered difficult, they must assuredly have thrown themselves into the arms of Brasidas with a feeling of thankfulness that any change must be for the better. But, as we have seen (pp. 4, 27), the imperial yoke of Athens pressed on the allies as a sentimental rather than as a real grievance; and it was precisely thus at Akanthos and Amphipolis. There was no positive love for Athens; but as they felt that their connexion with her was on the whole to their own benefit, they were not carried away by enthusiastic admiration of a stranger, who simply promised to leave them in a state of complete isolation; and the introduction of Brasidas was brought about only by the intrigues of a small but overbearing faction, which resolved to hurry the people into revolt under pain of ruin in case of refusal. Even thus, it is asserted, Amphipolis would have remained true to Athens, if there had been good reason for thinking that a few hours would bring to them the aid of Thucydides.

The tidings of the revolt of Amphipolis filled Athens with dismay. The place was, in fact, the key to their Thrakian possessions, and the loss of this position increased the readiness of the allies to revolt as much as it lowered the reputation of Athens. *Punishment of Thucydides.* The urgency of the peril seemed rather to paralyse the Athenians than to rouse them Nothing was done beyond despatching a few troops to reinforce the garrisons in the Thraceward cities; and further disasters were averted only by the reluctance of the Spartans to encourage schemes which probably they did not very clearly understand. The story went that Kleon accused Thucydides of incapacity or wilful mismanagement, and that the historian, failing to defend himself, was sentenced to banishment. From his own words, we do not learn that he was formally sentenced at all; but he admits that he spent twenty years in exile, and his silence on the share of Kleon in the matter seems to attest the self-condemnation of the general. Had he felt the injustice of the charge and the sentence, Thucydides was not the man to rest quiet under an iniquitous imputation. Far from defending himself, he leaves the facts to speak for themselves, and these show that he was one of the generals appointed to watch over the interests of Athens in Makedonia and Thrace; that his duty demanded his presence at Amphipolis, or at the least at Eion, which was only three miles further to the south; that he is found with his squadron off Thasos, an island which Brasidas could not attack, because he had no ships; and that he was cruising off Thasos because his personal interests attracted him to the Thrakian gold mines of which he was a proprietor. That on hearing of the loss of Amphipolis he hastened to prevent the loss of Eion, in no way lessens his fault. No one knew better than he that a general who had failed to keep a post intrusted to him when with common care he might easily have kept it, is in no way more deserving of acquittal because he succeeds in preserving another post which but for his previous negligence would never have been endangered. In this instance, if Kleon had anything to do with the matter, he was perfectly right. Amphipolis was lost only through the carelessness of Thucydides and his colleague; and the absence of Thucydides from his post must be set down to a preference of his own interests over those of his country.

The prospects of the Athenians were growing more and more dark; but the tale of the exploits of Brasidas was not yet full, and before the year ended they were to lose Torônê, a town lying on the slope of a steep hill at the extreme end of the Sithonian peninsula of Chalkidike. This place Brasidas won, chiefly by assuring the inhabitants

Truce for one year between Sparta and Athens.
B.C. 423.

that thus far they had not been free agents, that he was come to give them liberty whether they liked it or not, and that those who opposed him should share the blessing not less than his most zealous partisans. In the following year his schemes were damped by his countrymen, who feared that his success might be for them scarcely less disastrous than his failure. The latter would assuredly assign either to death or to hopeless captivity the Sphakterian hoplites, for whose rescue they were most of all anxious: the former would probably bring them nothing more than they could now win without risk. Eager, therefore, to do all that they could to bring about a lasting peace, the Spartans agreed to a truce for one year on the general principle that each side should retain its present possessions.

But if the Athenians hoped that the truce would tie the hands of Brasidas they speedily found themselves mistaken. The Spartan faction in Skiônê managed to coerce those who were opposed to revolt, and to send him an invitation which he eagerly accepted. The campaign of Brasidas had now acquired a romantic character; and when he told the Skionaians that their boldness in defying Athens would be rewarded by the special confidence and esteem of the Spartans, they were carried away by their enthusiasm. In the public assembly a golden diadem was placed on the head of the deliverer of Hellas: in private houses he was crowned as an athlete who had reached the highest standard of Hellenic humanity. In the midst of these rejoicings the Spartan and Athenian commissioners arrived to announce the truce. After reckoning up the time, the Athenian commissioners refused to recognize the revolt of Skiônê as coming within the terms of the treaty; and Brasidas boldly antedated the day of its defection. His falsehood was believed at Sparta: at Athens it

Revolt of Skiônê.

aroused an indignation which made it easy for Kleon to obtain a decree, carried out two years later, dooming the Skionaians to the punishment which had been all but carried out at Mytilene (p. 69).

From these enterprises among the subject-allies of Athens Brasidas was called away by the terms of his contract with Perdikkas, to an expedition against the Lynkestian chief, Arrhibaios. But Perdikkas, dismayed at learning that a force of Illyrians, whom he had hired to serve against the Lynkestai, had transferred themselves to his enemy, retreated in all haste, leaving Brasidas to shift for himself. Here, as before, Spartan discipline and bravery prevailed against overwhelming odds; but the revenge taken by the Peloponnesians on the beasts of burden and baggage train left behind by the Makedonians so alienated Perdikkas that he resolved once more to seek the alliance of the Athenians, whom he had more than once betrayed. During his absence the Athenians had stirred themselves to more vigorous action; and Nikias had arrived with a fleet of fifty ships before Mendê, which had followed the example of Torônê. His arrival gave strength to the philo-Athenian party; and when the Spartan commander ordered the Mendaians to sally out against the enemy he was met by passive resistance. In an evil moment he ordered the arrest of a citizen who cried out that he had no intention of serving against the Athenians, and that the war was only a luxury for the rich. This insult drove the demos to seize their arms; and the Athenians, admitted within the town, left to the judgement of the Mendaians those citizens whom they suspected to be the authors of the revolt.

Recovery of Mendê by the Athenians.

The defection of Perdikkas from the Spartan side came opportunely for the Athenians. His experience of his lies had shown Nikias how he should be dealt with.

He was therefore told that, if he desired the friendship of Athens, he must prove that he really meant what he said. Happily for the Athenians, he could do this and gratify his resentment against Brasidas at the same time. The reinforcement for which Brasidas had so long and so earnestly prayed was known to be on its way from the Peloponnesos; and a message from Perdikkas to the Thessalian chiefs cut short its march. *Alliance of Perdikkas with the Athenians.*

The year's truce had come to an end; but so anxious were both sides for peace, or so indifferent were the Spartans to the schemes of Brasidas, that nothing was done until after the celebration of the Pythian games. No sooner, however, were these ended than we find Kleon in command of a fleet which Perikles would most certainly have sent to Thrace two years earlier, before Brasidas had crossed the Thessalian border. The facts to be noted are these: that after an interval of three years a man, who, in the public assembly of Athens, had candidly confessed his incompetence for military command (p. 82), and who had been successful at Pylos merely because he had had the sound sense to subordinate himself to a leader of real genius, is now sent on a far more dangerous service without the aid of such a colleague as Demosthenes. Why Demosthenes did not accompany him we are not told. He may at this time have been on his old station at Naupaktos; and in this case the state of things at Athens becomes clear enough. Had Perikles lived he must have insisted that the full strength of Athens should be put forth instantly for the recovery of Amphipolis. But, throwing cold water on a policy which would have been not less prudent than vigorous, Nikias and his adherents had insisted that the schemes of Brasidas would most easily be foiled, not by sending out armies to fight him, but by *Expedition of Kleon to Makedonia. B.C. 422.*

making peace with Sparta. But Kleon cannot have failed to see that Brasidas had utterly disregarded the current truce, and therefore that there was no sound reason for thinking that he would respect a contract for a permanent peace. In truth, the mere fact that Kleon, whose non-employment since the capture of Pylos proves that he had not sought employment, was now sent to command on the Thrakian coasts, shows that the old trick (p. 82) of Nikias and his adherents was repeated. The shameful policy which regarded his downfall as of more importance than the welfare of Athens, had been openly asserted before he set off for Pylos ; and the language of Thucydides justifies the conclusion that they were prompted by the same disgraceful motives now. We may therefore safely infer that Kleon went to Thrace merely because Nikias would not go. Throughout the whole quarrel the conduct of Nikias forebodes the crimes and the misery of which oligarchical selfishness was soon to yield at Athens an abundant and fatal harvest.

Leaving Peiraieus long after the summer solstice, Kleon succeeded in wresting Torônê from Brasidas, the fall of the city being followed by the slaughter or captivity of the men and the selling of the women and children into slavery. But the real object of his expedition was the recovery of Amphipolis; and Kleon dared not attack the town without reinforcements from Perdikkas. While he was awaiting these at Eion, Brasidas took up his post on the hill of Kerdylion, on the western bank of the river facing the city. He knew that the Athenians had no confidence in their general, and that they resented his inaction; he could afford, therefore, to wait patiently for an opportunity of surprising him when discontent and want of discipline had thrown his army into sufficient disorder. Blunder after blunder followed ; but the disgrace of these blunders

Battle of Amphipolis. Death of Brasidas and of Kleon.

lies not with Kleon so much as with those who sent him on an errand which he would far rather have seen intrusted to others. Whatever they were, we see them at their worst, for he had a merciless critic in the historian whom he helped to drive away from his country. Kleon, it is clear, was wholly at a loss how to act. His men were becoming impatient, and he was driven at last to the course which led him to success at Pylos. This course was seemingly nothing more than marching uphill for the purpose of marching down again; and even this manœuvre, the historian adds with supreme contempt, Kleon regarded as a thing worth knowing. The wall of Amphipolis ran across the ridge which rises to the eastward until it joins the Pangaian range. This ridge Kleon ascended; but no sooner was his army in movement than Brasidas entered the city by the bridge over the Strymon, his object being to dupe Kleon by that semblance of inactivity and inability to act which for a wary general would carry with it the strongest suspicion. On reaching the top of the bridge, which commanded an unbroken view of the city and the river, Kleon was impressed by the silence and quiet of the scene. Through the vast extent of country which he surveyed no bodies of men were to be seen in motion; not a man was visible on the walls, not a sign betokened preparation for battle. Brasidas was offering sacrifice before sallying forth against the enemy. This ceremony was seen by the scouts of Kleon, who also told him that under the city gates they could discern the feet of horses and men ready to issue out for battle. Having satisfied himself of the truth of these tidings, Kleon fatally resolved to retreat to Eion. He had, in fact, no one to guide him, and his incompetence, which he had never sought to hide, now produced its natural result. Wheeling to the left, his army began its southward march, leaving the right, or unshielded, side open to the enemy. 'These men will never withstand our onset,' said Brasidas : 'look at their quivering spears and nodding heads. Men who are going to fight never march in such a fashion as this. Open the gates at once, that I may rush out on them forthwith.' The sudden onslaught broke the Athenian ranks; but in the pursuit of the Athenian left wing Brasidas fell, mortally wounded. On the right wing the resistance of the Athenians was more firm; but Kleon, it is said, had come without any intention of fighting, and he soon made up his mind to run away. Flight, however, is more easily thought of than accomplished; and Kleon, abandoning his men, was slain by a Myrkinian peltast. So says Thucydides; but the strong bias of his narrative may fairly lead us to suspect that his end was not so ignominious as he describes it to have been. Brasidas lived just long enough to know that the Athenians were defeated; and the career of this thoroughly un-Spartan champion of Sparta was closed with a public funeral in the Agora of Amphipolis, where he received yearly henceforth the honours of a deified hero. The buildings raised by Hagnon (p. 39) were thrown down; and Brasidas was venerated as the founder of the city.

Thus were removed the two great hindrances to peace between Athens and Sparta: but Thucydides makes no effort to show that peace, at the cost of sacrifices which Kleon was not willing to make, was at this time to be desired for Athens, or that the line taken by Nikias and his partisans was one which Perikles would have approved; nor, indeed, does he ask whether it is one against which Perikles would have protested as involving virtual treason. Happily the unswerving honesty which never allows him to suppress facts has shown us that, when Kleon charged the first Spartan envoys with deliberate duplicity, he was

Merits of the policy of Kleon.

disgracing himself and running a risk of fatally injuring Athens (p. 80); that, when the truce was once broken, he was perfectly right in insisting that at whatever cost the Spartan hoplites in Sphakteria should be brought prisoners to Athens (p. 82); that he was again wrong when, after they had been so brought, he hindered the settlement of peace by imposing conditions too exacting and severe (p. 84); and, finally, that he was from first to last more than justified in insisting that Brasidas must be encountered and put down in Thrace (p. 97). That he was left to carry out this policy by himself was his misfortune, not his fault: that he was feebly supported at Athens and sent without competent colleagues to Thrace, redounds not to his own shame but to that of his adversaries.

The negotiations for peace were now resumed in earnest; but it was not without difficulty that, according to the arrangement, probably, of Nikias, by whose name this peace is generally known, the contending parties agreed each to give up what they had acquired during the war. The Athenians thought that they should thus regain Plataia; but we have seen that the Spartans had provided against this by the subterfuge of a voluntary surrender (p. 70). They remembered, however, that if the Thebans had a right to hold Plataia, they had a right to retain Nisaia (p. 29), and they refused accordingly to give it up. By the terms of the peace, which was to last for fifty years, Sparta was to restore Amphipolis, while Athens was to leave independent all towns in Chalkidikê which had put themselves under the protection of Brasidas, subject to their paying to Athens the tribute due by the assessment of Aristeides (p. 18). On their part the Athenians, who were to receive back all prisoners in the hands of the Spartans or their allies, were to restore all captives

The peace of Nikias. B.C. 421.

belonging to Sparta or any city of her confederacy, as well as to surrender Pylos and Kythera. But it was now to be seen that though the Spartans might make promises in the name of their allies, they could not insure their fulfilment. The Boiotians, as being constrained to give up Panakton, (a fort which they had seized in the preceding year), the Megarians (as not recovering Nisaia), and the Corinthians, would have nothing to do with the treaty. More than all, the Chalkidians would not give up Amphipolis, and the Spartan general Klearidas declared that he had not the means of compelling them.

The Spartans were thus discredited with their allies, and they had a further cause for anxiety in the fact that the truce for thirty years with Argos was drawing to a close. It was, therefore, of great importance to prevent an alliance between Athens and Argos which might restore to the latter her ancient supremacy in the Peloponnesos. A special arrangement hurriedly made with the Athenians pledged Athens and Sparta to defend each the other's territories against all invaders, and bound the former to put down all risings of the Helots,—in other words, to put an effectual restraint on the Messenians at Pylos. Even this would have been a concession far too great for this practically worthless alliance which Sparta offered in mere fear of Argos; but so great was the value which Nikias and his partisans professed to put upon it that they induced the Athenians to surrender the hoplites taken at Sphakteria. Such were the firstfruits which Athens received from the philo-Lakonian policy of her oligarchic citizens. She was now practically ruled by those who prided themselves on being nobly born and nobly bred; and these statesmen set to work to deprive her of one advantage after the other, offering her in their stead

<small>Failure of the Spartans to carry out the terms for the peace.</small>

<small>Surrender of the Spartan hoplites taken at Sphakteria.</small>

apples of the Dead Sea. Nothing can excuse the weakness which could dispense with all tests for trying the sincerity of the Spartans. The continued detention of the Pylian prisoners and a demand that a combined Athenian and Spartan force should be sent to reduce Amphipolis, would at once have compelled the Spartans to show themselves in their true colours, or, as is far more likely, have secured to Athens all that she wanted. As it was, the terms of the peace were not kept on either side; and the period which followed until the open resumption of the war was at best no more than a time of truce. Hence the whole period of twenty-seven years from the surprise of Plataia by the Thebans to the surrender of Athens is rightly regarded by Thucydides as being taken up with one persistent struggle.

In the irritation of the moment the offended allies of Sparta turned naturally to Argos with the language of flattery to which the Argives had been long unaccustomed. The confederacy to which the latter accordingly invited all autonomous Peloponnesian cities was joined in the first instance by Mantineia, then by the Eleians, and lastly by the Corinthians, whose zeal was suddenly damped on learning that Tegea refused to share the new alliance. The politics of the leading Greek states now assume that complicated form which must result from the conflicting interests of a large number of autonomous cities seeking each its own supposed welfare alone. Among the tortuous intrigues which mark this time, we may note the engagement made privately between the Spartans and the Boiotians, who without this compact refused to surrender Panakton. The Spartans could not rest without regaining Pylos: and as the possession of Panakton was insisted on by the Athenians as an indispensable preliminary, the Spartans ended the

Formation of a new Argive confederacy.

eleventh year of the great struggle with a measure which looked like deliberate treachery to the Athenians, to whom they were pledged to make no engagements without their knowledge and consent. The Boiotians, however, were resolved that no Athenian force should occupy the fort, and they spent the winter in levelling it with the ground. Much as they were annoyed at a deed which vastly increased the difficulty of their task the Spartans still had the assurance to send envoys to demand from the Athenians the surrender of Pylos on the ground that the surrender of a site was equivalent to the surrender of the fort which had been built upon it. But the Athenians were not in the mood for further fooling, and the envoys were dismissed after a reception which showed the depth of their indignation.

This feeling was diligently fostered by Alkibiades, the son of Kleinias, who fell at Koroneia (p. 34), and the

Beginning of the public life of Alkibiades.

grandson of that Alkibiades who had been one of the most strenuous opponents of the Peisistratidai. To the possession of vast wealth this man added a readiness of wit, a fertility of invention, a power of complaisance, which invested his manner, when he wished to please, with a singular charm. Magnificent in his tastes, and revelling in the elegance of the most refined Athenian luxury, Alkibiades shrunk from no hardship in war, and faced danger with a bravery which was above cavil or question. He has been compared with Themistokles : but few comparisons could be more unjust. Professing no austere righteousness, Themistokles yet from first to last promoted the best interests of his country with unswerving steadiness, and carried out one uniform policy which laid the foundations of the Athenian empire, and continued to sustain its greatness. Alkibiades had no policy. Hating a demos in his heart, he was, nevertheless, as ready to destroy an oligarchy as to uproot a free constitution, and he was therefore justly dreaded by men of all political parties as one treading in the paths of the old Hellenic despots. To commit the people to his plans, he could act or utter a lie with only a feeling of self-complacence at his own cleverness. Utterly selfish and unscrupulous, Alkibiades, in company with scoundrels like Kritias, sought the conversation of Sokrates; but the society of this wonderful man only made him more dangerous; and if we are to believe the stories told of him, his youthful career was one unbroken course of gilded sensuality and of barbarous ruffianism, hidden by a veil of superficial refinement. Under any circumstances, such a man must be infamous; but Alkibiades had opportunities of committing crime on a vast scale, and he availed himself of them to the utmost.

To such a man a slight was a deadly offence, and Alkibiades had received a marked slight from the Spartans. His courtesies to their prisoners had not only called forth no public recognition, but had seemingly been forgotten even by the ransomed men. He therefore discovered that *Deception of the Spartan envoys by Alkibiades.* the true means for restoring the preponderance of Athens was to bring about an alliance with Argos. By his advice, accordingly, envoys from Argos appeared at Athens in company with others from Mantineia and Elis. At the same time came a counter-embassy from Sparta; and the fears of Alkibiades for his new scheme were roused by their saying before the senate that they had full power for the immediate settlement of all differences. Such a statement, made before the assembly, would jeopardise his alliance with Argos. It must not therefore be made. Warning them that this profession might subject them to troublesome demands and importunities, he pledged himself to secure for them the possession of Pylos and to plead their cause before the people, if they would claim no further mission than that of envoys charged only to report the wishes of the Athenians. The Spartans fell into the snare. The answer, given according to his prompting, roused the deep resentment of hearers who could hardly believe their senses. More vehement than all the rest, Alkibiades burst into invectives against Spartan shuffling and lying, and was proposing that the Argive envoys should at once be admitted to an audience, when an earthquake caused the adjournment of the assembly.

When the assembly met on the following day, Nikias insisted successfully that important interests were not to be rashly thrown aside, and that if alliance with Sparta was to the interest of Athens, it was their duty to send commissioners to ascertain the real intentions of the Spartans. Sent thither himself, he could obtain nothing more than the declaration that they were ready to renew the oaths of the covenant with Athens. Dispensing with a superfluous and useless ceremony, he returned to find the Athenians ready to effect with Argos, Mantineia, and Elis a defensive alliance which distinctly recognised the imperial character of each of these states, thus introducing into the Peloponnesos relations among the allies or former subjects of the Spartans which the Spartans could not consistently tolerate and the existence of which they would prefer not to acknowledge.

Defensive alliance between Athens, Argos, Elis, and Mantineia.

Under the guidance of Alkibiades, Athens was rapidly committing herself to schemes which completely reversed the policy of Perikles. New conquests alone could satisfy him, and the paramount need of re-establishing the Athenian empire in Chalkidikê was put aside for the acquisition of a new supremacy in the Peloponnesos. Of the schemes which he set on foot for this purpose, it cannot

Interference of Alkibiades in Peloponnesos. B.C. 419.

be said that any one brought any gain to Athens, while all tended to keep up and to multiply occasions of strife between the chief Peloponnesian cities. The first of these enterprises was the building of long walls to bring the Achaian Patrai within the protection of an Athenian fleet; the second the erection on the Achaian Rhion of a fortress which might serve as another Pylos. No sooner had both these schemes been foiled by the Corinthians and Sikyonians than Alkibiades discovered that the occupation of Epidauros would be greatly to the advantage of Athens, and therefore he stirred up the Argives to the invasion of its territory. Irritated with this warfare, which really broke while it nominally respected the peace, the Spartans during the winter smuggled a force into Epidauros; and the Argives complained at Athens that the clause of the treaty between them which asserted that neither side should allow hostile forces to pass through their territory had been violated. The Spartans had conveyed these men by sea, and the sea was specially the dominion of Athens. Pleased with this flattery, the Athenians readily adopted the suggestion of the Argives, that, by way of punishing the Spartans, the Messenians and the Helots should be brought back to Pylos, a note explaining the reason for this step being added to the inscription on the pillar of peace at Athens.

But the Spartans now saw that vigorous efforts were needed, if they would prevent their confederacy from falling to pieces; and they resolved accordingly to inflict summary chastisement on the Argives. A simultaneous invasion of Corinthian and Spartan forces from two different quarters caught the Argives in front and rear. *Spartan and Corinthian invasion of Argos. B.C. 418.* The latter, far from fearing the destruction which, if they fought, was really inevitable, saw in their desperate position only an opportunity for taking ample revenge upon their enemies, and were fiercely indignant when at the last moment two of their generals, who saw how they were placed, obtained from the Spartan king Agis a truce for four months. Thus, instead of paying the penalty for their misdeeds, the Argives were left free to listen to the oratory of Alkibiades, who urged them on, in spite of the covenant just made, to attack the Arkadian Orchomenos, which speedily surrendered to the combined forces of the Argives, Eleians, Mantineians, and Athenians. The Eleians now wished to attack Lepreon: the Mantineians were anxious to assail the more powerful town of Tegea, where a minority desired to throw off the alliance with Sparta. The Mantineians would not give way, and the Eleians went home. Thus hard was the task of securing the joint action of a number of autonomous city communities.

These events excited at Sparta so deep an indignation against Agis that he narrowly escaped a sentence fining him 100,000 drachmas and decreeing that his house should be razed to its foundations. Asking only that he might be allowed an opportunity of redeeming his past error before the punishment was inflicted, he hastened, with a rapidity never yet matched by any Spartan leader, to the aid of the Tegeans, who sent to say that only instant help could prevent the loss of their city to the Spartan confederacy. Finding the Argives posted on a steep and precipitous eminence, he was about to attack them without further thought, when a veteran cited in his hearing the old proverb of healing evil by evil. The retreat of the Spartan king again awakened the resentment of the Argives, who thought that their generals had been allowing their prey to slip once more from their grasp; and the latter, taught by the peril which they had lately escaped, led their forces down to the plain. On this ground on

The battle of Mantineia.

the following day was fought a battle which Thucydides describes with such singular minuteness and exactness of detail as to justify the conclusion that he must have been an eye-witness. The partial victory of the Mantineians, with the Argive regiment of One Thousand on the right wing, was followed or accompanied by a crushing defeat of the other allies, with the Athenians and their cavalry on the left. The result did away with the impression which the surrender of the hoplites at Sphakteria had almost everywhere created; and it was at once acknowledged that, although they may have been unfortunate, Spartan courage was as great and Spartan discipline as effective as ever.

The battle had further consequences at Argos. The Thousand Regiment had really been victorious in the fight: the demos had been shamefully beaten. The former, representing the oligarchic party, resolved on allying themselves with Sparta, and with their approval the Spartans offered the Argives either war or a treaty, which was sent to them already drawn up, binding them to restore to Sparta such hostages as might be in their keeping, and to evacuate Epidauros. A further covenant declared the autonomy of all allies whether of the Argives or of the Spartans, while questions of peace or war were to be decided by the common vote of Sparta and Argos, which was to be binding on their allies. This treaty, which nominally allowed the imperial character of the Argive state, re-established in fact the supremacy of Sparta; and the Mantineians, seeing that they could no longer inforce their claim to supremacy over their allies, joined once more the confederacy of Sparta. The year closed with the upsetting of the democratic constitution at Argos, and the establishment at Sikyon of a stricter oligarchy than that which had thus far prevailed there.

Establishment of oligarchy at Argos by the Spartans.

But the fabric thus raised stood on insecure foundations. The insolence of the Thousand at Argos became intolerable. The demos was restored; the alliance with Athens was renewed; and the people set to work to connect the city by long walls with the sea. The completion of this design would have enabled Argos to bid defiance to the attacks of any land army, as the Athenians could pour in from the sea any supplies which might be needed. But the oligarchic party was not rooted out; and receiving promises of help which were not fulfilled, Agis, unable to enter Argos, levelled the long walls with the ground.

<small>Restoration of democracy at Argos. B.C. 417.</small>

A seeming revival of vigour marked the conduct of the Athenians during the ensuing winter. Seeing now that Amphipolis, if it was to be recovered at all, must be recovered by force, Nikias and his adherents urged an expedition, subject to the co-operation of a chief whose only gifts to Athens had been confined, in the words of the comic poet, to shiploads of lies. Perdikkas, of course, failed to keep his engagements; the enterprise was abandoned; and the strength which might have recovered Amphipolis was put forth in the following year for the destruction of a petty township in the island of Melos. This place, a colony from Sparta, had never been included in the Athenian confederacy (p. 4); and if force was to be employed to bring them within it, this force should have been used in the days of Aristeides, and not now, when a long war with Sparta had materially altered the complexion of the case. But in the sixteenth year of the war Nikias appeared before the city, and on the refusal of the Melians to become allies of Athens, proceeded to blockade it. Time went on; no help came from Sparta; and plots were discovered for betraying the place to the

<small>Unsuccessful attempt of the Athenians to recover Amphipolis.</small>

<small>Massacre of Melos. B.C. 416.</small>

Athenians. The Melians resolved to anticipate them by unconditional surrender; and their recompense for so doing was the murder of all the grown men and the selling of the women and children into slavery. But the case of the Melians is obviously quite different from that of the Mytilenaians, who were threatened with the same punishment, or of the Skionaians, on whom it was actually inflicted (p. 96). The Melians had done the Athenians no specific wrong; and the worst charge that could have been urged against them was that they shared in the benefits arising from the Athenian confederacy and empire without sharing (if such was the fact) the burdens necessary for its maintenance. But according to the elaborate report given by Thucydides of the conference which preceded the siege, the arguments urged by the Athenians in justification of their attack were of a totally different kind. The Athenians had pre-eminently the reputation of people who were always disposed to call ugly things by pretty names; and even average Greeks sought to throw over deeds of wanton iniquity a veil of decency, even if they could not pass them off as righteous and equitable. Least of all in the history of Athens generally do we find the temper which glories in the exertion of naked brute force and delights to insult and defy the moral instincts of mankind. But in the conference which precedes the siege and massacre of Melos we have precisely this temper; and the Athenians are represented as trampling on all seemliness of word and action, as asserting an independence which raises them above all law, and as boasting that iniquity to the weak can do the strong no harm. In short, the whole spirit of this conference stands out in glaring contrast not merely with the earlier Athenian history but with that which follows it. When we remember, further, that the massacre at Melos was a political crime, greater, certainly, and more atrocious than any of which they had yet been guilty,—that it brought them no gain while it insured a bitter harvest of hatred,—and that this horrible and infatuated crime preceded only by a few months the fatal expedition to Sicily, we can scarcely doubt that in his account of this conference the historian has for once left us not a record of fact, but a moral picture such as that which Herodotos has drawn of the Persian despot in his overweening arrogance and pride. From this time forward the strength of Athens was to be turned aside to impracticable tasks, in which even absolute success could scarcely bring a gain proportioned to the outlay, and the affairs of the city were to be conducted in the gambling spirit which stakes continually increasing sums in the hope of retrieving past losses. The supposed conference vividly inforces this contrast; and although Thucydides nowhere mentions his name in connexion with this crime, the arguments put into the mouths of the Athenians are just those might have come from Alkibiades, who is said by Plutarch to have vehemently urged on the massacre. The conduct thus ascribed to him was a fitting prelude to the treasons of his after life.

CHAPTER V.

THE PELOPONNESIAN WAR—THE SICILIAN EXPEDITION.

THAT the empire of Athens depended on the maintenance of her supremacy in the Egean sea, and that this supremacy could not be maintained without a thorough hold on the Hellenic cities which studded its northern shores, and, therefore, that no efforts could be too great to reduce the towns that had revolted in that quarter,

Earliest interferences of the Athenians in Sicily.

no sober-minded Athenian citizen could have doubted for a moment. It was the lesson which Perikles had preached throughout his political career; and his warnings against the folly of attempting distant conquests simply expressed his conviction that slackness in the recovery of a place like Amphipolis would be a crime or a blunder not less mischievous and ruinous. But for a long time there had been signs that for a certain class of politicians in Athens the idea of interference in the distant island of Sicily had special attractions. Twelve years had passed since the celebrated rhetorician Gorgias had headed an embassy from Leontinoi to ask the aid of Athens against the Syracusans, who were at open war not only with them but with Naxos and Katanê. The argument on which he chiefly laid stress was that, if the Sicilian Dorians should be suffered to subdue their Ionian kinsfolk, the Spartans would not fail to receive from Sicily the succours on which the Corinthians had long been counting. The Leontine envoys found little difficulty in obtaining promises of help; but during the autumn of that year the Athenian generals sent to their aid accomplished little. In the following summer Messênê became a subject ally of Athens, hostages being taken for its fidelity; but, in spite of this caution, the generals of the next year found the place again in the hands of the Syracusans. They had been delayed on the way partly by the circumstances which led to the occupation of Pylos by Demosthenes, and partly by the frightful seditions which were at that time turning Korkyra into a shambles. Horrible as was the state of things there, and wantonly wicked as the conduct of Eurymedon, the Athenian general, may have been, the history of this desperate strife between the Korkyraian oligarchs and commons has no direct connexion with that

B.C. 427.

B.C. 426.

B.C. 425.

of the Athenian empire; nor had it on public opinion in Sicily anything like the effect produced by the success of Demosthenes at Sphakteria. The conception and execution of the plan which left Sparta almost helpless brought home to the Sicilian Greeks the likelihood that their incessant quarrels and wars might leave the whole island at the mercy of a people who had shown a power of resistance and a fertility of resource far beyond any with which at the beginning of the war their enemies would have credited them. This fear was first felt by the citizens of Kamarina and Gela, and probably was first expressed by the men of the weaker city. In a congress held at Gela the Syracusan Hermokrates, forgetting that the Sikeliot Dorians had seized on the beginning of the great struggle between Athens and Sparta as a convenient time for making an attack upon their Ionian neighbours, dwelt strongly on the necessity of settling their feuds in the presence of a danger which threatened all the Sikeliot Greeks alike. The peace which he desired was made; but it was not likely to last longer than the general fear of Athenian ambition, a fear which was speedily dispelled by the disasters of the Boiotian campaign and the crowning catastrophe of Delion (p. 89), while at the same time the suspicion was reawakened that in the city which Hermokrates represented the Sikeliot Ionians might have an enemy more dangerous than Athens.

B.C. 424. Congress at Gela.

But a quarrel between Selinous and Egesta, one of the two cities of the Elymoi, in Sicily, was destined to produce greater results than the appeals of Leontinoi for the help of Athens. The latter had come at a moment when the intrigues of Alkibiades to secure the supremacy of Athens by means of a new Argive confederacy (p. 106), and the expedition for the recovery of Amphipolis, which was begun only to be

Quarrel between Selinous and Egesta.

frustrated by the remissness or treachery of Perdikkas (p. 110), left to the Athenians no time for thinking of interference in Sicily. The envoys of Egesta appeared when only a small portion of the Athenian people were finding occupation in the siege which preceded the butchery of the Melians. The graciousness of their reception may also have been in some measure due to the fact that they rested their claim to help not simply on the Athenian feelings of compassion but on the more constraining grounds of expediency. They could not, as they admitted, stand alone; but they pledged their faith not merely to bring their own men into the field, if the Athenians should decide on helping them, but to take on themselves the whole costs of the war. *Embassy to Athens from Egesta. B.C. 416.*

Charmed at the prospect thus opened to them, the Athenians, instead of pausing to think whether under any circumstances they would do well to interfere further in Sicily, resolved to send ambassadors to test the resources of the Egestaians and their prospects of success in the war with Selinous. The Egestaians turned out to be impostors; but the trick was discovered too late. The envoys, of whom Nikias ought to have been, but was not, one, returned with glowing accounts of the wealth of Selinous; and the crew of the trireme which conveyed them were loud in their expressions of admiration at the magnificence of the hospitality which they had enjoyed. But the treasures of the temples were of silver, not gold; and the ornaments which made their feasts so splendid represented the collective wealth not of Egesta only but of other cities from which they were borrowed, the whole being transferred secretly from house to house for each successive entertainment. A trick like this clearly points to bribery. But the bribery of a whole ship's crew is a somewhat costly business; and if these are to be *Embassy from Athens to Egesta.* *B.C. 415.*

acquitted, the good faith of the ambassadors is still more seriously called into question. For the present, the Athenian people were convinced that the Egestaians had spoken the truth, when the envoys laid before them sixty talents of uncoined silver as a month's pay in advance for a fleet of sixty vessels; and a decree was passed appointing Alkibiades, Nikias, and Lamachos commanders of an expedition charged with maintaining the cause of Egesta, and with the general furtherance of Athenian interests in Sicily.

Resolution of the Athenians to send a fleet to Sicily.

Nikias had done what he could to knock the whole scheme on the head; but when the assembly met again to discuss the details of the expedition, his language lacked force, because, while he suspected the ambassadors, he was afraid to reflect on the sincerity of the men who had accompanied them on their mission. The life of Nikias, born though he was to high station and great wealth, was not, indeed, particularly fortunate; but of all his misfortunes none was greater than his strange inability to discern the road which almost at any given time would have led him out of his difficulties. It was also his misfortune that his habitual hesitation, caution, or timidity, deprived his language of all persuasiveness, even in cases where reserve or prudence became the highest wisdom. Most of all, it was his misfortune that he had never drawn out in his mind a definite policy founded on the real interests of his country. Had he done so, he might have told his countrymen that although in discouraging the enterprise of Demosthenes at Pylos he was setting his face against a plan which would have had the hearty approval of Perikles, still in deprecating any further interference in Sicilian affairs he would have had the unqualified sanction of that great statesman. As it was, he never uttered words more true

Opposition of Nikias.

than when he assured his countrymen that they owed no duties to barbarian inhabitants of a distant island; that the Spartans, only nominally at peace with them, would welcome the first opportunity for giving vent to their stifled wrath; that if Athens was bent on righting wrongs, her business was to redress her own; and that until Amphipolis was recovered and the Thraceward Chalkidians were again brought under obedience, it was madness to despatch fleets and armies to aid the Egestaians. With less prudence, unless he meant to persist in his opposition, he inveighed against the selfish ambition of men who outran their fortunes in the extravagant luxury of their private lives and in the splendour with which they competed for the prizes in the great Hellenic festivals. Expressing honestly the dread with which he saw this knot of disaffected citizens grouped together in the assembly, he besought the older men to discharge their duty by putting an effectual check on their folly, and lastly entreated the Prytanis, or president, to disregard an irregularity which would certainly be condoned, and once more to ask the assembly whether the expedition should be undertaken at all.

The latter part of the speech of Nikias had been aimed at Alkibiades, and roused his vehement indignation. Foiled in his notion of setting up an Athenian empire in the Peloponnesos, he had turned with eagerness to a scheme which seemed to promise a more tempting prize in Sicily: and therefore, making a virtue of necessity, he gloried in the acts which had called forth the censures of Nikias. He insisted that the splendour of his victories at Olympia had impressed the whole Hellenic world with a sense of the power and wealth of Athens, in which they had well-nigh ceased to believe. He had even the effrontery to boast of his Peloponnesian intrigues, and to assert that, although

Reply of Alkibiades.

Sparta had won the stake at Mantineia, she had not yet recovered the haughty confidence of the times preceding the disasters of Sphakteria. More especially he pleaded that the Athenians had attained their empire by bestowing their help on all, whether Hellenes or Barbarians, who chanced to ask for it; and slackness now in aggressive movements would be virtually an abandonment of the old imperial tradition. Sicily would supply a field for such action; the refusal to occupy this field would be followed by stagnation, and stagnation would end in death. It would have been well if his hearers could have seen through the assumptions and falsehoods of this impudent harangue. The insinuation that Athens must be devoured with idleness if she would not decree the expedition to Sicily, had already been met by Nikias; but unfortunately his own remissness in all that concerned Amphipolis had deprived him here of a strong vantage-ground. The assertion that the Athenian empire had been acquired by indiscriminate help bestowed on every applicant was a mere lie. In the first instance it had been forced upon Athens; and the Delian confederation, which had alone made her dominion possible, had sprung up from definite needs and was confined within fixed limits. With the protection of the Asiatic Hellenes from the Persian power the work of Athens began, and with the maintenance of their safety and welfare it ended.

The support which Alkibiades received from other orators was so great that Nikias, feeling himself virtually defeated, resorted to a device by which he hoped to disgust the people with the enterprise. Declaring plainly that he regarded the Egestaian professions of wealth as a falsehood, he insisted that they must be provided with no ordinary fleets or crews, and that they must go amply provided with everything that could insure the well being of an army under all possible acci-

The wishes of Nikias defeated by his own representations of the amount of force needed for the expedition.

dents of war. Far from succeeding in his purpose, Nikias united all parties by proposing a course which seemed to make failure impossible, while even the more sober-minded were led to think that what Athens undertook with a superfluity of resources she would assuredly be able to accomplish. When, then, one of the citizens started up and insisted that without further preface Nikias should say plainly what he wanted, the unfortunate general was caught in his own trap. Like one passing sentence, not on himself (for his personal bravery was never questioned), but on his high-spirited, although mistaken, countrymen, Nikias said that he must have at least 100 triremes, and, if possible, more than 5,000 hoplites, with light troops in proportion. The die was cast; and the efforts of Nikias to bring about the abandonment of the enterprise had secured to Alkibiades a victory far greater than any which he could have hoped for, while it staked almost the very existence of the state on the issue of the enterprise. But in justice to Nikias we must remember that his dissuasions were not founded on mere apprehensions of disaster. If he had made up his mind that the scheme must end in failure, we may be sure that he would have refused to command in it as steadily as he had refused to take charge of the reinforcements for Pylos (p. 82). His condemnation of the scheme was based on the ground that in such an enterprise victory would be not much less a calamity than a defeat. The latter might cripple Athens for a time; but success would extend her empire to an unmanageable size, would involve her in a network of difficulties, and lead to schemes of aggression which would sooner or later be avenged in her downfall.

The prospect for the present was singularly bright and alluring. An eager crowd of volunteers came forward where the generals had feared that they might have to constrain men for an irksome service. The trierarchs vied with each other in the lavishness with which they provided everything necessary for the comfort of their crews; and the cheerfulness of the people was at its height, when they awoke one morning to find that the figures of Hermes had, with scarcely an exception, been mutilated and defaced. These Hermai stood in the Agora, before the temples, the public buildings, the private houses; and the people comforted themselves with the thought that the reverence which they paid to him enlisted the god on their side, and pledged him, as the Master-Thief, to protect them against the robbers, of whom he was the most adroit and subtle. The event produced a profound sensation. No part of the city was free from the profanation thus offered to the god, and therefore all Athens had forfeited its right to the goodwill of the deity; nor was it possible to say how far his feelings might be shared by the great company of the gods. The religious fears of the Athenians had been roused, and no people on this point were ever more sensitive. The sacrilege had been committed by men belonging to an organized body; and hence the Athenians had in their midst a secret society which hated the existing constitution of their country, and which must have engaged in active conspiracy before it could venture on such outrage of law and decency.

The mutilation of the Hermai by a band of secret conspirators.

That some conspiracy existed, there is not the least doubt: whatever it was, it is equally certain that Alkibiades had nothing whatever to do with it. It is absurd to suppose that a man should set in motion schemes which would involve him in imminent danger, and that he would do this just when he was setting off on an expedition on which he had set his heart, and to which the discovery was likely to be fatal. Hence it may with equal safety be inferred that the end aimed at was the ruin of Alkibiades and the

Innocence of Alkibiades.

abandonment of the enterprise. The mutilation of the Hermai would appeal directly to the religious fears of Nikias, and might call forth the protests of men who were thus far afraid to break silence. As to Alkibiades, his career had raised up against him a band of bitter enemies; and there were good grounds for thinking that if he returned a conqueror from Sicily, he would return with an ascendency so prodigious as to render the possibility of a despotism renewed in his person no mere dream. The great thing, then, was to prevent him from going, and in this they very nearly succeeded; but the charge brought against him had, strangely enough, nothing to do with the mutilation of the Hermai. Rewards offered for the apprehension of conspirators brought forward witnesses who accused him not of mutilating statues, but of mimicking in private houses the ceremonies of the Eleusinian mysteries. Of this there is no reason to suppose him innocent; but there is no greater reason for inferring on this score his guilt in the matter of the Hermai. The demeanour of Alkibiades in this crisis was straightforward and commendable. He insisted on being brought to trial before he sailed, asserting, at the same time, his innocence, and professing his willingness to submit to any penalty if he should be found guilty. But his opponents saw that a large proportion of the army was on his side, and that his condemnation might send home in wrath or disgust the Argive and Mantineian allies whom he had persuaded to join in the expedition. It was therefore decided that his trial should be postponed to some time subsequent to his recall.

Alkibiades charged with profanation.

It was now midsummer, and the fleet was ready for sea; and never did a more magnificent force issue from Athens than when the hoplites left the city to embark on board the ships which were to bear them away to Sicily.

Its splendour lay not so much in the numbers whether of the men or of the triremes; nor was the day made memorable so much by the brilliancy of the military array as by the high hopes, troubled by some transient misgivings, which filled the hearts of all who had accompanied their friends from the city, and were now to bid them farewell. Almost the whole population of Athens had come down to the Peiraieus. Foreigners were there, gazing in wonder at the sumptuousness of the armament, while fathers, brothers, wives, and children felt their bright hopes fading away as they were brought face to face with the stern realities of parting. Thus far they had buoyed themselves up with the thought that the power of Athens was fully able to accomplish her purposes; but now the length of the voyage, their scanty knowledge of the island which they were going to conquer, and the certainty that in any case many were departing who would never see their homes again, threw a dark veil over the future, and many burst into bitter weeping. The trumpets gave the signal for silence, and while some prayed to a God and Father neither local nor changeful, the voices of the heralds rose in invocation of the gods of the city. Presently the pæan shout echoed over the waters, and the long line of triremes swept in file from the harbour.

Departure of the fleet for Sicily.

Even in Sparta, with its habitual wariness and secrecy, a plan so vast could not have been formed without giving rise to rumours which would reach the state against whom these preparations were being made. At Athens there could be no secrecy; but the tidings brought to Syracuse were received with an incredulity against which Hermokrates in vain raised his voice, urging them to man their triremes and wait for the Athenians on the shores of Italy,

Incredulity of the Syracusans.

and thus probably determine Nikias, whose dislike of the enterprise was notorious, to abandon it altogether. His opponent Athenagoras insisted, on the contrary, that the Athenians, noted as they were for sobriety of judgment, would never be so frantic as to leave a war unfinished in Chalkidikê in order to undertake a war on a huger scale in Sicily, and that the persons to be punished were, therefore, not the Athenians whom they would never see, but the orators who for their own selfish ends sought to scare them with imaginary terrors and to shut their eyes to more real perils at home. The speech of Athenagoras would have been followed, beyond doubt, by angry controversy, had not the Strategoi, or generals, interposing their authority, insisted that, as they were responsible for the safety of the city, so they would take the measures most likely to insure it.

While with the Syracusans the coming of the enemy was a matter of doubt and controversy, tidings were brought that the Athenians had already reached Rhegion. Their progress was not flattering to their hopes. The Tarantines and Lokrians would have nothing to do with them; the men of Rhegion insisted on maintaining a strict neutrality until they could learn the wishes of their fellow-Italiots; and the ships sent forward before the fleet returned with the news that the wealth of Egesta was a fiction, and that its treasury contained no more than the modest sum of 30 talents. *Discouragement of the Athenians on approaching Sicily.* The discovery greatly disconcerted Alkibiades. To Nikias it was no disappointment, and his mind was soon made up. He proposed to act according to the letter of his instructions (p. 116), and, having displayed the power of Athens before the cities on the coasts of Sicily, to return home unless any fresh events should open a way for further operations. *Plan of Nikias.* A course so honest had little attractions for Alkibiades, who urged that envoys should be sent to the Sikeliot cities in the hope of detaching them from Syracuse, and to the Sikel tribes in the hope of securing their friendship, as preliminaries to an attack upon Syracuse and Selinous. Taking the view of the mere general as distinguished from the statesman, Lamachos insisted that not a moment was to be lost while the impression made by their sudden arrival was still fresh. Syracuse was as yet quite unprepared for the struggle; and an immediate attack upon it would be followed by either complete victory or an important success. Of these three plans that of Nikias was the best from the statesman's point of view: from that of the general the counsel of Lamachos was both bold and able; that of Alkibiades was unworthy either of the soldier or the statesman. A more prudent and businesslike course than that which Nikias proposed can scarely be imagined; and the result would have been a return home, if not after brilliant success, yet without disgrace, and without that exasperation of feeling which would have followed the execution of the plan of Lamachos. That of Alkibiades was a trimming and vacillating compromise, which showed him to be as deficient in true military genius as he was prominent for the arrogance of his demeanour. Unhappily it was the plan which was inforced by the adhesion of Lamachos, who felt, as a soldier, that it was better to run the chance of victory with Alkibiades than at once to abandon it with Nikias.

Plan of Alkibiades.
Plan of Lamachos.

An attempt of Alkibiades to win the alliance of Messênê was unsuccessful. Overtures, not more fortunate, made to the men of Katanê, were followed by a display of Athenian ships in the Great Harbour of Syracuse; but nothing was accomplished beyond a survey of the fortifications. On

Occupation of Katanê by the Athenians.

their return to Katanê the generals were admitted to a conference within the city; and while Alkibiades was speaking, some Athenians found their way into the town through a postern which had been imperfectly walled up, and appeared in the Agora. The small minority which constituted the Syracusan party, seeing the enemy thus seemingly in possession of the place, hurried away: and in their absence the Katanaians, passing a decree of alliance with the Athenians, invited them to bring thither the forces which had been left at Rhegion. The news that Kamarina might be expected to join them, led the generals to sail thither. But they found only that the Kamarinaians were resolved on maintaining their neutrality; and on their return to Katanê they learnt that the Salaminian trireme had brought a summons for Alkibiades to return to Athens for his trial.

The departure of the fleet for Sicily had been followed at Athens by a religious excitement which speedily became intense; but although many were imprisoned, some put to death, and others sentenced, in their absence, for a share in the plot of the Hermokopidai, or mutilators of the busts of Hermes, evidence criminating Alkibiades in the affair was not forthcoming, and the charge on which he was summoned home accused him simply of mimicking the Eleusinian mysteries in his own house. But although the popular indignation against Alkibiades was thus carried to a high pitch, his enemies could obtain no order for his apprehension. It was felt that such a measure might drive away the Argive and Mantineian allies, and perhaps excite dangerous discontent among the Athenian troops themselves. The commander of the Salaminian trireme had, therefore, no further charge than to deliver to Alkibiades an order to return home in his own ship. He accompanied the trireme as far as

Recall and flight of Alkibiades.

Thourioi; but when the ships were to sail onwards, he was nowhere to be seen, and all attempts to search for him were fruitless.

Nikias and Lamachos were now joint commanders of the expedition; but the latter hesitated to place himself in opposition to a colleague whose influence with the army far exceeded his own. The fleet therefore sailed through the Messenian strait and coasted along the northern shore of the island without achieving any material success. The first feelings of awe and depression felt by the Syracusans had now given way to something like contempt, and the discovery of this fact suggested to Nikias a device for effecting an uncontested landing in the bay of Syracuse. A Katanaian informed the Syracusans that the men of his city would set fire to the Athenian fleet if on a given day the Syracusans would attack their lines. The bait was eagerly seized. The whole force of the city was dispatched to Katanê; but while they were on their march the Athenian fleet had sailed round the island of Ortygia into the Great Harbour, and had landed its troops on the western shore, near the inlet known as the bay of Daskon. Here a strong position was speedily fortified; and a battle, fought on the following day with the Syracusan army, which had returned, with unabated confidence, from Katanê, ended in a victory of no decisive importance for the Athenians. A real defeat might have led Nikias at once to give up the enterprise, to the unspeakable benefit of Athens; his insignificant success furnished him with an excuse for spending the winter in comparative idleness, and sending to Athens for troops and munitions of war. But even now the general prospect was almost as favourable as it had been at first. Between the Great Harbour and the bay of Thapsos lay the inner city on Ortygia, joined by a bridge to the mainland, and the outer city on Achradina to the north, each with its own walls. Between the two the Little Harbour afforded an unwalled landing-place; and there was no reason why the Athenians should not at once have drawn their lines within the circuit of the wall which, during the winter now beginning, the Syracusans threw up from the shore of the Great Port, taking in the precincts of Apollon Temenites. But now, as before, the golden hours were wasted. The fleet sailed to Messênê, and there they had the first practical experience of the hatred of Alkibiades. His countrymen had sentenced him to death; he had sworn that they should feel that he was alive. Warned by him of the intended betrayal of the town, the Syracusan faction put the Athenian partisans to death.

During the winter the envoys both of the Syracusans and the Athenians appeared at Kamarina; and it is especially remarkable that the Athenian Euphemos invites the adhesion of the Kamarinaians on just those grounds which Nikias had urged as reasons for abandoning the enterprise altogether, and which must have failed to awaken the enthusiasm of the Athenian people. For the time the Athenians were beyond all doubt smitten with the lust of conquest, and dreamt of an indefinite extension of their empire: but Euphemos nevertheless insisted that they had not come to effect any permanent settlement in Sicily, or to make the island a part of their empire. Their objects were twofold. The one they would be glad to attain; the other must at all costs be achieved. They earnestly desired the friendship of Kamarina and other Sikeliot cities; but they could not afford to leave the Dorians of Sicily in a position which would enable them to give important aid to the Dorians of Peloponnesos. The fact, however, still remained that the Athenians had no reason to fear

Presence of Athenian and Syracusan envoys at Kamarina.

aggression even from Syracuse, and that, therefore, the motives alleged by Euphemos for their presence in Sicily were not those which had really brought them.

The envoys on both sides were dismissed with courtesy; but Kamarina remained neutral, when the prompt action recommended by Lamachos might have secured her hearty friendship. In fact, during the winter the plan of action, such as it was, was that of Nikias; and it showed his incompetence as a general scarcely less than his previous career had shown his incompetence as a statesman. The fate of Athens at this time was indeed hard. Her aggressive instincts led her to put faith in the most profligate and lawless of men; the reverence which she paid to personal integrity seduced her into the not less fatal error of trusting a momentous task to a citizen whose only merit was his respectability.

<small>Inactivity of Nikias.</small>

Meanwhile the evil genius of Athens was busy at work elsewhere. Having received a solemn pledge for his safety, Alkibiades presented himself at the city whose power he had hoped to destroy on the field of Mantineia (p. 109). Not long after his arrival, came Corinthian and Syracusan envoys to urge an open resumption of the war with Athens. The ephors were placidly contenting themselves with the expression of a hope that the Syracusans would hold out, when Alkibiades broke in upon the debate with a vehemence for which he felt that some apology was needed. With matchless effrontery he took credit to himself for exceptional moderation and sobriety, for the prudence of his public counsels, and for his real love of oligarchy, which he had made up his mind to set up at Athens on the first convenient opportunity. Of his own share in originating the Sicilian expedition he said not a word: but he dared to tell the Spartans that schemes

<small>Treason of Alkibiades at Sparta.</small>

which even he had not ventured to put forth before the Assembly, were familiar to the minds of his countrymen generally, that they contemplated the subjugation of the whole Carthaginian empire, and intended to swamp the Peloponnesos with hordes of Iberians, and thus make themselves supreme in all Hellas. If Syracuse should fall, these visions would assuredly be realised. A Spartan force, then, should at once be sent to Syracuse; the presence of a Spartan general to organize resistance in that city was even more needful; but most needful of all was it to cripple the Athenians at home. The establishment of a permanent garrison within their borders would weight them with a burden scarcely tolerable; and at Dekeleia, in the lower ground between Parnes and Pentelikos, they would find a post which would give them the command of the silver mines of Laurcion, while it would do the Athenians mischief far more serious than the loss of a few cartloads of precious metal.

When we remember that Athens lay exposed to this deadly wound only because the flower and strength of the people had been drafted away on a distant expedition which Alkibiades himself had planned and urged on with frantic passion, we can scarcely avoid the conclusion that, whatever may have been his wrongs, treachery more dastardly has rarely been found in the annals of mankind. But what were his wrongs? His life at Athens had been one of enormous licence: yet even thus he had been enabled to repel an accusation for which the evidence of facts was not forthcoming. His recall had nothing to do with the mutilation of the Hermai: he had not even to answer any charge of political conspiracy. So great was the charm of his manner and such were his powers of persuasion that, had he chosen, on first being charged with complicity in the schemes of unknown conspirators, to make

Mission of Gylippos to Sicily. B.C. 414.

a clean breast of it, and, while asserting his ignorance of those plots, to express his regret for acts of profanity and irreverence which were never designed to be more than a private jest, and which ought not therefore to be regarded as an offence against the Athenian people or the public gods, the minor offence would in all likelihood have been condoned, and, promising greater care for the time to come, he would have departed for Sicily free from all accusations and from all suspicion. But the armour of traitors is seldom invulnerable, and Alkibiades insured his death-wound when he asserted that no man was bound to look upon a state as his country any longer than he received from that state the treatment which he regarded as his due. Such a doctrine could be tolerated nowhere, least of all, perhaps, by the state which had cut short the career of Pausanias ; and in due time it was remembered. But for the present his work was done. It was decreed that a Spartan army should seize on Dekeleia, and that Gylippos should at once be sent to take the command at Syracuse. The choice was fully justified by the event. While Alkibiades was thus rekindling the war in the Peloponnesos, the trireme sent by Nikias for more men and money reached Athens. Both were granted without a word to express the disappointment which the Athenians must have felt, and the strength of the state was more dangerously committed to an expedition which it would have been infinitely better if they had from the outset starved.

For the present Nikias, unenterprising and sluggish as he was, had the vast advantage of possessing a first-rate general in his remaining colleague Lamachos ; and the change which comes over the conduct of the siege immediately after the death of the latter justifies us in attributing to Lamachos such success as the besiegers had thus far achieved. The

Successes of the Athenians before Syracuse.

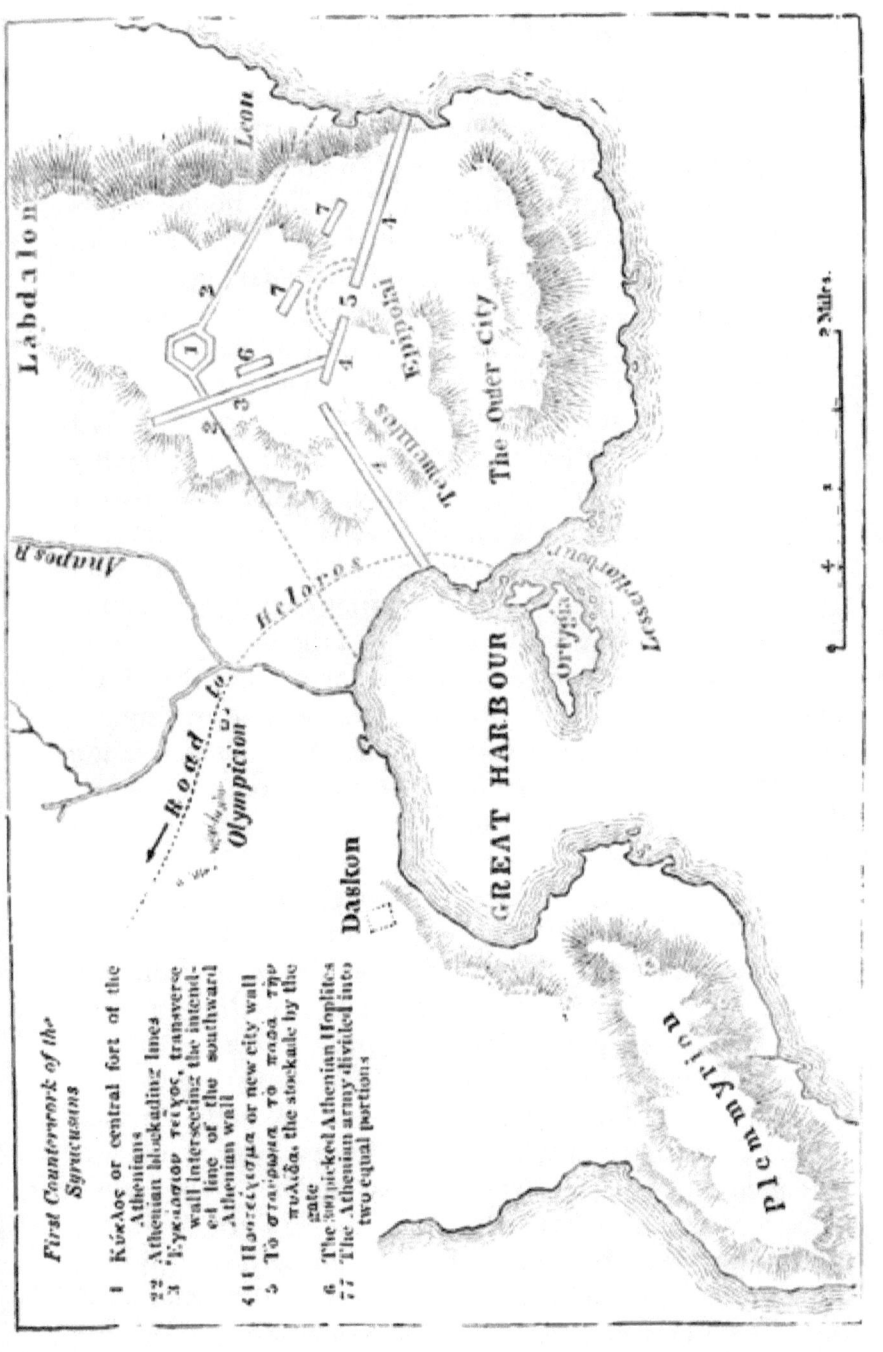

ATHENIAN OPERATIONS BEFORE SYRACUSE (PLATE I.)

occupation of the table land of Epipolai by the Athenians neutralized the effect of the wall built by the Syracusans inclosing the ground to the east of the temple of Apollon Temenites. The building of a fort on Labdalon was followed immediately by the erection of another work with a rapidity which amazed their enemies. This strongly-fortified inclosure was to serve as a stronghold for the army, and as a centre and starting-point for the blockading walls which were to run thence eastward to Trogilos and westward to the Great Harbour. The first counterwork of the Syracusans which, starting probably from Temenites and extending to the cliffs of Epipolai, cut the intended southern wall of the besiegers, was carried by storm, the wall itself was destroyed, and the materials were used by the Athenians in their work of circumvallation.

<small>First counterwork of the Syracusans.</small>

The Athenian generals now resolved that the Syracusans should not have the opportunity of throwing out fresh counterworks running, like the last, to the cliffs of Epipolai. The cliffs were themselves fortified, and the Athenians had thus an immense advantage in their task of carrying their southward wall to the Great Harbour. Meanwhile the Syracusans were busied on a second counterwork carried from the new wall of the city across the low and marshy ground stretching to the banks of the Anapos. The Athenians thus found themselves opposed by a fresh obstacle in their progress to the sea; and Lamachos determined to make himself master of this stockade and of the trench by which it was defended. The fleet was ordered to sail round from Thapsos into the Great Harbour; and an attack on the counterwork at daybreak was rewarded by the capture of almost the whole of it. The rest of it was taken later on in the day; but a picked body of Athenian hoplites having

<small>Death of Lamachos in the attack on the second counterwork of the Syracusans.</small>

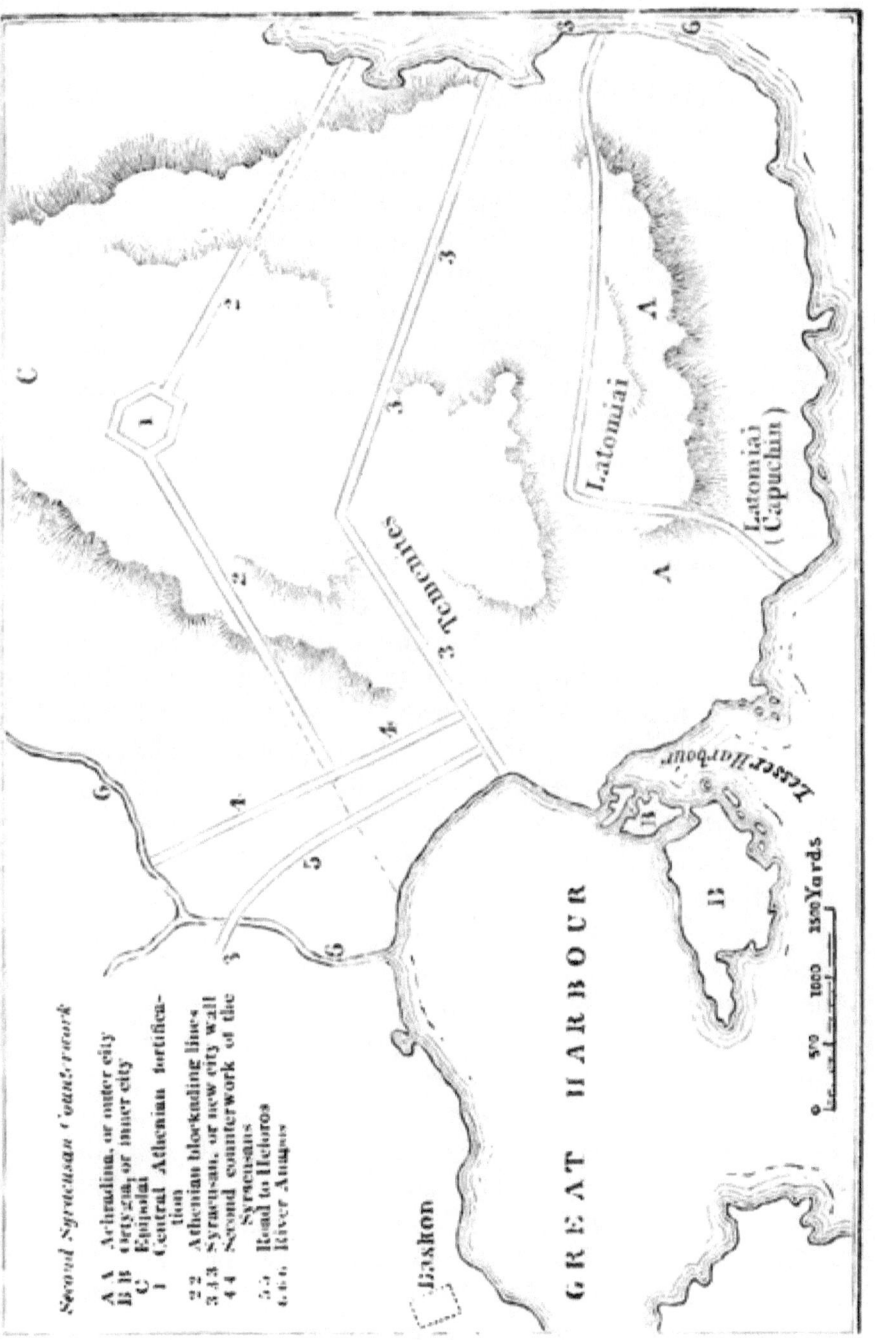

ATHENIAN OPERATIONS BEFORE SYRACUSE (PLATE II).

hurried to the bridge across the Anapos in order to cut off some of the Syracusan fugitives, was attacked by a body of the enemy's horse and thrown into disorder. Seeing their danger, Lamachos hurried to their aid, and, crossing a trench, was for a moment separated from his followers. In an instant he was struck down and killed: but the Syracusans gained no immediate advantage from his death, and the doom of Syracuse seemed to be sealed when the whole army retreated within the city, while the magnificent Athenian fleet, with all its splendid appointments, was seen sweeping round into the harbour which it was destined never to leave.

<small>Entry of the Athenian fleets into the Great Harbour.</small>

Some weeks were yet to pass before Gylippos could attempt to enter Syracuse; and the one thing of vital moment was that the city should be completely invested before that attempt should be made. A single wall, carried from the Great Harbour to the central fort and thence to the sea at the northern extremity of Achradina, would have amply sufficed for this purpose. But Lamachos was no longer at hand to urge the necessity of speed, and Nikias wasted time in building the southward wall double from the first, while much of the ground which should have been guarded by the north-eastward wall was left open. But although the Syracusans were thus able still to bring in supplies by the road which passed under the rock of Euryelos, their prospects were gloomy enough. They were beginning to feel the miseries of a state of siege, and their irritation was vented upon their generals. Hermokrates and his colleagues were deprived of their command; and the elation, and consequent supineness, of Nikias were increased when he learnt from the philo-Athenian party within the city that the Syracusans were on the eve of surrender. The prospect of this uncon-

<small>Further advantages gained by the Athenians.</small>

ditional submission probably made him turn a deaf ear to the proposals which were actually made to him for a settlement of the quarrel. The Athenians seemed, indeed, to be floating on the full tide of good fortune. Tyrrhenian ships were hastening to join their fleet, and Sikel tribes which had thus far held aloof were pressing forward to their aid.

Meanwhile Gylippos, sorely discouraged by reports which purposely exaggerated the difficulties of the Syracusans, was working his way to Sicily. Far from giving him the help which he expected, the men of Thourioi sent to inform Nikias that a Spartan general was approaching, more in the guise of a pirate or privateer than as the leader of a force which should command respect. The contempt implied in the phrase soothed the vanity of Nikias, who showed his sense of his own superiority by failing to send, until it was too late, so much as a single ship to prevent his landing in Sicily. But even when Gylippos had begun his land march, Nikias had only to block the roads by which he had himself seized Epipolai, and Gylippos must have fallen back to devise some other means for succouring Syracuse. Even in this he failed; and, by a strange irony of fate, the Syracusans were discussing definitely in their public assembly the terms for a pacification, when with a single ship the Corinthian Gongylos made his way to the city and told them that the aid of which they had despaired was almost at their doors. At once all thoughts of submission were cast to the winds, and they made ready to march out with all their forces to bring Gylippos into the town. To this Nikias interposed no hindrance. His workmen were busy on the few furlongs which remained unfinished at the end of the southern wall, where for the present there was no danger whatever, when Gylippos entered Syracuse

Entry of the Spartan Gylippos into Syracuse.

almost as a conqueror. The Athenians were at once made to feel that the parts of the actors had been changed. The Spartan general offered them a truce for five days, if they would spend this time in leaving not merely Syracuse but Sicily. The next day was marked by the loss of the fortress of Labdalon. At the same time, a third Syracusan counterwork was steadily advancing which would cut the northern blockading wall at a point about 500 yards to the east of the central fort; and the passing of this spot would render the whole work spent on the blockading walls mere labour lost. So far as Nikias could judge, the contest must be decided in the Great Harbour, and he resolved, while there was yet time, to fortify the promontory of Plemmyrion, which with Ortygia, from which it is one mile distant, formed the entrance to the port. As a post commanding the access to the harbour, it had great advantages; but it had no water, and the Syracusan horsemen harassed or destroyed the foraging parties, which were compelled to seek supplies from long distances. More fatal than all was the admission, implied by this change of position, that the Athenians were rather defending themselves than attacking. Henceforth their seeming victories were to do them no good: their slightest failures or blunders were to do them infinite harm. The Syracusans were successful in carrying their third counterwork across the enemy's lines, and all hope of blockading Syracuse except by storming this counter-wall faded finally away. But Nikias still had it in his power to guard the entrances to the slopes of Epipolai, and thus to keep the ground open for the work which the new force from Athens must inevitably have to do. Again the opportunity was allowed to slip, and the Syracusans were suffered to raise the further works without which Gylippos saw that the city could not be safe, if

Third Syracusan counter-work.

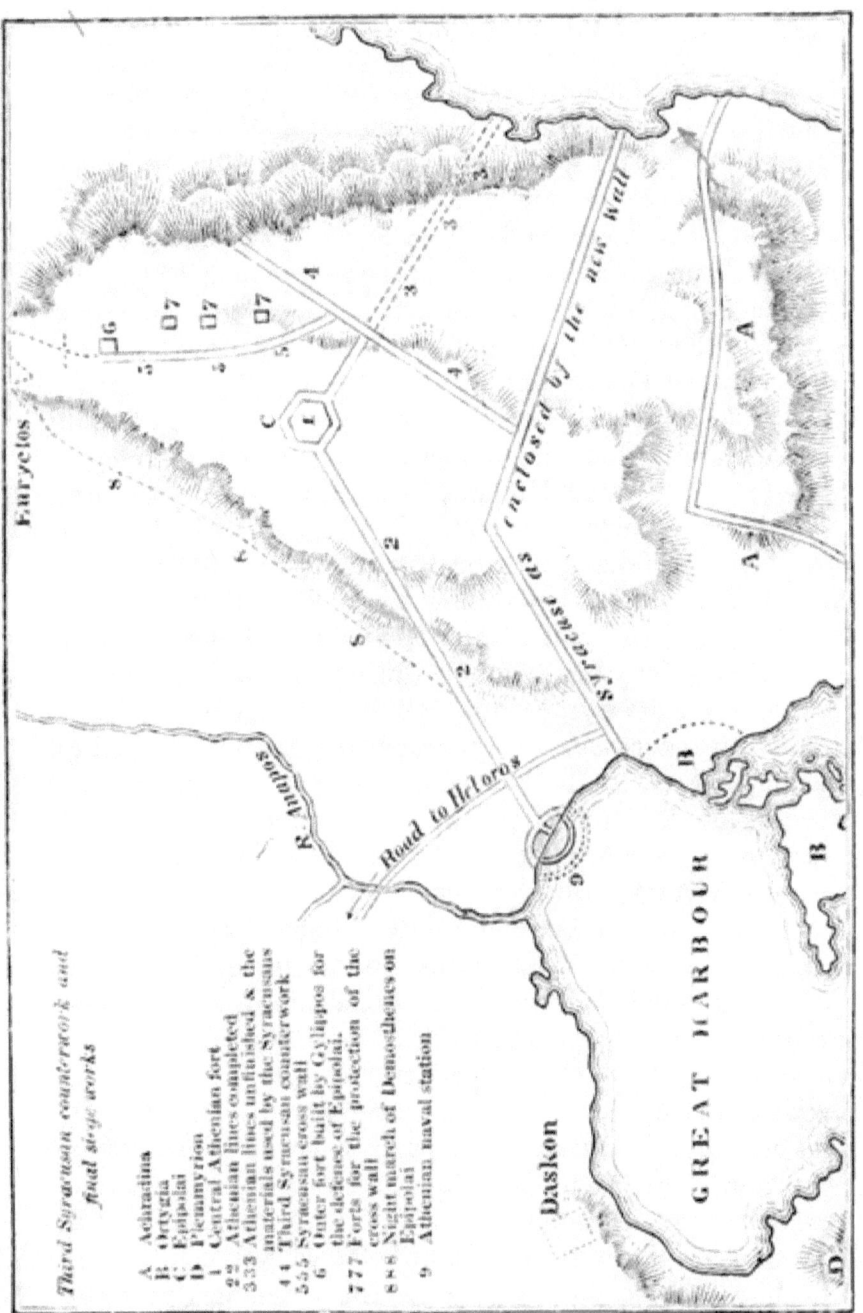

ATHENIAN OPERATIONS BEFORE SYRACUSE (PLATE III.)

an army of sufficient strength should occupy the heights under Euryelos. These works consisted of a strong fort (seemingly not far from Labdalon), joined with the third counterwork by a single wall. On the north side of this long wall were built three forts, to serve as guard-posts in the event of an attack on the long wall. So passed away the precious days, while the idleness of Nikias added to the colossal burden under which even the genius of Demosthenes broke down.

While Gylippos was thus bestirring himself on behalf of Syracuse, a messenger was bearing to Athens a letter in which Nikias professed to give a plain un-varnished report of all that had thus far befallen the fleet and army. Strict truth would have called upon him to confess that the first three months of his time in Sicily had been wholly wasted; that by his inaction during the first winter he had allowed the Syracusans to build a new city wall, thus rendering necessary an enormous extension of the be-sieging lines; that he had failed to turn to account the success of Lamachos in the destruction of the second Syracusan counterwork; that he had not prevented the entry of Gylippos into Syracuse with a formidable re-inforcement; that he had made no effort to hinder the construction of the final works and forts of the enemy which rendered the successful prosecution of the siege an almost hopeless task; that, having brought with him a fleet of unparalleled efficiency, he had dispirited the crews either by inactivity or by employing them on use-less errands; and that his ships, from being constantly in the water, were fast becoming unseaworthy. Far from making these admissions, Nikias, in the only two pas-sages in his letter in which he blames anyone, blames not himself, but the men under his command and the Athenians who had sent him as their commander. He

<small>Letter of Nikias to the Athe-nians.</small>

told them, in substance, that at first they had been uniformly victorious, until Gylippos came with an army from Peloponnesos; but he never told them that common care would have made his entrance impossible. He told them that not merely the splendid appearance but the usefulness of their ships was wretchedly impaired, forgetting that only through his own resistance to the counsels of Lamachos they had failed to do and to finish their work long ago. He told them that either the present army must be withdrawn or another army of equal strength sent to reinforce it, adding the expression of his own wish to be relieved from his command, for which he was incapacitated by a painful internal disease. He had always been incapacitated for it; but whether, when this ominous letter was read in the assembly, there were any who had the wisdom to see, and the courage to denounce, the monstrous misconduct of the expedition, we are not told. His resignation was not received; but two of his officers, Menandros and Euthydemos, were appointed his colleagues, until the generals should arrive with the reinforcements from Athens.

The disaster of Sphakteria had convinced the Spartans that they and their allies were under divine displeasure for the way in which they had brought about the war; and they acknowledged that in the crisis which preceded the outbreak of the struggle the Athenians were in the right and themselves wholly in the wrong. Hence they were especially anxious that the blame of renewing the strife should attach distinctly to the Athenians; and the landing of some Athenian ships with their crews at this time to ravage the territories of Epidauros and some other cities, seemed to furnish the overt breach of the peace which they wanted.

Occupation of Dekeleia by the Spartans.

B.C. 413.

Early in the spring, therefore, a Spartan army, marching to Dekeleia (p. 129), not merely renewed a war which had been only nominally interrupted, but seemingly without opposition built the fortress which gave its name to the ten years' struggle which followed its erection.

Meanwhile, at Syracuse, Gylippos was urging the people to attack the Athenians on their own element. His great object was to obtain possession of the entrance to the Great Harbour; and he therefore arranged a simultaneous attack on the Athenian fleet and the naval station at Plemmyrion by two divisions of the Syracusan fleet, while his land forces should attack the forts. Both in the harbour and at the naval station the Syracusans were at first victorious; but when the Athenians at last gained sufficient room for the manœuvre in which they were unrivalled, they speedily sunk eleven ships of the enemy at the cost of three of their own. The victory, however, came too late to do them any good. Plemmyrion was already lost. With astonishing want of caution the garrisons of the three forts had gone down to the beach to view the naval conflicts in which they could be of no use; and in their absence Gylippos fell on the forts with overwhelming force, and thus became master not only of the entrance to the harbour but of the large quantities of corn and money which had been placed there for safety, together with three triremes, which had been hauled up for repairs, and the sails and tackle of nearly forty ships. Henceforth, Athenian convoys could be introduced into the harbour only after a fight. Blow after blow now fell on the besieging force. Their treasure-ships were intercepted; the timber stored for shipbuilding was set on fire; and it was unfortunate for Athens that the Syracusans did not succeed in their larger scheme for the destruction of the Athenian fleet before any reinforcements should reach them. The ruin

Naval victory of the Athenians in the harbour of Syracuse, accompanied by the loss of Plemmyrion.

of the navy of Nikias would have furnished to Demosthenes sufficient excuse for taking off the army and forthwith returning home.

This attack was delayed by a disaster which befell a body of allies who, on their way to Syracuse, were, at the request of Nikias, cut off by some of the Sikel tribes. Had Nikias taken this step while Gylippos was on his march, the issue of the siege might have been different. As it was, 800 of these allies were slain, but the remaining 1,500 reached the city. Nor was this the only accession of strength on the Syracusan side. Akragas (Agrigentum) alone of all the Sikeliot cities insisted on remaining neutral; but apart from mere additions to their numbers the Syracusans were fast acquiring that power of making the best of circumstances to which the Athenians owed the rapid growth of their empire. They were well aware that for Athenian fleets ample sea-room was indispensable; and as they saw the Athenian ships cooped up at one end of their harbour, they drew the conclusion that the bulk and awkwardness of their own vessels would tell in their favour only so long as the Athenians were unable to resort to their peculiar tactics. A simultaneous attack by land and sea produced on the first day no decisive results. Two days later things were following much the same course, when a Corinthian suggested that the Syracusan crews should take their midday meal on the shore and then immediately renew the fight. Seeing their enemy retreat at noon, the Athenians thought that their work for the day was done. They were soon undeceived, and few of them had eaten anything when they saw the Syracusan fleet again advancing in order of battle. Even thus, in spite of the disorder arising from the hasty surprise, the Athenians had lost nothing until hunger compelled them to bring the matter to an issue.

Defeat of the Athenian fleet in the Great Harbour.

The result was precisely what the Syracusans had expected. The heavily-weighted bows of their ships crushed the slender prows of the Athenian triremes as these advanced rapidly to the encounter. Three Syracusan ships were lost; but seven Athenian vessels had been sunk and many more disabled, when 73 triremes, bringing with them 5,000 hoplites, with light troops in proportion, swept into the Great Harbour. The first feeling of the Syracusans at this fresh display of the resources of Athens, at a time when her enemies were establishing a permanent garrison at Dekeleia, was one of consternation; but Demosthenes, who commanded this reinforcement, saw at a glance that the temporary advantage gained by his coming must go for nothing unless some decisive success should justify the continuance of the siege. If the Syracusan cross-wall could be taken and the guards in the three forts fronting it (p. 138) be disarmed or slain, there might be some hope of storming their counter-wall and so of effectually investing Syracuse. Attacks by day could, however, have little chance of success, and Demosthenes resolved on a night assault.

Arrival of Demosthenes with reinforcements from Athens.

A moonlight night was chosen for the purpose. His men, in spite of all previous sufferings, were full of hope and even of confidence. They were now acting under a general whose sagacity in council and energy in the field had won him the highest reputation, and they carried with them everything which might be reasonably expected to insure their success. At first, all went well. Not only did the Athenians make their way along Euryelos, but the cross-wall itself was taken before any alarm could be given. The Athenian generals now led on a large proportion of their forces to the counter-wall, while others began to demolish the cross-wall; and the deter-

Night attack by Demosthenes on the Syracusan counterwork.

mined energy of their assault drove back Gylippos, who now came up with all the forces at his command. In fact, their work was already done, if they could only maintain their position: and had they set out an hour or two before dawn instead of an hour or two before midnight, they would in all likelihood have succeeded in doing so. They had turned the Syracusan lines, and the daylight would now be rather to their advantage than to that of the enemy. But Demosthenes was anxious to push the Syracusans at once as far back as possible; and success with Greek troops generally led to neglect of discipline. The Athenians in front were already in some disorder, when they were thrown into confusion by the sudden charge of some heavy Boiotian hoplites who had been recently brought to Sicily. From this moment the battle became a wild jumble.

Defeat of the Athenians.

As the disorder increased, the Athenians were no longer able to see in what direction their movements should be made, nor to distinguish in the uproar the words of command. The watchword, repeatedly asked for and given, became known to the enemy. The discovery was fatal; and the presence of Dorians in the Athenian army completed the catastrophe. The war-cry of the Argives and their other Dorian allies could not be distinguished from the Syracusans; and the Athenians, dismayed already, were bewildered by the suspicion that the enemy was in their rear, was among them, was everywhere. The defeat had become utter rout. In their efforts to reach their lines on the Anapos, hundreds were pushed over the precipices which bounded the slopes, and were either sorely maimed or killed. Others, belonging to the reinforcements of Demosthenes, who knew nothing of the nature of the ground, strayed away into the country, where they were found by the Syracusan horsemen, and slain.

The enterprise of Demosthenes had failed; and he now saw that, do what they would, the siege must be abandoned or end in their ruin. In such circumstances he was not a man likely to hesitate; and he discharged the duty which he owed as much to Athens as to himself with a manly frankness sullied by no mean or selfish feelings. For the present the fleet which he had brought made them once more masters of the sea; and he candidly assured Nikias that his business was to remove the army at once while the path lay open. The reply of Nikias betrays either a startling infatuation or a not less startling mental depravity; and we have to remember that it is preserved to us by an historian who reviews his career with singular indulgence and who cherished his memory with affectionate but melancholy veneration. He chose to speak of the philo-Athenian party as still strong in Syracuse: but his resolution was taken on other grounds. The Athenians, he asserted, were a people under the dominion of loud-voiced demagogues; and of the men who were now crying out under the hardships of the siege the greater number would, if they should again take their seats in the assembly, join eagerly in charging their generals with treachery or corruption. Nothing, therefore, should induce him to consent to their retreat before he received from Athens positive orders commanding his return. In truth, he was afraid to go home, and was a coward where Demosthenes, in spite of his failures, was honest, straightforward, and brave. He was even ungenerous as well as cowardly. He had no right to slander soldiers who had done their duty admirably; least of all was he justified in ascribing an exacting severity to a people whose sin it had been to place unbounded trust in his mere respectability. In vain Demosthenes again insisted that the siege must be given

Resolution of Demosthenes to return to Athens.

Opposition of Nikias.

up, and that even if they were to await instructions from Athens, they were bound in the meantime to remove their fleet to Katanê or to Naxos. So firm was the opposition of Nikias that Demosthenes began to think that he had some private grounds for his resistance which time in the end would justify. He had none; and when Gylippos returned to Syracuse with large reinforcements, Nikias admitted that retreat was inevitable and requested only that the order should be privately circulated, not formally decreed in a council of war.

This consent, even now reluctantly extorted, came to Demosthenes as a reprieve for which he had almost ceased to hope; and the preparations for departure were far advanced when an eclipse of the moon filled Nikias with an agony of religious terror. The prophets must be consulted, and their decision followed. According to Thucydides, they declared that no movement must be made for twenty-seven days. Diodoros tells us that they required no more than the usual delay of three days; and even Plutarch affirms that in insisting on the longer time Nikias went altogether beyond their demands. If this story be true, his infatuation assumes a blacker character. He had sealed the doom of the fleet and the army; for long before the twenty-seven days had passed away, this once magnificent armament had been utterly destroyed. *Eclipse of the moon.*

Through Syracuse the tidings flew like fire that the Athenians, having resolved on retreat, had been detained by the eclipse. The first decision was an admission of defeat and hopelessness; the second gave them ample time for securing their prey. An assault by the Syracusan fleet, when all was ready, ended in the destruction of the squadron commanded by Eurymedon. On land the Athenians had won some advantages over *Second defeat of the Athenian fleet in the Great Harbour.*

the Syracusans, and the rules of Greek warfare compelled them to treat this check as a victory; but they probably felt that the setting up of their trophy was but as the last flash of the sinking sun, which gives a more ghastly hue to the pitch-black storm-clouds around him. They had undergone a ruinous defeat by sea, and the hope that the new triremes of Demosthenes would restore the balance had failed them altogether.

For the Syracusans the result of the battle had changed the whole character of the struggle. A little while ago they had been fighting in the mere hope of compelling the enemy to abandon the siege: the prospect was now opened to them of sweeping away the Athenian empire. With the intoxication of men who from mountain-summits seem to look down on a world beneath them, they abandoned themselves to the conviction that henceforth they must fill a foremost place in the history of Hellas. They were now leaders, along with Spartans, Corinthians, Arkadians, and Boiotians, against the relics of the most splendid and efficient armament which had ever left the harbours of Athens. The epical conception which had led Thucydides to ascribe to the Athenians before the massacre of Melos language which belies their general reputation (p. 111) now leads him to enumerate, with a solemnity full of pathos, the tribes which were to face each other in the last awful struggle. Here, as at Marathon, the Plataians were present in the hope, perhaps, of avenging themselves on the Boiotian allies of Syracuse, but prompted still more by a devotion to Athens which had never wavered. Here Aigina was represented, not by the descendants of those who had conquered at Salamis, but by the Athenian citizens who had been thrust into their place (p. 53). Here with the Dorian allies of Athens were Messenians from Pylos and Naupaktos, and Akarnanians who were now to

Change in the popular feeling at Syracuse.

follow to their death the standard of their favourite general. On the side of the Syracusans were enrolled the Kamarinaians, for whose friendship the Athenian Euphemos had bidden largely (p. 127), and the men of Selinous who were to play their part in the closing scenes of the stupendous drama which had grown out of their petty quarrel with the barbarians of Egesta.

In the enthusiasm excited by their victory the Syracusans resolved that the whole Athenian armament should be destroyed like vermin in a snare. Triremes, trading ships, and vessels of all kinds were anchored lengthwise across the whole mouth of the harbour from Plemmyrion to Ortygia, and strongly lashed together with ropes and chains. *Closing of the mouth of the Great Harbour.* This was all that Nikias had gained by fostering silly scruples for which the men to whom Athens owed her greatness would have felt an infinite contempt; and fierce indeed must have been the indignation of Demosthenes when he saw the supreme result of the besotted folly of his colleague. Their very food was running short, for before the eclipse an order had been sent to Katanê countermanding all fresh supplies. Regret and censure were, however, alike vain. The lines along Epipolai must be abandoned and everything staked on a last effort to break the barrier which now lay between them and safety. If this should fail, the ships were to be burnt, and the army was to retreat by land.

So far as it regarded the lines on Epipolai, this decision seems to have been an error of judgement, not on the part of Nikias (for he had no judgement to exercise), but of the firm and sagacious Demosthenes. *Mistake of Demosthenes.* Past experience had taught him that in encountering the solid prows of the enemy's ships in a cramped space they were setting themselves the task of cutting wood with a razor; but the lines on Epipolai gave them free access to the country beyond and the power of effecting a deliberate and orderly re-treat. A few only of the twenty-seven days had passed when Nikias told the Athenians that all had been done which could be done to insure success in the coming struggle. Grappling irons were to fall on the enemy's prows and keep the ships locked in a fatal embrace until the combatants on one side or the other should be swept into the sea. In short, a hard necessity compelled them to make the fight as much as possible a land battle on the water; and he besought the Athenians to show that in spite of bodily weakness and unparalleled misfortunes, Athenian skill could get the better of brute force rendered still more brutal by success. He told them plainly that they saw before them all the fleet and all the army of Athens, and that if they should now fail, her powers of resistance were gone. A speech more disgraceful to himself and less likely to encourage his men has seldom been uttered by any leader. It was his fault that Syracuse had not been taken a year ago; it was his fault that everything had gone wrong since the death of Lamachos; it was his fault that Gylippos had entered the city; it was his fault that they had not retreated when retreat was first urged by Demosthenes; and it was his fault that they had not left the harbour before the barrier of ships had been stretched across its mouth. Yet this was the man who could beseech his soldiers to remember that on the issue of this fight depended the great name of Athens and the freedom which had rendered her illustrious.

Speech of Nikias.

The time for the great experiment had come, and the men were all on board, when Nikias in his agony made one more effort to rouse them, not to greater courage (for this had never failed), but to greater confidence. He cared nothing whether he repeated himself or dwelt on topics which

Ruin of the Athenian fleet.

might be thought weak or stale. They were, in fact, neither the one nor the other, and they had furnished the substance of the great funeral oration of Perikles (p. 54); but it may be doubted whether he was acting judiciously in drawing to this extreme tension, at a time when steadiness of eye and hand were most of all needed, the nerves of a people so highly sensitive as the Athenians. At length the signal was given; but, in spite of the rapidity of their movements and the strength of their assault, the Athenians had not succeeded in breaking the chains which bound the ships at the harbour's mouth when the Syracusan fleet, starting from all points, attacked them in the rear. The battle was soon broken into groups, while within their lines the Athenian army, advancing to the water's edge, surveyed with alternations of passionate hope and fear the fortunes of a fight on which the lives of all depended. All, however, were not looking in the same direction; and thus there might be seen in the Athenian camp some who, in the intensity of feverish suspense, were keeping time with their bodies to the swayings of the battle, others who were abandoning themselves to a paroxysm of agony on witnessing some disaster, others carried away by an unreasonable hope on seeing their own men drive back the enemy. At last brute force prevailed. The Athenians were pushed further and further back till their whole fleet was driven ashore. Amidst the piercing shrieks and bitter weeping of the troops, who hastened to give such help as they could, the crews of the shattered ships were landed, while some hurried to the defence of their walls, and others bethought themselves of providing only for their own safety.

The sun sank upon a scene of absolute despair in the Athenian encampment and of fierce and boundless exultation within the walls of Syracuse. Demosthenes was still anxious that one more effort should be made to break the barrier at the mouth of the harbour; but the men would not stir. The generals therefore determined to retreat by land: and if the retreat had been begun at once, the whole of this still mighty armament might have been saved. The roads were still unguarded, and the whole city was so given up to a frenzy of delight that Hermokrates abandoned as hopeless the idea of inducing them to start at once and break up the ground on the probable line of march. But if he could not do this, he might try the effect of stratagem to detain the Athenians as victims for the slaughter; and with Nikias, who was to be their evil genius to the end, his trick succeeded. Some Syracusan horsemen, professing to belong to the Athenian party, went down to the Athenian lines with the tidings that the roads were already blocked, and suggested that a careful and deliberate retreat on the following day would be better than a hasty departure during the night. Having remained over the first night, they thought it best to tarry yet another day: but early in the morning, while within the Athenian lines the flames which rose from burning ships showed that the naval war was already ended, the Syracusan troops had set out into the country, to break up or to guard carefully the roads, the forts, and the passes in the hills.

Stratagem of Hermokrates to delay the retreat of the Athenians.

With the morning of the second day after the battle the retreat which was to end in ruin began with unspeakable agony. The cup of bitterness was indeed filled to the brim and running over. They had looked their last on the rock and shrine of the Virgin goddess with the expectation that they were going to make Athens the centre and head of a Panhellenic empire; they were now marching ignominiously, after irretrievable defeat, perhaps to slavery or to death. But although they could take their food (its weight would now be no oppressive burden), they

Departure of the Athenians from their camp.

could not take their sick. Hundreds were pining away with the wasting marsh fever; hundreds were smitten down with wounds. All these must now be left, and left, not as in the less savage warfare of our own times, with the confidence that they would be treated with some humanity, but to the certainty of servitude, torture, or death. As the terrible realities of departure broke upon them, the whole camp became a scene of unutterable woe. Brothers and sons were here to be forsaken whom parents and kinsmen had accompanied with affectionate pride from the gates of Athens to the triremes at Peiraieus. Comrades in the same tent were now to be separated, happy if, after a brief pang here, they should be reunited in the world unseen. In the agony of the moment the fever-stricken sufferers clung to their companions as these set out on their miserable march, and mangled wretches crawled feebly on, intreating to be taken with them, until strength failed and they sank down by the way.

In this desperate crisis Nikias did his best to cheer and encourage the men whom his own egregious carelessness had brought into their present unparalleled difficulties. His words were chiefly a comment on the homely saying that the lane must be long which has no turning, and that the evils which they might still have to suffer must in some degree be lightened by the consciousness that they were shared alike by all. Suffering from a painful malady, accustomed during his life to the ease of a wealthy Athenian, and, more than this, scrupulously exact in his religious worship and blameless in his private life, he had now to bear up under the same toils and privations with themselves. This is not the language of a man who dreads the physical dangers of war; but it is the language of one who, even in the direst extremity, cannot be brought to see that the misery which he is

Efforts of Nikias to sustain the courage of the Athenians.

striving to alleviate is the result strictly of his own folly in wasting a series of golden opportunities.

The horrors of the march, for which they had chosen the road to Katanê, may be faintly imagined from the fact that, in spite of fearful exertion, with little food, and almost without water and without sleep, they accomplished in five days a distance which, if unhindered, they could have traversed easily in two hours. Convinced now that the northward journey was impracticable, they set forth at dead of night on the Helorine road leading to the southern coast. A panic separated the division of Nikias from that of Demosthenes, who, being in the rear, had to think more of keeping his men in order of battle than of getting over the ground. Thus constrained to mass his troops, he found himself presently hemmed in between walls in an olive garden with a roadway on either side, where his men could be shot down by an enemy who was himself exposed to no danger. For hours the fearful carnage went on, until at length the Syracusans invited the surrender of Demosthenes and his troops, under a covenant which included the general not less than his men, and by which the captors pledged themselves that none should be put to death either by violence, or by bonds, or by lack of the necessaries of life. The summons was obeyed, and four shields held upwards were filled with the money still possessed by the troops of Demosthenes, who were now led away to Syracuse.

<small>Surrender of Demosthenes.</small>

Nikias, five miles further to the south, had crossed the Erineos, when, early on the following day, the Syracusan messengers informed him of the surrender of Demosthenes, and summoned him to follow his example. The counter proposal of Nikias, that in exchange for the men under his command Athens should pay to the Syracusans the whole cost of the war

<small>Surrender of Nikias.</small>

would have filled their treasury with money sorely needed; but the delight of trampling a fallen enemy under foot was more enticing. The terms were rejected, and all day long the harassing warfare was carried on. At night the Athenians made an attempt to escape under cover of darkness; but the war-shout which instantly rose from the Syracusan camp showed that they were discovered, and with a feeling of blank dismay they remained where they were. On the following morning they reached the little stream of the Assinaros. The sight of the sparkling water banished all thoughts of order and discipline, all prudence and caution. Instead of turning round to the enemy and so covering the passage of those who had to cross first, each man sought only to plunge into the water himself, to quench his thirst, and to gain the other side. In an instant all was hopeless tumult, and the stream, fouled by the trampling of thousands, was soon reddened with their blood. Still the Peloponnesians mercilessly drove the masses before them upon the crowds already struggling in the water, and still the men drank on, almost in the agonies of death. To put an end to the slaughter which had become mere butchery, Nikias surrendered himself to Gylippos personally, in the hope that the Spartans might remember the enormous benefits (p. 102) which in times past Sparta had received from him. The number of prisoners finally got together was not great. The larger number were hidden away by private men, and the state was thus defrauded of the wealth which an acceptance of the offer of Nikias would have insured to it.

Forty thousand men had left the Athenian lines on the Great Harbour; a week later 7,000 marched as prisoners into Syracuse. What became of the sick and wounded in the camp we are not told. We can scarcely doubt that all were murdered; and murder was mercy in comparison with the treatment of the 7,000, who were penned like cattle in the stone-quarries of Epipolai. The Syracusans had promised to Demosthenes that no man belonging to his division should suffer a violent death, or die from bonds or from lack of necessary food; but they insured the deaths of hundreds and of thousands as certainly as Suraj-ud-Dowlah murdered the victims of the Black Hole of Calcutta.

Confinement of the prisoners in the stone quarries of Epipolai.

The Athenian generals were happily spared the sight of these prolonged and excruciating tortures. Both were put to death; and unless the terms of the convention were to be kept, Demosthenes could, of course, expect no mercy. Next to Perikles and to Phormion there was no leader to whom Athens in this great struggle owed so much, and none, therefore, whom the Spartans and their allies regarded with more virulent hatred. In flagrant violation of a distinct compact, the victor of Sphakteria was murdered. He died, as he had lived, without a stain on his military reputation, the victim of the superstition and the respectability of his colleague.

Death of Nikias and Demosthenes.

So ended an expedition which changed the current of Athenian history and therefore, in a greater or less degree, of the history of the world. In the Athenian people such a project as the conquest of Sicily was a political error of the gravest kind. They had been warned against all such undertakings by the most clear-sighted of their statesmen; they had been enticed into the scheme by one of the most insolent and lawless men with which any country ever was cursed. They had allowed their plans to be enormously extended by a general who wisely advised them not to go to Sicily, and who did them a deadly mischief by consenting to go against his will

Influence of the catastrophe on the subsequent history of Athens.

They had hazarded on this distant venture an amount of strength which was imperiously needed for the protection of Athens and the recovery of Amphipolis; and instead of a starvation which, as things turned out, would have been wise, they fed the expedition with bounty so lavish that failure became ruin. The power of trampling on Sicily as Gylippos and his allies trampled on the defeated armament would have done no good to Athens or to the world; but if the isolating policy which seeks to maintain an infinite number of autonomous units be in itself an evil, then it is unfortunate that the victory of Gylippos insured the predominance of this policy. The empire of Athens, if it could have been maintained, might have prevented the wars of many generations, and might have kept within narrower bounds the empire of Rome itself. To a vast extent she could offer to her allies or her subjects common interests and common ends. Sparta could offer none: but the system of Sparta fell in with instincts in the Hellenic mind which may have been weakened but were never eradicated; and against this instinct the wisdom and prudence of Athenian statesmen strove in vain.

CHAPTER VI.

THE PELOPONNESIAN, OR DEKELEIAN, WAR, FROM THE FAILURE OF THE SICILIAN EXPEDITION TO THE SUPPRESSION OF THE OLIGARCHY OF THE FOUR HUNDRED AT ATHENS.

THE Athenians were still feeding themselves on bright hopes of Sicilian conquest while the walls of the Spartan fortress of Dekeleia were daily gaining height and strength. There was, in truth, need of encouragement. Previous invasions had lasted but a few weeks at the utmost; now the whole country lay permanently at the mercy of the enemy. Each day they felt the sting of the monster evil of slavery; and the desertion of 20,000 men left Athens almost destitute of skilled workmen. Athens had, in truth, ceased to be a city. It was now nothing more than a garrison in which the defenders were worn out with harassing and incessant duty. The very magnitude of their tasks savoured of madness or infatuation. Athens was herself in a state of siege; and all her fleet, with the flower of her forces, was besieging a distant city, scarcely less powerful than herself. When at length, after weeks of dreadful silence, their hopes of success in Sicily were dashed to the ground, they turned in the first burst of despairing grief on the speakers who had urged on the expedition and on the soothsayers and diviners who had augured well for the enterprise; but such revenge was a poor consolation for the failure of a scheme which they had themselves decreed. Their thoughts were soon drawn away to more practical matters. Their army had been cut off; their fleet was either burnt or in the enemy's hands; their docks were almost empty of ships. There was nothing to hinder their enemies from attacking the city, or to keep the subjects of Athens from joining them. But in spite of this sea of troubles one feeling only pervaded the people. The idea of submission crossed no man's mind. The struggle must be carried on vigorously and economically. Wood must be provided for shipbuilding, and all movements among their allies must be carefully watched. With the rapidity which had astonished the Syracusans (p. 132) the promontory of Sounion was strongly fortified to protect the passage of merchant vessels, while a further force was rendered

Effects of the disaster in Sicily on popular feeling at Athens.
B.C. 413.

available by abandoning the fort on the Peloponnesian coast facing the island of Kythera (p. 85).

As for the enemies of Athens, they regarded the struggle, not unnaturally, as all but ended. It had taken long to shatter the fabric of her empire; but now it was falling to pieces of itself, and the golden age in which every Greek city should be absolutely autonomous had all but begun. Nor had the winter come to an end before some of the allies made efforts to transfer their allegiance to Sparta. The first deputation came from Euboia; the second from Lesbos. After these came envoys from Chios and Erythrai, and with them ambassadors from Tissaphernes, the Persian satrap of Lydia, who had received notice from the Persian king that the tributes due from the Hellenic cities within his jurisdiction must be paid into the treasury. The mere fact that the weakness of Athens should at once call forth such a claim might have taught the Asiatic Greeks that in seeking to be free of the Athenian yoke they were, like the frogs, simply changing king Log for king Stork. Tissaphernes, at least, knew that without Spartan aid he could not break up the Athenian empire, and that until this work could be done, he must remain a debtor to the king for a sum the magnitude of which was every day increasing. While the envoys of Tissaphernes were pleading the cause of the Chians, the representatives of Pharnabazos, the viceroy of the Hellespont, came to ask that his satrapy might be made the scene of the first operations. Thus was presented the singular sight of two Persian satraps beseeching the Spartans to undo the work which they had left Athens to carry out (p. 4), and which she had carried out for nearly seventy years. That the satraps should be anxious to win the royal favour by being foremost in pulling down the Athenian empire, was natural enough; that the Spartans, who in the day of need had solemnly adjured the Athenians not to betray their kinsfolk to the barbarian, should now deliberately reopen the way for Persian aggression, was a treason against the liberties not only of Hellas but of Europe. But looking merely to the mode in which treachery might be made to yield its fruits most readily, they were right in inclining to the side of Tissaphernes. The contest was decided by Alkibiades, who with all his strength urged the claims of the Chians as being the highest bidders.

So passed away the winter which ended the nineteenth year of the war. The spring had come; and the Chian conspirators still waited impatiently for the promised succour. They were in a fever of anxiety lest their plans should become known to the Athenians; and the refusal of the Corinthians to sail until after the celebration of the Isthmian games gave the Athenians time to verify in some measure the suspicions which they had already formed. Aristokrates was accordingly sent to Chios, and on being assured by the government that they had no intention of revolting, he demanded a contingent of ships by the terms of the alliance. The demand was complied with, we are told, only because the conspirators desired not to call the people into their council; and seven Chian triremes sailed for Athens.

Mission of Aristokrates to Chios. B.C. 412.

The defeat of a Peloponnesian squadron by the Athenians off the Epidaurian coast first made the Spartans think that the task before them might be less easy than they had anticipated; and they at once issued an order for the recall of Chalkideus, who with five ships was taking Alkibiades to Chios. In this resolution Alkibiades saw the death-

Revolt of Chios from Athens.

blow to his whole scheme. Chios could be added to the Spartan confederacy only through the success of the oligarchic plot; and he was well aware that the conspirators, although ready to revolt, were not ready to run the risk of ruining themselves. If these plotters should learn that Chalkideus had been recalled because the Athenians had won a victory, they would at once seek to pacify the Athenians by an increased profession of zeal for their service. He insisted that the original plan should be carried out, and pledged himself that, if he could but reach the Ionian coast, he would bring about the revolt not only of Chios but of the other allies of Athens. His influence gained the day; but it was necessary now to hoodwink the conspirators as well as the demos of Chios. The council was assembling when, to the dismay of the people, the Spartan triremes approached the landing-place; and Alkibiades, appearing at once before the senate, assured them that the little squadron now in their harbour was but the van of a large fleet already on its way. The plotters, convinced by this lie that they might trust to Sparta for prompt and efficient help, resolved to risk the solid benefits of a prosperity unbroken for half a century for the sake of gratifying an unreasoning instinct of isolation,—an instinct which made even the demos place but little value on a connexion from which they yet knew that they had received much good and no harm. Chios revolted from Athens; and her example was followed first by Erythrai and then by Klazomenai. Thus had Alkibiades once again changed the history of his country. Spartan tardiness would have allowed the Chian conspirators to learn the real state of the case, and to take in the full extent of the risk which they were running; and their refusal to revolt would have insured the fidelity of the other allies.

The energy of the traitor turned the scale, and the voyage of Chalkideus with his five ships bore fruit in the final catastrophe.

Having once committed themselves to the venture, the Chian oligarchs espoused the cause of their new friends with impetuous ardour. They were not blind to the benefits which they received from Athens, and while they wished to weaken her, they had no desire to impoverish themselves. Any such result they trusted to avert with the aid of Sparta. They found themselves quite mistaken; but for the present their act had given a startling impulse to the centrifugal instincts of the allies, and had awakened at Athens feelings bordering on despair. Her present resources were wholly inadequate for the crisis; but there was yet the reserve fund of 1,000 talents which Perikles had stored up in the Akropolis (p. 53). The sanctions forbidding its use were now removed; and the money was employed to send a fleet, probably of inferior ships, to take the place of the blockading squadron off the Epidaurian coast, from which eight ships, under Strombichides, were sent to Chios, while the seven Chian ships were taken to Athens, where the free men among the crews were imprisoned, the slaves being set at liberty.

Employment of the Athenian reserve fund.

The example set by Chios was soon followed by Miletos, which revolted on the arrival of Alkibiades. At the same time, a treaty was ratified between the Spartans and the Persian king, which declared the latter to be the rightful owner of all lands which he or his forefathers had at any time possessed,— in other words (according to Persian theories of possession), not only of the lands lying to the east of the Egean, but of Thessaly, Boiotia, Phokis, Attica, and even Megara which for a few days had been held by Mardonios.

Revolt of Miletos.

First treaty of the Spartans with the Persians.

There seemed, indeed, to be little or nothing to encourage the Athenians. The cities of Lebedos and Erai were induced by the Chians to join in the revolt, while the blockade off the Epidaurian coast was broken by the beleaguered ships. *Revolution at Samos in favour of Athens.* But at this time an event occurred which seemed even to make it likely that Athens might yet be victorious over her enemies. A revolution took place in Samos, not against her but in her favour. So little had Athens interfered with the internal affairs of the island since the suppression of the first revolt (p. 40) nearly thirty years before, that the Geomoroi, or oligarchical landowners, had regained their preponderance and deprived the demos of all right of intermarriage with the dominant class. The demos had probably been for some time watching for an opportunity for deposing their rulers, when the presence of three Athenian ships, of which Thucydides speaks as purely accidental, determined them to act at once. The oligarchy was probably taken by surprise, but they made an obstinate resistance. Two hundred were slain in the struggle; four hundred were banished, their property being divided among the demos, who, with studied irony, treated the Geomoroi as an inferior class by forbidding the people to contract any marriages with them. These were measures which, if they cannot be justified, must be severely condemned. But it is admitted that these oligarchs intended to follow the example of their Chian brethren; and unless it can be maintained that the people were bound to be passive while a foreign enemy was being brought in, and a yoke put upon them far harder than the mere sentimental grievance (pp. 4, 27, 65) which formed their one ground of complaint against the Athenians, then it must be granted that they took the only course open to them. The violence of the struggle was owing to the power of the dominant party; and the punishment dealt out to them after their defeat was certainly not so heavy as that which they would have inflicted on a demos against which they might themselves have risen in successful revolt. The Samian people had given signal proof of their fidelity, and Athens rewarded them by raising them at once to the rank of an autonomous ally.

The effect of this revolution soon became felt. If the Athenians were to continue the struggle at all, they must have a safe base of operations; and such a post they now had in Samos. The Chian oligarchs, dreading to stand alone in their revolt, were making strong efforts to detach Lesbos from Athens. Thirteen Chian ships sailed to Lesbos, where Methymna and Mytilene had thrown off their allegiance to Athens. Not many days afterwards, a fleet of twenty-five Athenian ships took Mytilene by surprise, and the Athenians were soon masters of the whole island. If the Lesbians now escaped the punishment which was all but inflicted on the Mytilenaians in the days of Kleon, the difference was owing rather to the weakness than to the magnanimity of the conquerors. But there was nothing to prevent the Athenians from retaliating on their enemies those evils which the fortification of Dekeleia had so bitterly aggravated for themselves, and their vengeance was directed first against the conspirators of Chios. A series of defeats reduced the Chians to a state of siege within their walls, and compelled them to look passively on the ravaging of those fruitful and happy lands on which no invader had trodden since the days of Xerxes. The losses thus occasioned roused naturally the indignation of the demos against a struggle of which they had never approved, but by which they were sufferers not less than the oligarchs. The fortification of Delphinion by the Athenians, some-

Abortive revolt of the Lesbians.

Ravaging of Chios.

what to the north of the city, made all alike feel the miseries which Sparta, by fortifying Dekeleia, had inflicted upon Athens. The number of slaves in Chios was unusually great, and the harshness of their treatment led many to escape to the mountains, and there live by systematic plundering. To these men the fort of Delphinion furnished an irresistible temptation to desertion, and few slaves remained in the city. But these fugitives knew the country well, and their defection was followed by calamities which almost reduced the Chian government to despair. This was all that the plotters had gained by intrigues warily carried on and schemes carefully matured. Thucydides, indeed, tries hard to show that if they had committed an error of judgement, it was one which might easily be pardoned. To all appearance the power of Athens was broken at Syracuse; and they were backed, as they thought, by an adequate body of supporters. But unless it be maintained that a patrician class would be justified in bringing foreign enemies into the land against the known wishes of a whole people, these Chian oligarchs must stand condemned. The demos, throughout, had had no desire to join them. They must have known that they at least had little benefit to look for from Spartan Harmostai and Persian tribute-gatherers, with whom these Spartans seemed to maintain so suspicious a friendship. The singular prosperity of the island for more than half a century proved that the islanders had not only no real ground of complaint against Athens, but were indebted to her for happiness and wealth, which in like measure they would never know again. There was enough in the conduct of the Chian government to excite the indignation of Englishmen at the present day. Had it not been for Athens, they must have remained subject to the degrading yoke and arbitrary exactions of the Persian king. As her free allies, they had been called upon only to furnish their yearly quota of ships for the maintenance of an order from which they derived benefits fully equal to any which Athens herself received. It is not, indeed, too much to say that this order was the greatest political blessing which the world had yet seen. It reflected on the humblest members of this great confederacy the lustre of the most considerable states inrolled in it; and the inhabitants of insignificant Egean islands were thoroughly aware and not a little proud of the importance thus attached to them both in the Hellenic and in the barbarian world. If they were injured by the men of other cities, they could appeal, as we have seen (p. 4), to the great assembly of the Athenian citizens, in whose courts, as they well knew, there was little difficulty in obtaining justice even against distinguished Athenian generals. To this order, in spite of the sentimental grievances shaped by unwholesome dreams of autonomy, the people in most of the allied or subject cities were honestly attached; and in Chios their attachment was so strong that the oligarchs had to work in fear and trembling lest their plots should come prematurely to the knowledge of the Athenians.

State of parties in Chios.

A victory gained at this time by the Athenians on Milesian territory might have been of the greatest benefit to them in their intended investment of Miletos, had not tidings come that a large fleet from Peloponnesos and Sicily might at any moment be looked for. In this fleet the Syracusan squadron was commanded by Hermokrates, who was as earnestly bent on breaking up the empire of Athens in the Egean as he had been on destroying her forces on the soil of his own city. Joining him at Teichioussa in the gulf of Iasos, Alkibiades, who had fought in the battle recently won by the Athenians, told

Arrival of a Syracusan fleet under Hermokrates.

him in few words that unless Miletos could be relieved their whole work in sapping the empire of Athens must be frustrated. A resolution was taken to go at once to its aid; but their mere approach did the work. The Athenian commanders wished at first to meet the Peloponnesians in open fight; but they were opposed with determined energy by Phrynichos, who insisted that the one thing which Athens in her present need could not afford to incur was defeat. For himself, he assuredly would not allow the safety of Athens to be imperilled from any fancied notions of honour or self-respect. From Samos they might at a more convenient season become assailants in their turn.

The events of the ensuing winter told more, on the whole, for the Athenians than for their enemies, although in the powerful fleet assembled at Miletos the Spartan admiral Astyochos read the condemnation of the disgraceful treaty made by Chalkideus with Tissaphernes (p. 160). It was not *[Second treaty between Sparta and Persia.]* that he had any definite grievance; but the covenant seemed to be too much in the interests of the Persian king, and accordingly he insisted on a revision of the terms. The result was a compact which formally bound the Spartans not to injure any country or city which might at any time have belonged either to the reigning Persian monarch or to any of his predecessors. From such territories or towns they were forbidden to exact any tax or tribute whatever. On his part, the Persian despot condescended to give the Spartans such help as he might be persuaded to afford, and to guarantee them to the best of his power from invasion on the part of any of his subjects. It may be seen at a glance that this treaty simply substituted an absurdity in place of an insult. The former covenant had secured to the king all lands which he or his forefathers might at any time have possessed, and thus owned him as lord of Thessaly, Boiotia, Attica, and Megara (G.P., p. 188): the latter pledged Sparta to do no mischief to any of these lands or cities. But there was no clause declaring that Athens was in a state of rebellion and must be brought back to her allegiance; and therefore this treaty formally pledged the Spartans to immediate peace with the enemies against whom they were now fighting to the death. This fact alone proves the hollowness of the league to which neither side intended to adhere so soon as it had become inconvenient to do so. But the uselessness of these compacts was made known to Tissaphernes, when the Spartan commissioner Lichas, feeling himself adequately backed by the combination of two Spartan fleets, told the satrap that he had not the least intention of abiding by covenants so humiliating not only to Sparta but to the Greeks generally. If the Persian king thought that Sparta would own him as lawful master of Thessaly, Lokris, and Boiotia, he was much mistaken. Taken aback by the frank avowal that under the present arrangement Sparta would not condescend to accept Persian subsidies, the satrap turned away and went off in a rage.

The retreat of the Athenians to Samos left Rhodes exposed to the full force of Spartan influence. The three cities of the island, Lindos, Ialysos, and Kameiros, were inhabited by a Dorian population; and it might be supposed that they would therefore be eager to shake off the yoke of an Ionic power. But it was not so; and the fact speaks volumes for the general spirit of the imperial administration of Athens. Here, as elsewhere, revolt was the work not of the people but of the oligarchs. On the approach of the Peloponnesian fleet of nearly a hundred ships the demos fled in dismay to the mountains; and the conspirators, thus left free, declared Rhodes a member of the Spartan

Revolt of Rhodes from Athens.

confederacy. For three months the fleet lay drawn up on shore in the harbours of the island. The Spartans were here, as they wished to be, out of the way of Tissaphernes; and, in the hope of being able to carry on the war without Persian subsidies, they levied a tribute of thirty-two talents on the Rhodians, who found thus early that freedom from the yoke of Athens was a blessing which must be paid for. But another cause for their inaction lay in the intrigues of Alkibiades. For a man who had made treachery his trade there could obviously be no alternative but that of pre-eminence or ruin; and pre-eminence could be retained only by constant success. His treasons had indeed destroyed the Athenian fleet and army in Sicily, and had inflicted a terrible blow on Attica itself by the fortification of Dekeleia: but in the waters of the Egean things began to wear a different aspect. It was true that he had brought about the revolt of Chios, and that this had been followed by the defection of other cities on the islands and on the Asiatic continent. But Chios had been miserably ravaged: Lesbos had been reconquered (p. 162); and they had to contend everywhere with the passive resistance of the people, who were sadly indifferent to the freedom held out for their acceptance by Sparta. They were still more irritated by the rising of the people in Samos (p. 161) and by the airs of superiority assumed towards them by the Persian satrap. An order to kill Alkibiades was therefore sent out to the admiral Astyochos; but the Athenian exile was more than a match for the stupid treachery of the Spartans, and he made his way to Tissaphernes, contrasting probably the secret assassinations of an oligarchic community with the open courts and straightforward decrees of a vulgar demos.

Order from Sparta for the assassination of Alkibiades.

From this new counsellor Tissaphernes received the

suggestion which led him to reduce the pay of the Peloponnesians from a drachma to half a drachma daily, and to stifle the discontent which might be thus roused by bribing their generals and trierarchs. The acceptance of these bribes at once enabled Alkibiades to come forward as the agent of Tissaphernes and adopt towards them a tone which they dared not openly resent. To the satrap he insisted that in the interests of Persia the movements of the war should be slow and that Persian aid should be so thrown into the balance that the contending parties might gradually wear each other out. He urged, further, that if either side was to be victorious the victory of Athens would be more to the advantage of the Great King, whom she would willingly leave master of the continental cities, her object being confined to the task of bringing the Egean islanders into absolute subjection to herself; whereas the Spartans might be compelled even against their will to secure to the Asiatic Hellenes the autonomy which they had so long promised them. To this string of glibly-uttered falsehoods Tissaphernes listened probably with the quiet incredulity of a man who knew himself to be in debt to the king, because for more than half a century Persian tax-gatherers had been shut out from the continental not less than the insular allies of this state, which was now described as ready to abandon the former to Persian slavery. But in his turn Alkibiades knew that, although his advice might for the present be followed, his position must be fearfully precarious; and he resolved to make an effort to bring about his return to Athens by upsetting her political constitution. If anything in his life could be amazing, it would be the impudence of the message which he sent to those of the oligarchic party who were serving in the armament at Samos. Although

Counsels of Alkibiades to Tissaphernes.

Overtures of Alkibiades to the oligarchy in the army at Samos.

he was certainly guiltless of the mutilation of the Hermai (p. 120), no one knew better than himself that that crime had been perpetrated by oligarchs provoked by his own unbearable insolence. He knew also that if he had been innocent of the crime for which he was summoned from Sicily to take his trial, or if, frankly confessing his guilt, he had promised that the offence should not be repeated, his influence with the demos would not have been impaired. Knowing all this, he could yet dare to tell them that he owed his banishment to the demos, and that so long as this vagabond society continued to exist he would not set foot in the streets of his native city. This message was, of course, not made known to the army generally; and the oligarchs alone were assured by him that if he could return to an oligarchic Athens he could and would secure for her the active friendship of Tissaphernes. When the envoys from the camp of Samos appeared before Alkibiades in answer to his letter, he went on to tell them that the Persian king was anxious to ally himself with Athens, but that it was her democratic constitution which made it impossible for him to trust her citizens. The envoys were duped. Instead of asking for some evidence that the Persian despot took this deep personal interest in the domestic concerns of Athens, they hastened back to deliver themselves of the tidings that the treasures of the Persian king were within their grasp, on the small conditions that the banishment of Alkibiades should be annulled and the democracy of Athens put down.

One man only, it would seem, saw through these glaring falsehoods, and this was the general Phrynichos. With convincing clearness he pointed out to them the absurdity of supposing that the Persian monarch could care whether Athens was or was not governed by a democracy. If he had any predi- *Protest of Phrynichos.*

lection for either side, it must be for the Peloponnesians, who had done him little or no harm, rather than for the Athenians, who had deprived him of some of his best possessions; nor could the warnings inforced by the history of three generations be effaced from his mind by the occurrence of an internal revolution, of which he did not know the cause and could not forecast the results. Even more earnestly Phrynichos sought to dispel the wretched delusion that the establishment of oligarchy at Athens would tend to maintain and strengthen her maritime empire. It was worse than ridiculous to count on retaining for their own benefit an order of things the suppression of which was the one object of the enemies of Athens. The revolution would not bring back one revolted city to its allegiance or render any one of the allies more trustworthy. Speaking from his own experience, he assured them that under the exclusive regimen of oligarchs the allies would be only more troublesome and unruly, for these high-born rulers were most of all bent on securing what they called their freedom, while they hounded on the people to acts of violence which they hoped to turn to their own profit. Nay more, he knew that it was the Athenian demos alone which could hold the allies together at all. The citizens of the allied states were well aware that from an oligarchical government they had nothing to expect but capital sentences without fair trial or hearing, or perhaps the more summary method of secret murder; and even those which were already under oligarchies rejoiced most of all in the fact that the Athenian demos was for them a haven of refuge against their masters, who stood in wholesome terror of an arraignment before the tribunal of the sovereign people. No more triumphant or emphatic eulogy of the imperial government or of the political constitution of Athens could have been pronounced than the simple statement of facts by which Phrynichos sought to warn the assembled oligarchs against a step likely to involve them and the whole state in ruin. The further fact that Phrynichos did not belong to the school of Perikles or Ephialtes (p. 36) adds only to the strength of his words, and makes his warning more memorable. If we may, as we unquestionably may, take the account of Thucydides as an exact report of the case, Phrynichos opposed the revolution only because he was resolved on keeping Alkibiades away from Athens; and the protest with which he wound up his speech did not prevent him from furthering and joining the oligarchical movement when he had no longer any reason to fear his rivalry.

In spite of his warnings the conspirators determined to send Peisandros with other envoys to Athens; and Phrynichos, feeling that the offer of Persian help would in the present impoverishment of the city come with irresistible force, resolved to cut short the intrigues of Alkibiades by informing the Spartan admiral Astyochos of his plots. But Astyochos, who, like all his colleagues except the Syracusan Hermokrates, had sold himself to the Persian satrap, (p. 168), went straight to Magnesia and laid the letter before Alkibiades and his patron; and Alkibiades wrote in his turn to his friends at Samos, desiring them to put Phrynichos at once to death. Why the deed was not done, we are not told; and Phrynichos wrote again to Astyochos, upbraiding him with his breach of confidence, and offering now to betray the whole Athenian armament into his hands and so put an end to the war. This letter, he knew, would be also shown to Alkibiades. Announcing, therefore, to the army that the enemy was about to attack the camp, he insisted on its being fortified with all speed. The walls were finished, when a letter from Alkibiades announced that Phrynichos had

Counterplots of Phrynichos and Alkibiades.

betrayed the army and that the enemy would immediately be upon them. The only result of his letter was, of course, the acquittal of Phrynichos from the charge on which in his previous letter Alkibiades had demanded his assassination.

At Athens the proposals of Peisandros and his fellow envoys were met by vehement opposition, some pro-testing against the constitutional change, others exclaiming against the restoration of a man who had defied the laws, while the officers of the Eleusinian mysteries denounced it as an insult to the gods. Disregarding the clamour, Peisandros went up to each speaker and quietly asked him how he proposed to carry on the war if the whole weight of Persia should be thrown into the scale against them. The speakers were silenced; and Peisandros went on to assure the assembly that the change of constitution would win for them the confidence of the Persian king; that constitutional forms were matters of small moment compared with the safety of the state; and that if after fairly trying oligarchy they found that they did not like it, it would be easy for them to restore the democracy. He spoke to a people worn down by a series of disasters coming upon a struggle which had now lasted for nearly a generation; and the dulness which is the common result of long-protracted anxiety led them to believe the mere word of a man who told them that the resources for carrying on a struggle in which they could not make up their minds to confess themselves beaten would be supplied by Persia. No one asked what reason there might be for ascribing to the Great King so strange a hankering after a good understanding with a state which had destroyed Persian fleets and armies, had effectually checked the course of Persian conquest, and taken away for more than half a century the tribute which would have

Progress of the revolution at Athens.

found its way into the royal coffers at Sousa. In this credulous temper they resolved to send Peisandros with ten commissioners to settle matters with Alkibiades and the Lydian satrap. But before he could set off, Peisandros knew that he had much to do at Athens. The demos was not yet put down, and the army at Samos was strongly opposed to the change. It was therefore necessary to set in order the oligarchic machinery without which the foundations of democracy could not be overthrown. These foundations rested on freedom of speech; and if this could be repressed, the constitutional forms to which they were so much attached would be found most useful in riveting their chains. Going round to all the political clubs or Hetairiai, as they were called, Peisandros concerted with them a plan of action to be carried out by the leaders who should remain behind him. At the head of these was the Rhetor Antiphon, whose occupation, if it brought him large gains, had stood in the way of a singularly ambitious disposition. The Assembly felt jealous of the professed rhetoricians who, it was supposed, gave their minds to devising tricks of debate and advocacy, and with whom, therefore, ordinary citizens stood at an unfair disadvantage. Disliking the demos, partly, perhaps, because popular feeling had thus debarred him a public career, but more, probably, from a genuine oligarchical temper, Antiphon threw himself into the conspiracy with an energy equal to his ability, and for this end worked with consummate skill the machinery of assassination. In private life, we are told, he was a man of genial character, kindly in his relations with his family and affectionate in his intercourse with his friends. He had, in short, the estimable qualities of Nikias; and for the oligarchic Thucydides this was enough. Antiphon becomes in his eyes a man second to none of his age in virtue. This employer of murderous bravoes was ably seconded not only by Theramenes, son of Hagnon, the founder of Amphipolis (p. 39), but by Phrynichos, who seems to have convinced himself that a man may do anything to save his life, and who, when it became clear that Alkibiades had lost his chance of returning with the oligarchs, began to fear his enmity as leader of the democracy.

The arrival of Peisandros at Magnesia with the other envoys disconcerted Alkibiades, who saw that he was caught in a trap; the fact being, as he had now discovered, that Tissaphernes had no intention of making any definite covenant with the Athenians. One course only remained open to him. To confess that he could not get the satrap to do what he wanted would be to destroy his chance of returning to Athens under any form of government; and he already began to see that he had a second string to his bow in the democracy. He must then make it appear that the failure of the negotiation was owing to the envoys, and he did this by raising the terms for Tissaphernes at each conference. With the first proposal, which demanded the surrender of all Ionia to the king, and with the second, which involved the cession of the islands lying off the eastern shores of the Egean, the commissioners expressed their readiness to comply; and Alkibiades was almost at his wits' end to devise conditions more humiliating, when it struck him that his end might be gained by insisting that the king should be allowed to keep in the Egean as large a fleet as might suit his purposes. The commissioners, thoroughly angered by a proposal which swept away contemptuously the real or so-called convention of Kallias (p. 32), departed with the feeling that they had been both insulted and cheated by

[margin: Rupture between the oligarchy and Alkibiades.]

Alkibiades. Unfortunately this rebuff of the oligarchic commissioners led the Athenian army to the conclusion that in his heart Alkibiades leant to the democracy, and that he had both the power and the will to bring Tissaphernes into active alliance with it.

That satrap was, however, veering of his own accord to the Peloponnesian side. The Spartans and their allies, if starved or lacking money, might become dangerous neighbours, while a victory of the Athenians might re-establish their maritime supremacy. He therefore proposed a convention, which simply assigned to the king such of his possessions as were in Asia, reserving to him the freedom of taking such measures 'about his own country' as might seem to him best. Less humiliating in appearance, these terms left the real state of things practically unchanged. The sovereign of Persia was free, if he chose so to put it, to consult the true interests not only of Athens (p. 166) but of Thessaly, Lokris, and even of Boiotia; in other words, he might at any time invade them, the implied compact being that in the way of this work the Peloponnesians would place no hindrance. *[Third treaty of Tissaphernes with the Spartans.]*

For Athens the year was to come to an end with the betrayal of Oropos to the Boiotians. The next, the twenty-first of this weary war, was to begin with the revolt of Abydos and Lampsakos. The latter, as being unfortified, was speedily recovered by Strombichides, whose efforts to win back Abydos either by persuasion or force were unsuccessful. But the work of Sparta was being done more effectually by the conspirators at Samos, who, on learning from Peisandros that no aid must be expected from Tissaphernes, and that in Alkibiades they had an open enemy, affected to feel special satisfaction in being rid of a man so little likely to work in harmony with them. *[Revolt of Abydos and Lampsakos. B.C. 411.]*

The tidings only made them more resolved to do by themselves what they had hoped to accomplish by his aid. They had extorted from the people of Athens an unwilling sanction for political changes by false promises of foreign help; and they resolved that the demos should be held to the terms of surrender, although this aid was not forthcoming. There was, in truth, no end to their folly and madness. They would have it that oligarchy must strengthen an empire which Phrynichos had solemnly warned them (p. 170) that it would assuredly dissolve ; and under this delusion they sent Peisandros with five of the commissioners to complete the work of revolution at Athens, and to establish oligarchies in any towns which they might visit on their way. With the remaining five Diitriphes was sent as general to operate in the Thraceward regions. His first exploit was to suppress the government of the people in Thasos and to place the oligarchs in power. Two months later the oligarchs showed their gratitude for the boon by fortifying the town and openly joining the enemies of Athens. To his statement that the same result followed this notable experiment in many other places, Thucydides adds a remark which, from a different point of view, agrees closely with the warning of Phrynichos. The sobriety of temper, created by oligarchic government, inspired, he tells us, a desire for true freedom, and not for the mere sham of liberty which was all that the Athenian oligarchs had destined for them. In other words, the latter did not act up to their own principles, their duty being to release all the allied subjects of Athens from their allegiance and to carry back Athens herself to the political state from which she first began to rise in the days of Solon

Revolt of Thasos.

At Athens the dagger soon put an end to freedom of speech. The first blow was inflicted on a man who had been prominent among the accusers of Alkibiades before his departure for Sicily; and by a strange irony of fortune this victim was offered up for the special purpose of winning his favour just when that restless schemer was throwing his weight into the opposite scale. Political assassinations at Athens. The work of murder once begun was not allowed to flag until it had served its purpose. Not a subject was proposed for discussion in the assembly except after the dictation of the oligarchs; the men who rose to speak on these subjects belonged to their faction, and the very words of their speeches were pre-arranged. At the same time, beyond the walls of the assembly, young men, hired for the work of murder, struck down citizens whose presence might be inconvenient, and picked off all the popular speakers. The man who ventured to oppose a measure soon disappeared; and the order of society was for the time broken up. Reign of terror. No man could trust even those whom he had looked upon as his friends. A knot of men striking swiftly and surely had brought about a collapse of authority and that extreme depression of the people which must follow this collapse. The council of the Five Hundred (G.P., p. 88) still held their meetings: and if some had spirit enough to absent themselves from the senate-house, there were others who felt that even their absence would tell as much against them as a speech in opposition to oligarchic innovations. Their presence was, indeed, all that Antiphon wanted, for if they were present they must vote; and by their vote they must be bound. Whatever was done, therefore, was done by the vote of the people; and if the people chose to pass decrees without debate, the responsibility of so doing must rest with themselves. Thus was the highest and best characteristic of the Athenian people—their respect for law and order—ingeniously used as an instrument for establishing and keeping up a reign of terror. While this terror was at its height, Peisandros, with his colleagues, arrived. Their first proposal was to appoint ten commissioners, Peisandros being one, with absolute powers, to prepare a plan by a given day for the better government of the city. On the day named the assembly was held, not in the Pnyx, but in the Temenos, or precinct, of Poseidon at Kolonos, about a mile beyond the city gates. Without preface or comment the commissioners proposed that anyone attempting to put in force the Graphê Paranomôn (a writ or indictment brought against any citizen who proposed or carried measures contrary to existing laws) should be visited by heavy penalties. The next proposition swept away all existing offices and all pay, except for military service, while it empowered the commissioners to choose five men, who should in their turn choose one hundred, these hundred again nominating each three. These Four Hundred, invested with absolute powers, were to take their place in the senate-house, taking counsel whenever they might wish to do so, but not otherwise, with the Five Thousand citizens to whom the franchise was to be limited, and whose abode was not in Athens but in the Aristophanic Land of Clouds and Cuckoos. The whole thing was meant to be an insolent mockery, and it was received, as such, with the silence which oligarchs loved as the best sign of popular docility. All that now remained to be done was the installation of the tyrants into the chamber of the senate which represented the Kleisthenean tribes (G.P., p. 87). Attended by a goodly band of assassins, carrying each his hidden dagger, the Four Hundred marched from Kolonos to the senate-house, and commanding the senators to depart, tendered them their pay for the fraction of their official year which was still to run out. The money was taken; the democracy of Kleisthenes died in self-inflicted

Usurpation of the Four Hundred.

ignominy; and in its place was set up the religious association of the old Eupatrid polity. The work begun by Solon and ended by Perikles was swept away to make room for the intolerance of the old Aryan civilization, which had proved a very upas-tree to all healthy political growth.

But the traitors who had thus undone the work of a century were to receive forthwith some hard and wholesome lessons. Now that the demos was put down and the oligarchs were supreme, there could surely be no difficulty in adjusting the quarrel with Sparta. *Unsuccessful attack on Athens by Agis.* Overtures were accordingly made in full confidence to Agis at Dekeleia, and by him were treated with silent contempt. Unable to believe that the work was quite so well done as they asserted it to be, he marched to Athens in hopes of being able to carry the walls by storm; but he found himself mistaken. A second embassy from the Four Hundred, sent after his return to Dekeleia, was more graciously received, and obtained his sanction to send envoys to make their wishes known at Sparta.

But the tyrants knew that practically they had achieved nothing, so long as they failed to secure the co-operation of the army at Samos. Prudence therefore required the oligarchs to assure them that they had acted only from a disinterested generosity which looked exclusively *Suppression of the oligarchic movement at Samos.* to the interests of the city and the empire; that by limiting the franchise they had effected a great saving in the public expenditure; and that the governing body, still being 5,000, fully represented the whole mass of the people. But before the envoys charged with this message could reach Samos, the traitors had set in motion there the machinery which Antiphon had worked at home. Their task would probably have been successfully carried out, had it not been for the precautions taken by Leon and Diomedon, the commanders sent out, on the suggestion of Peisandros, to supersede the oligarchic Phrynichos (p. 169). Honestly attached to the constitution of Athens, these men never quitted Samos without leaving behind them some ships to keep guard against oligarchic intriguers When, then, the oligarchs ventured to trust the issue to the sword, they were met by a determined and successful resistance; and thus by a righteous retribution this conspiracy against law and order was suppressed by leaders sent out to supersede a man who, on being deprived of his command, had joined the ranks of the plotters. In the enthusiasm of the moment the Paralian trireme was dispatched with Chaireas to Athens with a report of what had taken place. They sailed into the lion's den. As soon as they landed, some of the men were thrown into prison: the rest, placed in another ship, were ordered to cruise round Euboia. Making his escape, Chaireas hastened to Samos to inform the army that Athens was in the hands of tyrants who were scourging the citizens and insulting their wives and children. The picture may possibly have been over-coloured; but the historian, who has not a word of censure for the crimes of Antiphon, charges Chaireas indignantly with heaping lie on lie, because his report was not scrupulously exact down to its minutest details.

<small>Resolution of the citizens at Samos to treat Athens as a revolted city.</small>

The results which followed the escape of Chaireas showed that the tyrants had blundered in not putting him to death. An oath inforced by the most solemn sanctions was taken by every soldier in the army at Samos that he would maintain harmony under the ancient constitution of Athens, and that he would have no dealings with the Four Hundred, whom they denounced as public enemies. But the citizens assembled at Samos did even more. In a formal assembly it was ruled that, as the demos at

Athens had been violently put down, the lawful administration of government devolved upon themselves, and that they in fact constituted the true Athens. Exercising thus their rights of citizenship, they deposed such of their generals and trierarchs as were suspected of sharing in the oligarchic conspiracy; Thrasyboulos and Thrasylos being among the officers chosen in their place. With memorable terseness they declared that Athens had revolted from them, and that this fact could not humiliate and should not discourage those who had nothing to do with her apostasy. A lawless minority was in rebellion against the established polity of Athens; but, although they might fancy it otherwise, they stood at a terrible disadvantage with the citizens at Samos. Here was gathered the whole force of the city in an island which in the time of its revolt (p. 40) had done more than any other ally to shake the foundations of her empire. There was no need to change their position to carry on the war. Nay, because her army and fleet had found a refuge in Samos and friends to be trusted to the uttermost in the Samians, therefore, and only therefore, was the mouth of the Peiraieus kept open for the conveyance of supplies to a town which must otherwise soon be starved out. In short, the conspirators at Athens had sinned by setting at naught the laws of their fathers: it was the business of the citizens at Samos to keep those laws and to compel these traitors to keep them also.

Such was the attitude of the Athenians in Samos when the envoys of the Four Hundred, reaching Delos, heard that the army would have nothing to do with the oligarchic usurpers. Their fears of the influence of Alkibiades restrained them from going further; but at first it seemed that their apprehensions were groundless. The main

Election of Alkibiades as general by the army in Samos.

body of the Athenians at Samos were strongly opposed to his restoration; and it needed all the eloquence and energy of Thrasyboulos to induce them to consent to his recall. The narrative of the introduction of Alkibiades to the assembly at Samos is painful, not so much for the glibness of the lies strung together by this arch-traitor as for the pitiable credulity of his hearers. To the oligarchs he had said that nothing should induce him to set foot on Attic soil, until the demos which had driven him into exile should be put down: speaking to the people, he laid the blame of his calamities only on his own unhappy destiny. To the oligarchs he had insisted that the suppression of the democratic constitution was the indispensable condition for winning the thorough confidence of the Persian king: to the people he described in moving terms the absorbing anxiety of Tissaphernes to secure the close friendship of democratic Athens. If only Alkibiades were restored, the Athenians should never lack food so long as a Dareik remained in the satrap's purse; nay, he would provide money, if so it must be, by turning his silver couch into coin. No one, it would seem, asked why, if Tissaphernes was thus pining for the friendship of Athens, he should be so late in expressing his desire; and so greedily were the words of Alkibiades received by his hearers, that before the assembly dispersed he was appointed general, and a strong wish was expressed to sail at once to Peiraieus and punish the men who had subverted the constitution. But sincere though Alkibiades may for the moment have been to help his countrymen, he was much more eager to impress on Tissaphernes his greatness as an Athenian general; and he therefore strongly dissuaded the citizens from the course on which they had set their hearts.

Before his departure for Magnesia, the oligarchic envoys, who had been kept for a time, by their fears, at

Delos, appeared before the citizens at Samos. They were received with a storm of indignation which placed their lives in danger; but when at length they were suffered to speak, they protested with special earnestness against the lies with which, as they insisted, they had been cheated by Chaireas. There was no intention, they said, of harming their wives or their children: but their lame and stumbling apology, which preserved a discreet silence on the murders of men honestly attached to the Athenian constitution, rather inflamed than soothed the angry feelings of their hearers, of whom a large majority insisted on an immediate return to Peiraieus to undo the work of the traitors. But this plan, as we have seen, clashed with the designs of Alkibiades, by whose advice they contented themselves with bidding the envoys go back and tell their masters that they must yield up their power to the Five Hundred whose place they had usurped; that to the rule of the Five Thousand, if these were a reality and not a sham, they would make no objection; and that for any retrenchments which might enable them to carry on the war more vigorously the Athenians at Samos could feel only gratitude to their kinsmen at home.

Dismissal of the envoys of the Four Hundred from Samos.

At Athens, the usurpers feared that the ground beneath them was already becoming insecure. They felt that the people in Athens were anxious to shake off their yoke; they knew that in the people at Samos they had to deal with uncompromising enemies. Among them, also, were some (and the most prominent of these was Theramenes) who had already found that for themselves personally oligarchy had not been quite so profitable as they thought that it would be. But, as oligarchs, they belonged to a society in which each man avowedly was strictly for himself; and it was only natural

Fortification of Eetionia by the Four Hundred.

that the eyes of these men should now be opened to the need of making the Five Thousand a reality,—in other words, of restoring the old democracy, for as these Five Thousand had been thus far an indefinite quantity, so an indefinite quantity they would remain. The oligarchy, in short, was falling; and while Theramenes was considering how he might best place himself at the head of a popular opposition, those of his colleagues who were hopelessly committed to the usurpation of the Four Hundred, felt that if the resistance with which they were threatened was to be put down at all, it must be put down by force. Envoys, headed by Phrynichos and Antiphon, were sent to Sparta to conclude a peace on whatever terms and at whatever cost, while their accomplices at home set to work to prepare a place for the enemy. A mole, known by the name of Eetionia, artificially narrowing the mouth of the Peiraieus, presented an open space capable of fortification. To the tyrants it was especially convenient, not merely because strong works erected here might enable them to admit the Spartans within the harbour, but because they might be made not less serviceable against the greater danger of assault from within. A further precaution was taken by running a wall through a large covered space, open perhaps on both sides, the greater portion of which was thus included in the oligarchical stronghold. Into the part so shut off was carried all the corn brought to the harbour; and the city became dependent on the will of the Four Hundred for the daily purchase of their food.

The Spartans had, indeed, nothing to do but to take possession on their own terms; but the very abjectness of the envoys may have made the ephors fearful of being caught in some trap, and they could obtain nothing more than a promise that a fleet on its way to Euboia should pass the

Assassination of Phrynichos.

Athenian harbour. Having heard that this fleet was coming, Theramenes publicly inveighed against the erection of the fort on Eetionia as part of a scheme arranged in concert with the Spartans. The return of the ambassador stirred the people still more deeply. In the open market-place and in the middle of the day Phrynichos was struck down by a murderer, who made his escape; and Theramenes, rendered bolder by the impunity which attended this crime, insisted that the Spartan fleet, which had come to Aigina and thence fallen back on Epidauros, could not be going straight to Euboia. In ungovernable excitement the hoplites set to work to throw down the fortress which they had helped to raise, and all were invited to join in the task who wished that the Five Thousand should be put in the place of the Four Hundred. It was needful even now to use this mysterious formula, for it might be rash to deny positively the existence of this unseen company and thus to create antagonists where they hoped to have only friends.

Demolition of the fort on Eetionia.

On the following day the hoplites from Peiraieus took their station in the Anakeion, or sacred ground of the Dioskouroi, at the base of the Akropolis on its northern side. With singular moderation the people accepted a compromise by which the Four Hundred pledged themselves that the list of the Five Thousand should be published, and that the appointment of the senate should be in the hands of the larger body. A day was fixed for the assembly of the people in the theatre of Dionysos; and on that day the debate had all but begun when it was announced that the Spartan fleet was off the coast of Salamis. The people rushed with furious haste to the Peiraieus; but seeing that a surprise was not to be thought of, the Spartan commander pursued his voyage eastwards, and

Revolt and loss of Euboia.

the Athenians now saw that his squadron was intended to cover the revolt of Euboia. Now that Attica was itself beleaguered, Euboia was to them everything; and at all risks they must hasten to its defence, sick at heart at the miserable treachery of the oligarchs, which had cut them off from the aid of that noble army at Samos, which would have rejoiced to strike a blow for the city now restored to its right mind. The fleet of thirty-six Athenian ships, hastily got together, reached Eretria a few hours after the Spartan leader had landed at Oropos; and Thymochares hoped that he might be in time to refresh his weary and hungry crews. But the Agora of the Eretrians was purposely empty; and when his men had straggled for food even to the end of the town, a signal raised at Eretria called the Spartans to the attack. Hurrying back to the shore, the Athenians hastened as best they could to the encounter, in which two-thirds of their ships fell into the hands of the enemy, their crews being all killed or taken prisoners. The fleet was, in fact, destroyed; and the revolt of Euboia crowned the work of the murderers, who looked down calmly from their council chamber on their awful handiwork.

According to their own philosophy, oligarchs might afford to do so; but for the people, whose life-blood they had poured out like water, the revolt of Euboia seemed to bring with it the day of doom. The fleet at Samos could not desert its post, and scarcely a trireme now remained in the desolate harbour of Peiraieus. The town was indeed defenceless; but the great catastrophe was to be delayed yet a little longer, and the respite came through the singular slowness and dulness which made the Spartans the most convenient of all enemies for the quick-witted and prompt Athenians. Only twenty ships were they able to bring together; but happily they were not called upon to en-

Suppression of the Four Hundred at Athens.

counter any enemy, and the Athenians were enabled to fix their minds on the restoration of order. In an assembly held in the Pnyx the Four Hundred were solemnly deposed, and the so-called Five Thousand put in their place. No attempt was made to publish any list of the men included in this number; and the phrase by which the oligarchical conspirators had thought to rivet their own authority was made to cover the whole body of the people. The miserable conspiracy was at last put down; and Athens once more lived under the polity of Kleisthenes and Perikles. Thus was accomplished, seemingly amidst the death-throes of the state, a change which re-asserted the supremacy of law; and it was accomplished with a sobriety and calmness which calls forth the enthusiastic eulogy of Thucydides. For the Four Hundred, indeed, it was a fortunate thing that their usurpation was suppressed in some part by the co-operation of men belonging to their own side. If Theramenes and his helpers had not been concerned in restoring the democracy, the people would have been free to search out and punish the real murderers of the victims who had fallen by the hands of hired bravoes. As it was, the one act laid to their charge was the sending of the last embassy to Sparta to offer a peace clogged by no conditions; and on this charge Theramenes, to his own future cost, came forward as the accuser. But of the men thus accused, Phrynichos had passed beyond the reach of earthly law; others, with the most prominent leaders of the oligarchy, had taken flight when they saw that their house was falling. Three only remained at Athens, and of these two may have thought that their sins might be condoned. The hardihood of Antiphon, who must have known that he at least had sinned unpardonably, is scarcely consistent with his sagacity and practical wisdom. The

Restoration of democracy.

decree was passed for the apprehension and trial of these three; but before the writ could be served one of them made his escape. Antiphon and Archeptolemos were tried, condemned, and executed.

Trial and execution of Antiphon.

Many a speech delivered before Athenian tribunals had been written by the illustrious rhetorician who now stood at their bar. The first speech which he delivered in his own person was that in which he pleaded for his life. It was more than worthy of his great reputation, and Thucydides asserts that eloquence so magnificent had never marked the defence of a criminal on a capital charge. The poet Agathon, it is said, expressed to Antiphon his enthusiastic admiration of his splendid oratory, and was assured by the condemned man that his praise more than compensated him for the adverse judgment of the people. His eloquence may have impressed, it failed to convince, his judges; and if ever an orator deserved that he should not convince his hearers, that orator was Antiphon.

Meanwhile the relations of Tissaphernes and his Spartan allies exhibited the working of suspicion on the one side and of discontent fast passing into rage on the other. For nearly three months the Peloponnesian fleet had remained inactive at Rhodes; and the men were the more indignant that their hands were thus tied, as they had heard of the contentions between the oligarchic faction and the main body of the Athenians at Samos. Astyochos at length found himself compelled to move, and, with one hundred and twelve ships, to challenge the enemy to battle. The Athenians, with eighty-two vessels, declined the engagement.

Inactivity of the Spartan fleet at Rhodes.

Tired out with Tissaphernes, the Spartans now sent Klearchos, with forty ships, to the Hellespontine satrap Pharnabazos; but although his squadron was driven back to Miletos, he himself went on by land to the Hellespont, while his Megarian colleague, sailing with ten ships to Byzantion, brought about the revolt of that city. The departure of these two commanders in no way improved the state of things in the Peloponnesian camp at Miletos. Not by Hermokrates only, but even by others whose silence had been thus far secured by bribes, Astyochos was told that in the state of starvation to which the men were reduced they must inevitably desert. The Sicilian allies showed that they were no longer to be trifled with; and Astyochos, making the blunder of lifting his stick to strike the Rhodian Dorieus, who commanded the ships from Thourioi, saved his life only by taking refuge at a neighbouring altar. The Milesians averred frankly that they had counted on autonomy,—that is, on more thorough independence than Athens had allotted to them; and protection against Persian tax-gatherers was an essential condition of this independence. With these views the Syracusans heartily agreed, and against them the Spartan Lichas not less earnestly protested. So long as the war lasted, they must, he said, if need be, even truckle to the Persian satrap. He had money, they had none; and until they had put down the empire of Athens, the Asiatic Greeks must be content to fawn upon the man who could pay them if he would. If the Milesians were indignant at the cheat thus put upon them, the Spartans at home were also wearied out with the inaction of their forces in the East; and Mindaros was sent out to take the place of Astyochos.

<small>Discontent in the Spartan camp at Miletos.</small>

Cool and collected while his friends were thus waxing wroth, Tissaphernes now invited Lichas to accompany him to Aspendos for the purpose of returning with the Phenician fleet. This fleet was indeed there; but the proposal of Tissaphernes was, nevertheless, only a fresh trick to gain time. After

<small>Intrigues of Tissaphernes and Alkibiades.</small>

keeping the ships for a time on the Pamphylian coast, he sent them away again. But if Tissaphernes thus cheated both Lichas and Mindaros, he in turn overreached himself. It was no part of his plan to exasperate further the resentment already felt in the Spartan camp, if that result could be avoided; but Alkibiades was resolved that it should not be avoided. Well knowing that the satrap had no intention of bringing the Phenician fleet into action, he eagerly availed himself of the opportunity to promise the Athenians at Samos that he would either bring up the Phenician ships to their help or prevent them from coming to the help of their enemies. Sailing to Aspendos, he took care to parade ostentatiously his intimacy with the satrap; and as the fleet was sent away, the Athenians believed that the measure was due to his influence. Sharing this belief, the Peloponnesians became more indignant at the treachery of Tissaphernes, and for the time Alkibiades remained the most important personage in the theatre of the war.

The departure of the Phenician fleet made Mindaros resolve on transferring his forces to the satrapy of Pharnabazos; but a severe storm carried him southward and detained him for a week before he could sail to Chios, and the Athenian commander Thrasylos thus hoped to be able to intercept him on his northward voyage. He was, however, himself summoned away to the Lesbian town of Eresos, which had again revolted from Athens, and he made his preparations for vigorously besieging it, in full confidence that the movements of Mindaros would be carefully reported to him. He was mistaken; and beacon fires suddenly warned the Athenian squadron stationed at Lesbos that the enemy's fleet had passed the mouth of the strait at Sigeion. This squadron escaped destruc-

Voyage of Mindaros to the Hellespont.

tion, only because the orders of Mindaros kept at their post the sixteen ships which were on guard at Abydos. The Athenian triremes were thus enabled to make their way unmolested to Elaious. Four were here cut off from the main body by the ships of Mindaros; the remainder, joining the squadron of Thrasylos, raised the number of the Athenian ships to seventy-six. Five days were spent in preparations for a battle which strikingly proves the decay of Athenian science. Pent up in a strait nowhere two miles in width, they proposed to fight with eighty ships in a space which Phormion would have regarded as quite inadequate for the proper manœuvring of twenty (p. 62); and the details of the battle are, as we might expect, much on a par with the early tactics of the Persian wars. On both sides the main object was to outflank the enemy. The action was begun by Mindaros, who sought to work round the Athenians to the west: but Thrasylos anticipated his movement, and at the same time Thrasyboulos, in his effort to outflank the Syracusan squadron, had doubled the headland of Kynossêma, and thus passed out of sight of the battle which raged to the west of the promontory. The Athenian centre was thus left dangerously weak; and on the ships so left exposed the Peloponnesians fell with a vehemence which became the means of punishing them later on in the day. In the end the Peloponnesian fleet was driven back, leaving twenty-one ships in the hands of the enemy, who, having lost fifteen vessels, were gainers only by six. *Victory of the Athenians at Kynossêma.*

Compared with the great exploits of Phormion and Demosthenes, the victory was poor indeed; but on the Athenians, to whom it came at a time when they were depressed by an almost endless series of disasters, it exercised a moral influence scarcely *Exaltation at Athens.*

less than that of the victory of Mantineia on the Spartans (p. 109). In either case a people whose reputation had been discredited were restored to their self-respect; and to the Athenians the result was the more encouraging, as it seemed to be the just fruits of the restored polity of Athens after the murderous usurpation of the Four Hundred. The trireme sent home with the tidings was received with unbounded delight. The depression which had so long hung about them was suddenly dispelled, and they felt that the hope of a successful issue to the war was no longer a presumptuous and unreasonable delusion.

CHAPTER VII.

THE PELOPONNESIAN (DEKELEIAN OR IONIAN) WAR, FROM THE BATTLE OF KYNOSSÊMA TO THE SURRENDER OF ATHENS.

THE battle of Kynossêma was not the last victory won by Athenian fleets in the war which was now gradually drawing to its close. But the whole history of the struggle after the Sicilian expedition shows that Athens had reached a point beyond which even brilliant successes produce no permanent results. It was not merely that her fleets and armies had been destroyed, and that her revenues had become precarious. Against such difficulties she might have struggled successfully. She might even have repaired the mischief arising from the decay of that nautical skill which had made her name dreaded from the Hellespont to Sicily and Africa. But she could not do this, unless she was seconded by the goodwill of the great body of

Declension of the Athenian character.

her allies; and if these were not honestly convinced that alliance with Athens was to their own interest, there could clearly be but one issue to the struggle. This conviction was strong only in Samos; and the principle of isolation, against which her confederacy was a protest, had even for the democratic communities of Greece the charm which brings the moth to the flaming candle. But in all the allied states there was a party which hated as well as feared her, knowing that her courts would give redress for the crimes which they dearly loved to commit. This alone would have sufficed to shake her empire to its foundations: but all hope of preserving it was gone when Athenians themselves became traitors to their own constitution, when they set at defiance the laws which dealt out equal justice to all the citizens, and employed the dagger to put down opposition in a city for which freedom of speech was the very breath of life. Through the resolute resistance of the citizens at Samos this infamous conspiracy had been put down; but the wounds left behind it were never healed, and among the most fatal of these was the lessening of that respect for forms and processes of law which in earlier days had distinguished Athens from every other Greek city, and, therefore, from every other city in the world. From the first, indeed, the idea of the Athenian empire was one which could not be realised without reversing the most cherished principles of the ancient Hellenic and Aryan civilisation; and for this change the Greek tribes were assuredly not prepared. Athens, therefore, fell, but not until she had exhibited to the world a polity which might be the means of overcoming the miserable feuds of isolated clans and of cementing into a single people the inhabitants of cities spread over many lands.

Nothing, indeed, could prove more clearly that the fall of Athens was due to the moral corruption of some, whether few or many, of her citizens than the wonderful series of victories which began with the battle of Kynos-sêma. Taken singly, each of these might perhaps have been little thought of some thirty or forty years earlier; but collectively they showed a power of recovery such as has seldom been seen in any age or country. In great alarm the satrap Tissaphernes hastened to the Hellespont, in the hope of recovering the influence which seemed to be fast slipping away from him. For the present his crafty schemes had told only in favour of Alkibiades. The dismissal of the Phenician fleet had enabled him to say that the satrap was better inclined to the Athenian cause than he had ever been. On Halikarnassos he was able to impose a heavy fine. At the Hellespont he was enabled to decide in favour of Athens a battle which had begun in the early morning by the defeat of Dorieus in the bay of Dardanos and which had been continued during the day by the fleet of Mindaros. With thirty ships of the enemy the Athenians, having recovered their own captured triremes, sailed away to their station at Lesbos, where, however, they kept only forty of their ships, the rest being sent to gather money where they might and as they could. The necessities of war had substituted arbitrary and indefinite exactions for the orderly collection of tribute; and the indifference and even the kindly feeling of the allies gave way to active dislike or fiercer indignation.

Journey of Tissaphernes to the Hellespont.

Victory of Alkibiades over the Spartans in the bay of Dardanos.

Twenty years earlier a victory even such as this might have been followed by momentous consequences. All that Thrasylos could now do was to go to Athens to ask for more help both in ships and men. The fleet sent to aid him was compelled to rove about among the allied or other cities, exacting contributions or plundering with little respect

Victory of the Athenians at Kyzikos. B.C. 410.

to law; and when Theramenes reached Kardia, on the northern side of the Thrakian Chersonesos, he found there Alkibiades, no longer as a friend of Tissaphernes or of the king his master, but as a fugitive from his power. The Athenian generals, accompanied by Alkibiades, now resolved on attacking Mindaros, who was busied with the siege of Kyzikos. Sailing past Abydos at night to evade the Peloponnesian guardships, they took the further precaution of seizing all passing vessels, to prevent the news of their approach from reaching the Spartan admiral. On the next day Alkibiades, candidly telling the men that all hope of Persian help was gone, warned them that they must undertake simultaneously the tasks of a sea fight, of a land battle, and of a siege. The issue of the day was decided, it is said, by a trick of Alkibiades, who, by a pretended flight, concerted with his colleagues, lured the squadron of Mindaros to some distance from the rest of the fleet and then turned fiercely round on the hoisting of a signal. However this may have been, the victory of the Athenians was complete. Mindaros was slain, fighting bravely on shore; and more important, in the present exhaustion of resources, than the seizure of the Peloponnesian ships was the vast plunder in slaves and other booty taken in the Spartan and Persian camps. But if the victory was to have permanent fruit, the Athenians must command the gates of the Black Sea as well as those of the Egean. With Byzantion and Chalkêdon, which were both in revolt, they could for the present do nothing; but by fortifying Chrysopolis, the port of the latter city, the Athenians were enabled to levy tolls on all ships entering the Propontis, and thus again become masters of the most important road for the introduction of supplies to Athens.

A few hours after the battle of Kyzikos, Hippokrates,

the secretary of the Spartan admiral, addressed to the ephors the following letter :—'Our glory is gone; Mindaros is dead; the men are famishing; we know not what to do.' The despatch was intercepted and carried to Athens, where the joy of the people found expression in magnificent religious processions and displays. It is said that a Spartan embassy soon reached Athens with proposals for peace : but the Peloponnesians cannot have been greatly depressed by their defeat if their terms were limited to a mere exchange of prisoners and the withdrawal of hostile garrisons on either side—in other words, to the proposal that the Spartans should quit Dekeleia and the Athenians give up Pylos. But if they were in any measure discouraged, Pharnabazos certainly was not. Promising unbounded supplies of ship timber from Ida, he gave a garment to each of the soldiers of Mindaros, with provisions for two months, issuing at the same time orders for the building of a fleet equal to that which had been lost at Kyzikos.

Effects of the victory.

The events of the following year made no essential change in the position of the combatants. The Athenians were defeated near Ephesos, and victorious near Methymna over the Syracusans, and again over Pharnabazos at Lampsakos, which they strongly fortified. These efforts of the Athenians to retrieve their losses in the East led the Spartans to think that a determined attack on Pylos might now be successful. Sent out with thirty ships to its aid, Anytos, the future accuser of Sokrates, came back with the tale that stormy weather had prevented him from doubling cape Maleai (G. P. p. 19). He was brought to trial for his failure, but acquitted ; and his escape, possibly not altogether without reason, was attributed to the corruption of the jury. The absence of so

Recovery of Pylos and Nisaia from the Athenians. B.C. 409.

many citizens on foreign service may have reduced the numbers of each dikastery within limits not unmanageable for bribers, and the long-standing pressure of poverty may have done the rest. Thus deserted, the Messenians held out at Pylos for a time; and when they were compelled to surrender, they were able to secure their safe departure from a land which, if the Spartans could have had their will, they would never have left alive. The loss of this outpost was followed by that of Nisaia; and these two disasters affected Athens more seriously than the ruin of their colony at Herakleia (p. 73) affected the Spartans.

The following year began for the Athenians with two successes, which seemed to augur well for the result of the struggle. Chalkêdon was reduced, and compelled to become a tribute-paying ally, making up all arrears due for the period spent in revolt. The surrender of Byzantion left Athens mistress of the highway which brought to her harbours the wealth of the corn-lands bordering on the Euxine; and the convention, by which Pharnabazos of his own free will offered to send Athenian envoys to Sousa, was a still better omen of a settlement in their favour. The sober report of a man who had thrown himself heartily into the Spartan cause, and who now was obliged to say that even with Persian subsidies the Spartans were losing rather than gaining ground, could not but have great weight with a monarch to whom, after all, money was the chief object. Unhappily for Athens, the envoys were met on their journey by Spartan ambassadors bearing a letter with the royal seal, which named the king's younger son Cyrus lord of all his armies in Asia Minor; and Cyrus was pledged to aid the Spartans to the utmost of his power.

<small>Reduction of Chalkêdon and Byzantion by the Athenians. B.C. 408.</small>

<small>Arrival of Cyrus on the Egean coast.</small>

In the Persian prince now sent down to the coast

Lysandros, the Spartan admiral, found not an ally only but a friend. When Lysandros expressed a hope that the war might now be carried on with real vigour, Cyrus replied by assuring him that if the 500 talents which he had brought with him should not suffice, he would, according to the Persian metaphor, turn his silver-gilt throne into coin (p. 182). Obtaining from him, not without difficulty, an increase of pay for his men, together with all unpaid arrears, Lysandros was careful to send for the chiefs of the oligarchical factions in the several cities allied with Athens, and to form them into clubs pledged to act by his orders. He thus became the centre of a wide-spread conspiracy, which he alone was capable of directing.

Lysandros and the oligarchical clubs. B.C. 407.

Alkibiades, in the meanwhile, was working for his return to Athens. He had sailed to the Lakonian port of Gytheion, to ascertain what amount of ship-building might be going on there, and was still hesitating as to his future course, when he received the news that he had been elected strategos by the Athenians, while his friends assured him that the way before him was both open and safe. Having entered Peiraieus, the exile, whose memory must have recalled the long series of his treasons, stood for a time on the deck of his trireme, not daring to land until he saw his friends waiting to guard him on his way to the city. These would probably lose no time in letting him know the temper of the vast multitude now gathered to look upon the man who seven years before had sailed from that harbour with the most splendid armament ever sent forth by the imperial city. If they could not but admit that some denounced him as the cause of all the disasters which Athens had suffered since his departure, and of all the dangers which still threatened her, they would dwell with more satisfaction on the belief ex-

Return of Alkibiades to Athens.

pressed by others, that to him alone they were indebted for the victories which had turned their despair into something like cheerful confidence; that during his years of exile he had been the unwilling slave of men at whose hands his life was daily in danger; and that through the whole of this weary time his one grief had arisen from his inability to do for Athens the good which he would gladly have achieved for her. But amazing as must have been the effrontery of men who could thus speak of one who had done what he could to destroy the Athenian fleets and armies at Syracuse, who had fixed a hostile force on Athenian soil, and who had lit the fire which burst into flame in the usurpation of the Four Hundred, all moderate men must have felt that, unless he was still to be treated as an enemy, his past career must not be thrown in his teeth. If they could place no real trust in him, they ought at least to put no hindrances in his path so long as he continued to do his duty as a citizen, a statesman, and a general. Before the assembly Alkibiades played his part so well that his confiscated property was returned to him, and the tablets containing the decrees condemning him to death were thrown into the sea. The recurrence of the Eleusinian mysteries furnished him with one of those opportunities for display of which he would avail himself with eager delight. For seven years the procession along the Sacred Road had been necessarily given up, and the communicants, with their sacred vessels, had been conveyed to Eleusis by sea. It should now be said that under the man who had been charged with profaning the mysteries the procession should follow its ancient path as safely as in a time of profound peace. The pomp issued from the gates of Athens, guarded by all the citizens of military age; but no attack was even threatened by the garrison of Dekeleia.

Alkibiades left Athens with a head turned by the enthusiasm of his reception. The tidings which he re-
Defeat of Antiochos by Lysandros.
ceived on reaching Samos informed him of the arrival of Cyrus, and of the energy displayed by him on the Spartan side. Having in vain besought Tissaphernes to impress upon the prince the need of holding an even balance between the contending parties, he joined Thrasyboulos, who was fortifying Phokaia, leaving his fleet in charge of his pilot Antiochos, with strict orders to avoid all engagements with the enemy during his absence. He had scarcely departed before his deputy sailed out with only two triremes, and passed insultingly before the Spartan fleet at Ephesos. Lysandros came out and chased him with a few ships: Antiochos brought out more. But the Athenian ships advanced carelessly and in disorder, and the result was the loss of sixteen triremes and the death
Alkibiades deprived of his command.
of Antiochos himself. Even more unfortunate for Alkibiades was his attack on the people of Kymê, a town belonging to the Athenian confederacy. The Kymaians laid their complaints before the Athenian assembly, and Alkibiades, deprived of his command, betook himself to his fortified posts on the Chersonesos.

On reaching Samos, Konon, who had been sent to take the place of Alkibiades, was struck by the great
Difficulties of Kallikratidas, on succeeding Lysandrus. B.C. 406.
depression of the men. Their ships were becoming daily more inefficient, and for pay they had little more to depend on than plunder. He therefore cut down the number of his triremes from a hundred to seventy, picking out for these the best oarsmen and sending the rest of the crews away. But he was saved, perhaps, from some great disaster by the fact that the command of Lysandros expired at this time. In his successor, Kallikratidas,

Konon found an antagonist who had not convinced himself that the ruin of Athens would be cheaply purchased at the cost of prostration before the throne of the Persian despot. Kallikratidas had even learnt that the Hellenic tribes had something better to do than to tear each other in pieces for the benefit of the barbarians against whom, scarcely eighty years ago, they had pledged themselves to maintain a perpetual warfare. Thus deploring the miserable strife which had now dragged itself on through four and twenty years, he found himself face to face with men who practically refused to obey him. Summoning his officers, he told them that he was there by no will of his own; that, having come, he must do the bidding of the state which had sent him; but that, if they thought otherwise, he would at once go back to Sparta and report the state of matters at Ephesos. An appeal so manly and straightforward could be met only by the answer that he must be obeyed. Going, then, to Cyrus, he demanded the pay needed for the seamen. Cyrus kept him two days waiting; and Kallikratidas, in the agony of his humiliation, bewailed the wretched fate of the Greeks who, for the sake of silver and gold, were compelled to crouch before the Persian tyrants, and declared that if he should be spared to return home he would do all that he could to bring to an end this unnatural quarrel between Athens and Sparta.

The generous hopes and desires of Kallikratidas had made him none the less formidable to his enemies. Chased by his fleet to Mytilênê, Konon lost thirty out of his seventy triremes, their crews happily escaping ashore, and found himself blockaded in a situation where, from total lack of supplies, he must soon surrender, unless his position could be made known at Athens. Picking out the best oarsmen of the fleet, he placed them on board two triremes, and then waited vainly

Blockading of Konon at Mytilênê.

through four days for an opportunity of sending them forth with any chance of success. On the fifth day the dispersion of the Spartan crews at the time of the noon-tide meal seemed to justify the attempt. The two ships therefore started, making the utmost haste, the one for the southern, the other for the northern entrance of the harbour. With all their efforts one only escaped to tell the tale, first to Diomedon at Samos and then at Athens. Diomedon, hastening rashly with only twelve triremes to the aid of his colleague, lost ten of his ships. At Athens the news roused only a more determined spirit of resistance. All persons, whether free or slaves, within military age, were drafted into 110 triremes, and within a month this prodigious force was on its way to the Egean. Strengthened at Samos by ten ships, and on their onward voyage by thirty more, furnished by allied cities, the Athenian generals took up their position off the islets of Argennoussai with 150 triremes. Leaving Eteonikos with fifty vessels to blockade Konon, Kallikratidas had posted himself with 120 ships off the Malean cape, distant about ten miles to the west of Argennoussai. An attempt which he made to surprise the enemy at midnight was frustrated by a severe storm of thunder and rain. Early in the morning he advanced to the battle, in which the great effort of the Athenian officers was to prevent the Peloponnesians from performing those manœuvres which had once secured the most brilliant victories of the Athenian fleets. After a time, as in the last terrible conflict in the harbour of Syracuse, the combatants were broken up into detached groups. In one of these groups the ship of Kallikratidas came into contact with an Athenian vessel with such force that the Spartan admiral was hurled into the water and never seen again. At length the left wing of the Spartan fleet gave

Battle of Argennoussai.

Victory of the Athenians, and death of Kallikratidas

way; the flight soon became general, and the whole fleet was virtually destroyed.

According to one account the Athenians spent some time in chase of the flying enemy; another tells us that the generals intrusted the trierarchs Theramenes and Thrasyboulos with the charge of recovering from the wrecked and disabled ships as many of the crews as might still be living, while they themselves were anxious to sail at once against the blockading squadron of Eteonikos at Mytilênê. A heavy tempest compelled them, it is said, to give up this enterprise: but unless they had started immediately, they would have found Eteonikos already gone. As soon as the issue of the fight was decided, the admiral's pinnace carried the news to Eteonikos, who, with consummate presence of mind, bade the crew go back to sea and return singing the pæan of victory. Gravely offering the sacrifice of thanksgiving, he then ordered his crews to take their meal at once, and sail to Chios with the trading ships. Then, setting fire to his camp, he withdrew his land force to Methymna. The wind was blowing fair—that is, nearly due north—when they set out for Chios; and its violence may be inferred from the fact that although Konon suddenly found his way open before him, he could not venture to join the Athenians on their return from Argennoussai until the wind had somewhat gone down. Having at length joined his colleagues, he went with them first to Mytilênê and then to Chios in the hope of recovering the city which had done them enormous mischief by its revolt. The failure of the attack betrays their extreme exhaustion. Lysandros could do nothing after his victory over the pilot Antiochos; and now the whole Athenian fleet was so baffled at Chios as to be obliged to return, practically beaten, to Samos.

The tempest which followed the battle of Argennoussai

Departure of the blockading squadron from Mytilênê.

was to prove fatal to Athens. Twenty-five vessels belonging to the Athenian fleet had been more or less disabled during the action. Twelve, by the admission of Euryptolemos, one of the generals, were still above water, when the order was issued for sending forty-seven triremes to their rescue; and thus, by the lowest possible reckoning, it would seem that 1,500 men were allowed to die who might have been saved, if the generals, instead of debating, had at once set to work to recover them. In their first despatch the generals announced their victory, stating the amount of their loss, and adding that the severe storm immediately following the battle had put it out of their power to rescue the crews of the disabled triremes. In a second despatch they stated that the task of visiting the wrecks had been deputed to Theramenes and Thrasyboulos. By these two men, who had already come to Athens, this second despatch was treated as a mere trick to transfer to others the blame of inaction for which the generals were themselves wholly responsible. They boldly denied the facts both of the storm and of their own commission. The inquiry resolved itself therefore really into the one question, whether certain men were ordered to visit the wrecks or whether they were not. If the officers of forty-seven ships received this command, the responsibility of the generals was at an end; and if any punishment was needed, it should fall on those who had failed to obey their orders. But the Athenian people thought that the case justified the recall of all the generals, who were accordingly bidden to hand over their command to Konon. Suspecting mischief, two followed the example of Alkibiades after receiving his summons in Sicily. The other six went back with the confidence of men who had only deserved well at the hands of their countrymen. On being brought before the assembly all

Accusation of the Athenian generals by Theramenes and Thrasyboulos.

agreed in asserting that, with the other trierarchs, Theramenes and Thrasyboulos had been charged to visit the wrecks, adding that they would not allow the accusations of Theramenes to tempt them into a falsehood. They had no intention of retorting his imputations. The storm had rendered all action impossible, and neither they nor the trierarchs, their deputies, were to blame for results beyond their power. In proof of this fact, they relied on the evidence of their pilots and of many others who were present; nor had Theramenes and his partisans the hardihood to deny before the assembly, as they had denied before the senate, the fact of the commission with which they had been charged. This simple and straightforward answer, backed by the testimony of witnesses whom they had no grounds for mistrusting, produced its natural effect. The people were fast becoming convinced of their innocence, and Theramenes stood convicted of a lie. But it was now late in the day, and the discussion was postponed to the next assembly, the senate being ordered to consider how the trial of the accused should best be conducted.

<small>Favourable impression made on the Athenian assembly by the generals.</small>

Thus, without going further, the conclusion is definitely established that the statements of the generals are consistent and substantially true; that they may have been to blame for debating a matter in which action should have been spontaneous and immediate; that their council ended in telling off a large number of ships for the rescue of the distressed crews; and that before these could set off on their task, the wind, which had been gaining strength from a time probably preceding the end of the battle, had become a tempest which the triremes could not face. If it be true that Theramenes was busy at Athens inflaming the public feeling against the generals before their return, the conclusion seems to follow that he had come back

<small>Falsehoods of Theramenes.</small>

bent on bringing about their disgrace, if not their death. What his full motive may have been it is scarcely worth while to ask. His whole career reeked of villainy. He had been a traitor to the constitution and laws of his country. He had been the willing instrument of Antiphon and his abettors in their work of organized murder; and because he had failed to get from them the recompense which he regarded as his due, he had betrayed his confederates and thrown in his lot with men whom he hated. Lastly, we may turn to the closing scene of his life, when Kritias reviled him as the murderer of the generals, and mark his vehement reply, that he had never come forward as their accuser; that, having laid on himself and others the duty of rescuing the drowning men, the generals had charged them with disobedience to orders because they failed to do so; that they failed only because the storm made it impossible for them even to leave their moorings; and therefore that the generals deliberately laid a plan for their destruction by insisting on the practicability of the task and then taking their departure. Theramenes forgot that if the storm was so frightful as he chose to represent it to Kritias, the generals could not have left him to his fate in case of failure to obey orders and then at once have sailed away themselves over the raging waters.

The postponement of the debate had this result, that the matter could not be opened again till after the Apatouria, a feast celebrated by the ancient Eupatrid phratriai (G. P., pp. 6, 7), and therefore most closely connected with the polity of pre-Solonian Athens. In it the Athenian was carried away to a region of sentiment in which the family was everything, the state nothing; and here was the hearth on which Theramenes might kindle the flames which should devour his victims. The clansmen of the dead,

Conspiracy of Theramenes.

he insisted, would be bringing shame on their ancient houses if they failed to stand forth as the avengers of murder. The generals must die; and the kinsfolk of the men whom they had slain should besiege the assembly, clad in the garb of mourning and with their heads shorn, until the people should decree the great sacrifice. The drama was well got up. In the senate Kallixenos carried the monstrous proposal that without further discussion the people should at once proceed to judgement, on the ground that the accusers and accused had been heard at the last meeting. When the hour for the assembly came, the dark-robed mourners were there, like beasts of prey howling for the blood of their victims. The excitement caused by their cries and tears was aggravated to fury when a man came forward to say that he, too, had been among the drowning seamen, till he had managed to escape upon a meal-tub, and that, as he floated away, the last sounds which he could hear were intreaties that he would, if saved, tell the Athenians how their commanders had abandoned the bravest of their countrymen.

Proposition of Kallixenos.

Athenian law demanded that no citizen should be tried except before a court of sworn jurymen; that the accused should receive due notice of trial; and that, having had time to prepare his defence, he should be brought face to face with his accusers. All these forms were summarily set aside by the proposition of Kallixenos. But the proposer of unconstitutional measures was liable to indictment under the writ Graphê Paranomôn (p. 178); and Euryptolemos, with some others, interposed this check on the madness which was coming over the people. But it was too late. The shaven mourners, in their black raiment, raised the cry, taken up by the majority of the citizens present, that the demos had a right to do what they liked. Thera-

Amendment of Euryptolemos.

menes had indeed triumphed. The frenzy which Euryptolemos could not restrain was the natural result of the teaching of Peisandros (p. 172). A spirit was abroad in the assembly which was determined that, notwithstanding all laws and usages to the contrary, the generals should drink the hemlock juice that day; and Euryptolemos was told that, unless he withdrew his threat, he, with his helpers, should share the draught. It was decided that the proposition of Kallixenos might be submitted to the people; but the question could not be put without the consent of the Prytaneis, or ten presiding senators, and some of these protested against its shameless illegality. These also were told that continued resistance would only insure their doom. Of the ten, one only withstood this menace; and that one was Sokrates. His opposition was simply overruled: the question was put: and Euryptolemos rose to urge its rejection. Of the accused generals Perikles was his kinsman, and Diomedon his intimate friend; but he had no wish to screen any who should be lawfully found guilty of any well-defined crime against the state. Only, in the name of law and constitutional usage, he demanded that a day should be given to the discussion of each case separately. To his warnings he added a short account of the facts as, in his belief, they had really taken place; and lastly, he reminded them that they were about to pronounce judgement on men who had won for them a victory which had all but settled the war at a stroke, and which might easily be made to lead to the re-establishment of their empire; and these men, he asserted, deserved not to be put to death, but to be crowned as conquerors and honoured as benefactors of the city.

The amendment of Euryptolemos, on being put to the vote, was declared by the Prytaneis to be carried: but so clearly did the people see through the trick by which the presiding senators had hoped to prevent the commission of an enormous crime that they insisted on its being put to the vote again. It was so put, and rejected, and there remained only the task, as they phrased it, of judging the generals by one vote. The result was, of course, that for which Theramenes and his fellow conspirators had so persistently striven. All six generals were condemned; all six on that night were murdered; and thus Athens requited the lifelong labours of Perikles by slaying his son. To show still further the impartiality of the massacre, the same sentence was passed on Diomedon, who had urged that everything should be postponed to the visiting of the wrecks, and on Erasinides, who had held that everything must give way to the aiding of Konon at Mytilênê. No long time passed before the Athenians repented of their madness and their crimes: but, yielding still to their old besetting sin, they insisted, as they had done in the days of Miltiades and after the catastrophe at Syracuse, on throwing the blame not on themselves but on their advisers. *Condemnation and murder of the generals.*

This great crime began at once to produce its natural fruits. The people were losing confidence in their officers, who, in their turn, felt that no services to the state could secure them against illegal prosecutions and arbitrary penalties. Corruption was eating its way into the heart of the state, and treason was losing its ugliness in the eyes of many who thought themselves none the worse for dallying with it. Such men found it to be their interest to keep up underhand dealings with the enemy; nor could any feel sure that the man whom he most trusted might not be one of the traitors. The Athenian fleet had fallen back upon Samos; and with this island as a base, the generals were occupying themselves with movements, not for crushing the enemy, but for obtaining money. These leaders *Return of the Athenian fleet to Samos.*

were now six in number, for to Philokles and Adeimantos, who had been sent out as colleagues of Konon, there had been added Kephisodotos, Tydeus, and lastly Menandros (p. 139).

The Spartans, whether at home or on the Asiatic coast, were now well aware that one more battle would decide
<small>Activity of Lysandros.</small> the issue of the war; for with another defeat the subsidies of the Persians would be withdrawn from them as from men doomed to failure, and perhaps be transferred to the Athenians. In the army and fleet the cry was raised that Lysandros was the only man equal to the emergency. Spartan custom could not appoint the same man twice to the office of admiral; but when
<small>B.C. 405.</small> Arakos was sent out with Lysandros as his secretary, it was understood that the latter was really the man in power. Early in the year the scribe set vigorously to work, appointing trusty trierarchs to the ships of Eteonikos, bringing together such vessels as had survived the wreck at Argennoussai, and ordering others to be built at Antandros. He had work of another kind to do in Miletos, where two oligarchical bodies, it seems, were in antagonism, one of them wishing to maintain the policy of Kallikratidas. Against these more moderate men their antagonists employed both secret assassination and public massacre. About forty of the most prominent, we are told, were murdered privately; 300 of the wealthiest were cut down in the Agora at the busiest time of the day; and Miletos thus remained completely in the hands of the clubmen of Lysandros.

When at length Lysandros sailed from Rhodes to the Spartan station at Abydos, and thence advanced to the
<small>Arrival of the Athenian fleet at Aigospota-moi.</small> assault of Lampsakos, the Athenian fleet followed him, keeping on the seaward side of Chios. The tidings of the fall of Lampsakos reached them at Elaious, while they

were taking their morning meal. In the evening of the same day they supped at Aigospotamoi, the Goat's Stream, from which that goodly fleet of 180 triremes was never to return. In dealing with his enemies, Lysandros resolved to confine himself to strictly defensive operations, which might sooner or later throw them off their guard. He could not, indeed, have been ignorant of the cause which defeated the great enterprise of Demosthenes on Epipolai (p. 143); and in any case he was well aware that Athenian discipline, unlike that of Sparta, was always apt to grow slack with success. At daybreak he had his ships manned, strict orders being given that the line of battle was not to be broken by advancing to attack the enemy. The evening was closing when, having faced the Peloponnesians to no purpose all day, the Athenian fleet fell back on Aigospotamoi. The squadron which followed them was under strict orders not to return until the crews of the Athenian triremes were all fairly landed. For four successive days these tactics were repeated, each day being marked by increasing carelessness in the Athenian camp, which was merely on the open beach, the nearest town, Sestos, being nearly two miles away. Over this wide extent of ground the men were every day scattered to get their food, and the ships were left dangerously unguarded. The Spartan fleet was supplied from Lampsakos, and could be moved almost at a moment's warning. From his forts on the Chersonesos Alkibiades could see distinctly the dangers to which his countrymen were thus exposing themselves: but his advice and his warnings were rudely rejected, and by Tydeus and Menandros he was dismissed with the rebuff that they were now generals, not he. On the fifth day the Spartan squadron, which, as usual, followed the Athenian fleet as it fell back on its camping ground at Aigospotamoi, was ordered to wait until the enemy was thoroughly scattered over the country, and then, as they came back, to hoist a shield as a signal. On seeing this token, Lysandros gave the order for instant and rapid onset. Every man was at once in his place, and in a few minutes the work was done. Konon alone was at his post, and Philokles perhaps may have been close at hand: but these could do little or nothing. Of the triremes some had only two banks of rowers, some only one: most of them were quite empty. The whole fleet was insnared, but there was no battle. While the enemy was busied in capturing the ships and surrounding the prisoners on the shore, Konon, seeing at a glance that the case was hopeless, hastened with nine ships, the Paralian trireme being one of them, to Abarnis, the promontory to the east of Lampsakos, and thence took away the large sails of the Peloponnesian fleet, thus greatly lessening their powers of pursuit. Then, making his way down the Hellespont, he hastened to his friend Euagoras in Kypros (Cyprus), while the Paralian ship went on its miserable errand to Athens. The captured vessels with their crews were taken to Lampsakos, where Lysandros proceeded to sit in judgement on the Athenian prisoners for crimes which, as it was said, they intended to commit if they had been victorious at Aigospotamoi. All were condemned to death, and Philokles, who had arrayed himself in white garments, was taken away at the head of the long procession to the ground of slaughter. The last words addressed to him by Lysandros charged him with opening the gates to lawless wickedness against the Hellenes, because, in spite of the opposition of Adeimantos, he had thrown the crew of a Corinthian and an Andrian vessel overboard. Lysandros well knew that Hellenic usage gave the

Snaring of the Athenian fleet by the Spartans.

Escape of Konon with nine ships.

Massacre of the Athenian prisoners by Lysandros.

conqueror absolute power over his prisoners. If Philokles
had had a spear thrust through the bodies of these
Corinthian and Andrian captives, he would have done
nothing more than Spartan commanders were in the habit
of doing in every war, and not unfrequently in times of
peace. He chose, in fact, whatever may have been his
motive, a less painful mode of putting them to death ;
and he was charged with offending against the military
usage of Hellas by a man who was about to insult the
universal religious instincts of all the Hellenic tribes by
refusing burial to the crowd of prisoners who were still
standing alive before him. The fact is that Philokles was
faithful to his country : his name is, therefore, blackened.
Adeimantos was spared from the slaughter because, as
many felt sure, and some said openly, he had betrayed
the fleet to Lysandros ; and as it was needful to cloke his
treachery and to assign a decent pretext for his escape,
it was said that he opposed himself to the alleged
brutality of his colleague. But if the surprise was brought
about by Persian gold on the one side and Athenian greed on the other, the treachery could not be confined to one man alone. The constant and factious opposition of a single *Treachery of some among the Athenian generals.*
traitor could scarcely fail to excite the suspicions of his
colleagues ; but if the number of the traitors were more
nearly equal to that of the faithful generals, the action of
the latter might be neutralised without any appearance
of dishonesty or disaffection. Adeimantos seems to have
had even the better fortune of being in a majority. Of
the six generals, Philokles and Konon are beyond
suspicion : of none of the rest are we told that they were
put to death after the battle. According to the geographer
Pausanias, Tydeus was bribed not less than Adeimantos.
As to Menandros, it is significant that he should have
associated himself with Tydeus in his insolent rejection

of the counsel of Alkibiades. Of Kephisodotos alone, nothing can be said, because nothing has been recorded: but it was the conviction of Konon that Lysandros planned and Adeimantos deliberately wrought the destruction of the Athenian fleet. If he was right in so thinking, the whole narrative of this horrible catastrophe becomes luminously clear: on any other supposition, it is a bewildering and insoluble riddle.

But treachery on so vast a scale can spring only from wide and deeply ingrained corruption. If out of six generals three, if not four, could be found to betray the Athenian fleet to the enemy, then Athens was no longer the Athens of Aristeides or of Perikles. The only possibility for the success of Adeimantos in his treason lay in his being joined by a sufficient number of his colleagues to paralyse the action of the rest without drawing on themselves a dangerous suspicion. Nothing more was then needed than to place the fleet in a position of extreme danger under the pretence of holding at bay an enemy conscious of his own weakness. The challenge given every day by the Athenian fleet, and refused with seeming timorousness by the Peloponnesians, would be used as a theme for exciting in the men a profound contempt for the enemy, and the fatal confidence thus fostered would bring about the state of things most desired by the wolves to whom the hirelings had bargained to betray the fold. For the general corruption, without which such a scheme could not have been matured, many causes were at work: but all may be resolved into that neglect of law and that disregard of constitutional forms which had marked the history of Athens since the catastrophe in Sicily. The Athenian demos had been persuaded into decreeing away its own powers on the very ground that forms of government were of little consequence in comparison

Causes leading to this treachery.

with the independence of the state from foreign coercion (p. 172); and when they had put down the tyranny which had convinced them that government by an oligarchy meant simply submission to Sparta, they still believed or asserted that the demos was free from the duty of obeying the law, and could in fact do as it liked (p. 207). If Konon and Philokles had been supported by colleagues like themselves, the defeat of Lysandros must probably have been as signal as that of Mindaros or Kallikratidas, and another disaster must have taught Cyrus that in supporting the enemies of Athens he was playing a losing game. It was clear that either on the one side or on the other one more defeat would end the war in the Egean and the Hellespont. Athens could not produce another fleet; if she was victorious, it was unlikely that the Persian king would continue to subsidise men who failed to show anything for his bounty; and it was certain that without his aid Sparta could not maintain the contest by sea, if the result at Aigospotamoi had repeated the disaster at Argennoussai.

The tidings of the catastrophe came upon the Athenians with the suddenness of a thunderbolt. The cry of agony and despair, which on the arrival of the Paralian trireme passed along the double line of walls, rose into a piercing wail when it reached the city. All that night the mourning went up to heaven, for none could close their eyes in sleep. In this hour of overpowering dismay their thoughts recalled with terrible distinctness their own misdeeds in the days which were past. The wide prospect revealed not a gleam of comfort; but an unconditional surrender, which would enable the Spartans to slay every Athenian citizen and send their wives and children into slavery, was still not to be thought of. A decree was passed for blocking the en-

Dismay at Athens.

Preparations for undergoing a siege.

trance to the harbour, and for making every preparation for undergoing a siege.

But Lysandros was in no hurry to begin the blockade. He knew that Athens must yield or starve, and he took care that the Athenians should be made to feel the sting of famine at once. The Athenian garrisons in Chalkedon and Byzantion were sent straight to Athens, their lives being spared only on the condition that they should take up their abode within the city walls. His own immediate task was the establishment of that Spartan supremacy which the members of the Athenian confederacy had been exhorted to regard as the greatest of blessings. He had now no hindrances in his path. Nowhere was the least opposition offered except in Samos, where the citizens, feeling themselves too deeply compromised by their suppression of the oligarchy (p. 161), determined to hold out.

Operations of Lysandros in the East.

At last Lysandros set out for Athens. A force of 150 ships, having ravaged Salamis, appeared before the harbour from which scarcely more than ten years before had issued that fleet, more magnificent if not so large, which was to establish the supremacy of Athens over Sicily and to win for her a Panhellenic empire. Now it was a question whether she could insist on any terms at all, or whether she must submit herself unconditionally to the conqueror. The first embassy sent to Agis offered free alliance with Sparta, reserving to Athens the possession of Peiraieus and the Long Walls. By him they were referred to the Ephors, who bade them go home and return with more reasonable conditions. To the beleaguered people, in their appalling misery, this rebuff seemed to show that nothing less than their complete destruction would satisfy the Spartans; but whatever doubt there might be on this point, there

Blockade of Peiraieus by Lysandros.

Fruitless efforts to obtain peace.

was none that hundreds or thousands must starve before
any arrangements could be proposed or made. One condition there was on which the Spartans had declared their
readiness to treat; but the Athenians could not yet bring
themselves to pull down one mile in length of each of the
Long Walls. Still the increasing intensity of the famine
convinced them that something must be done. Theramenes was sent on a second mission; but three Mission of
months of frightful misery had passed before Thera-
he was seen again, and even then he brought menes.
from Lysandros no further answer than that terms of
peace could be considered only by the Ephors. Further
hesitation would be absolute ruin. The victims of famine
were lying unburied throughout the city; and Theramenes with nine colleagues was sent to Sparta, authorised
to make peace on any terms. There they were brought
face to face with the representatives of the great Dorian
confederacy, to which the power of Athens had long been
a rock of offence. The voices of the Corinthians and
Thebans were raised for her destruction; but if the
Spartans declared that they would never allow a city to
be inslaved which had done so much good to Hellas, we
may not unjustly ascribe their mercy to a consciousness
that at no very distant day the existence of Athens might
be of more value to them than that of Thebes, even if
Athens should not be needed to help them against
Thebes. The discussion ended with the Final terms
decree that the Athenians must pull down granted by the Spar-
their walls, must yield up all their ships tans.
except twelve, receive back their exiles, and follow im-
plicitly the biddings of Sparta. As Theramenes and
his colleagues made their way with these tidings from
Peiraieus, crowds thronged round him to learn whether
their miseries were now to end, or to be borne until none
should be left to bear them. They were told that their

lives and their freedom were safe; but not until the following day were the precise terms of the peace made known. A few still protested against the last humiliation, but they were overborne by the vast majority. The submission of Athens was made, and the long strife was at an end. Into that harbour from which but a little while before had issued the fleet which Adeimantos had decoyed to its own ruin and the ruin of Athens, Lysandros now entered with the fleet of Sparta, bringing with him those exiles whose crimes had made their names infamous. While the arsenals were dismantled and the unfinished ships in the docks burnt, the demolition of the Long Walls was begun to the music of flute-players and the measured movements of dancing women. Twelve ships only were left in the desolate haven of Peiraieus; and so began, according to Spartan phrase, the first day of freedom for Hellas.

Surrender of Athens.

Demolition of the Long Walls.

Thus passed away the great Athenian empire which Themistokles had shaped, and which Perikles sought to surround with impregnable safeguards; and thus was brought to nought (for that empire was never really revived) the work of these two great statesmen. No other end could be looked for, so soon as it became clear that the great Dorian state with its allies was determined to resist to the uttermost the idea which underlay the polity of Athens, and that in Athens itself a powerful minority was not less resolved on pertinacious opposition to it. This polity, even in its crudest and most imperfect form, was a protest against that spirit of isolation under which the old Eupatrid houses had grown up to power. To the form of society thus created the Spartan clung with vehement tenacity; and in this attitude he had the sympathy of the Hellenic world generally. Even

Causes leading to the fall of the Athenian empire.

when the Athenian empire had reached its greatest extension, and her power seemed most firmly established; when moreover her allies must have felt that from her they received benefits which they could never have secured for themselves, they still felt a certain soreness at her interference with those autonomous instincts which they invested with an inviolable sanctity. These allies, although they could prove no positive grievance (p. 65), could never be brought to rejoice in the good fortune which had connected them with Athens, and they regarded the idea of separating from her with cool indifference, if not with a more active desire.

But the empire of Athens, as her enemies asserted and as her friendssometimes maintained, was aggressive. It could not be otherwise. The same political instincts which maintain the union of Great Britain with her vast and scattered colonies led the statesmen of Athens to build up that coherent fabric which, so far as it was carried, exhibited a singular likeness to the polity of our own country. The necessities which gave birth to the Delian confederacy, and, through it, led to the more highly developed supremacy of Athens, compelled the imperial city to interfere to a certain extent with the freedom, or rather with the license, of those states which, although they might be able to do little good, could yet be powerful for mischief, and which, if they did nothing, would reap the same benefits with those members of the confederacy who did everything. How slight, on the whole, that interference was, how jealously Athens guarded the liberty and rights of her allies even against her own citizens, how great a protection her courts afforded to those allies in their disputes with one another, and how carefully she shielded them against the attacks of foreign powers, the whole course of this history has shown.

Character of the Athenian empire.

Briefly, with all their faults and crimes, the Athenians were fighting for a law and order which, they felt, could not be maintained at all if it was to be confined within the bounds of a single city. So far as they went, they were working to make a nation; but into a nation the Hellenic tribes and cities were determined that they would not be moulded. The resistance which Athens encountered compelled her to keep her allies more thoroughly under control, and imparted to her government an appearance of despotism which, however, was at its worst a slight yoke indeed when compared with the horrors of Spartan rule. She had attempted great things, for which the world was not yet ripe; and the cities which had been induced to band themselves against her awoke for the most part to the conviction that they had suffered themselves to be cheated with a shadow. Henceforth there was to be no sovereign people to which the allies might appeal against the violence or injustice whether of other allied cities or of Athenian officers (p. 4); no Demos which inspired the oligarchic citizens with a wholesome fear; no supreme assembly which was ready to hear complaints even against the most distinguished generals, and to punish with impartiality men of the highest or the meanest lineage. Above all, there was to be no ruling state in which everything was done by open process of law, after the confronting of the accuser with the accused, and a patient and careful examination of evidence. In place of this the members of the Athenian confederacy were now to feel the contrast of a system which imposed on every city the regimen of oligarchs, which governed these oligarchs by means of commissioners sent from Sparta, and which refused redress even for the most monstrous iniquities of these commissioners or their myrmidons. Henceforth they were to carry to Sparta complaints such as at Athens had brought a swift retribution to a general so eminent as Paches (p. 66), and to be dismissed unheard. Above all, they were to be subject to a government which condemned without trial, which struck without warning, and which for open law courts substituted the arbitrary action of irresponsible magistrates who through the Harmosts, or governors, of the subject cities exercised everywhere a power practically absolute. Henceforth, therefore, there was to be no political growth, no generous emulation for the promotion of common interests, no legitimate pride even in the power of a confederacy which existed for the benefit of all its members. In short the Hellenic cities were to feel under their Dorian lords that the freedom promised by Sparta was a privilege strictly confined to masters who demanded from their subjects the unquestioning submission of slaves.

CHRONOLOGICAL TABLE.

B.C.	PAGE		
479	10	Athens	Rebuilding of the city, and fortification of Peiraieus.
			Mission of Themistokles to Sparta.
478	12	Byzantion	Pausanias sends to Xerxes the prisoners taken in the city.
	13		Pausanias recalled to Sparta and deprived of his command.
	14		
477		Asia Minor	Withdrawing from all interference in the affairs of the Asiatic Greeks, the Spartans leave the ground open for the formation of the Athenian confederacy.
	14	Sparta	Treason and death of Pausanias.
		Athens	Developement of the Kleisthenean constitution.
471	17		Ostracism of Themistokles.
465	28	Thasos	Revolt of Thasos, which is reconquered after a siege of two years.
464	29	Peloponnesos	Revolt of the Helots. Dismissal of the Athenian troops by the Spartans. Alliance between Athens and Argos.
461			Alliance of Megara with Athens. Building of the Long Walls of Megara.
? 460	30	Athens	The Athenians send a fleet and army to aid the Egyptians against the Persians.
		Aigina	Siege of Aigina by the Athenians.
	31	Peloponnesos	Defeat of the Corinthians by Myronides
		Athens	Building of the Long Walls of Athens.

B.C.	PAGE		
457	31	Boiotia . . .	Defeat of the Athenians at Tanagra.
?			Victory of the Athenians at Oinophyta.
			Greatest extension of the Athenian empire.
		Athens . . .	Banishment of Kimon.
? 456	38		Reforms of Ephialtes, followed by his murder.
455	52	Peloponnesos . .	The expelled Helots placed by the Athenians in Naupaktos.
	31	Aigina . . .	Siege and conquest of Aigina by the Athenians.
		Egypt	Destruction of the Athenian fleet at Memphis.
	32	Kypros (Cyprus)	Final victories and death of Kimon.
			Alleged convention of Kallias.
447	18	Magnesia . . .	Death of Themistokles.
	34	Boiotia . . .	Defeat of the Athenians at Koroneia under Tolmides: Evacuation of Boiotia.
446		Euboia . . .	Revolt of Euboia and Megara from Athens.
? 443	39	Athens . . .	Ostracism of Thoukydides, son of Melesias.
			Public works of Perikles.
			Extension of Athenian settlements to Lemnos, Imbros, Skyros, and Sinope.
440	40	Samos	The revolt of Samos, effected by the oligarchical party, is followed by the revolt of Byzantion.
			The Samians ask help from the Spartans. The Corinthians insist on the right of every independent state to manage its own affairs.
437	39	Amphipolis . .	Founding of Amphipolis by Hagnon.
436			
	40	Korkyra . . .	The Korkyraians refuse to help the demos of Epidamnos, who apply to the Corinthians.
	41		A Corinthian army admitted into Epidamnos.
436		Korkyra . . .	The proposal of the Korkyraians to submit the question to arbitration is rejected by the Corinthians.

B.C.	PAGE		
433			Surrender of Epidamnos.
	43		Defensive alliance of Korkyra with Athens.
432			Defeat of the Korkyraians by the Corinthians. As the Korkyraians are aided by the Athenians, the result is adduced as the

FIRST ALLEGED CAUSE OF THE PELOPONNESIAN WAR.

	44	Potidaia	. .	Embassy from Potidaia to Sparta, asking for help against Athens.
				The Corinthian Aristeus forces his way into Potidaia.
				Blockade of Potidaia by the Athenians. Hence the

SECOND ALLEGED CAUSE OF THE PELOPONNESIAN WAR.

	44	Megara	. . .	The Megarians excluded from all Athenian ports.
	45	Sparta	. . .	In an assembly of Peloponnesian allies the Corinthians insist on war with Athens. Counter-arguments of Athenian envoys who happen to be present in Sparta.
	46			In a secret debate the ephor Sthenelaïdas puts aside the pacific arguments of Archidamos, and a majority in the assembly decides on war.
	47			Autumn. In a congress held at Sparta the question is put to the allies, and answered in the affirmative by a large majority.
431				Efforts of the Spartans to bring about the banishment of Perikles.
	48			The final demands of the Peloponnesians are rejected by the Athenians, who express their readiness to submit to arbitration.
		Athens	. . .	Prosecutions of Anaxagoras, Pheidias, and Aspasia.
431	50	Plataia	. . .	Surprise of Plataia by a party of Thebans invited by some Plataian citizens.

A.H.

B.C.	PAGE		
	51		The Thebans in their turn surprised by the Plataians, who, in direct breach of promise, slay their prisoners.
	52		The Plataian families remove to Athens.

PELOPONNESIAN WAR. FIRST YEAR.

B.C.	PAGE		
	52	Attica . . .	The Peloponnesian forces assembled at the Isthmus are led on into Attica by Archidamos, and attack Oinoê. Ravaging of the demos of Acharnai.
		Peloponnesos . .	The Athenians attack Methônê, which is saved by the Spartan Brasidas.
	53	Aigina . . .	The inhabitants of Aigina, expelled by the Athenians, are allowed by the Spartans to settle in the Thyreatis.
		Megara . . .	The Athenians ravage the Megarian territory.
		Athens . . .	A reserve fund of 1000 talents placed in the Akropolis.
	54		Funeral oration of Perikles.

SECOND YEAR.

B.C.	PAGE		
430	56	Athens . . .	Second invasion of Attica. Outbreak of the plague at Athens.
	57		Unpopularity of Perikles consequent on the ravages of the disease. He is fined, but re-elected Strategos.
		Potidaia . . .	Terrible losses by the plague in the Athenian camp.
	44		Surrender of Potidaia.

THIRD YEAR.

B.C.	PAGE		
429	59	Plataia . . .	The Spartan army invades the territory of Plataia. On the rejection of his proposals for the neutrality of the Plataians, Archidamos invests the place.

PELOPONNESIAN WAR. THIRD YEAR (*continued*).

U.C.	PAGE		
429	61	*Akarnania* . .	Wishing to detach Akarnania from Athens, the Spartan Knemos determines to attack Stratos with a force of Chaonian, Molossian, and Thesprotian allies.
			Disorderly advance of the mountaineers against Stratos.
			Defeat of the clans, and retreat of Knemos.
	62	*Naupaktos* . .	Phormion intercepts the Corinthian fleet, and wins a splendid victory.
		Krete	Fruitless Athenian expedition to Krete.
	63	*Naupaktos* . .	The Peloponnesian fleet contrives to entice Phormion into the Corinthian gulf; but the success of the Spartans at the first is turned into a second victory for Phormion.
		Salamis . . .	Raid on Salamis by Brasidas and Knemos, who are compelled to give up the plan of a night attack on Peiraieus.
	64	*Makedonia* . .	Abortive expedition of the Thrakian chief Sitalkes into Makedonia.

FOURTH YEAR.

428		*Lesbos*	Revolt of Lesbos.
	65		On the prayer of the Lesbian envoys who appear at the Olympic festival, a fleet of forty ships under Alkidas is ordered to support the revolt.
	66		The Lakedaimonian Salaithos contrives to enter Mytilênê and encourages the oligarchs to hold out.

FIFTH YEAR.

427		*Attica*	Invasion of Attica by the Peloponnesians under the Spartan Kleomenes.
		Lesbos	The oligarchs arm the demos, who insist on a distribution of corn, threatening in default to throw open the gates to the Athenians.

PELOPONNESIAN WAR. FIFTH YEAR (*continued*).

B.C.	PAGE		
427	66	Lesbos	The Mytilenaian oligarchs make a convention with Paches. Alkidas arrives too late, and being resolved to return home, massacres his prisoners by the way.
	67	Athens	The Mytilenaian prisoners, about 1000 in number, are sent to Athens, along with Salaithos, who is at once put to death. In the debate which follows, Kleon proposes the slaughter of the whole Mytilenaian people. The sentence is passed, but revoked on the next day, chiefly through
	68		the exertions of Diodotos. The prisoners at Athens are slain; but the trireme sent to arrest the
	69		execution of the decree arrives just in time.
	70	Plataia	Upwards of 200 Plataians escape from the city. The rest are com-
	71		pelled to surrender through famine, and, in accordance with the Theban plan, are all put to death.
	113	Sicily	Embassy from Leontinoi to Athens to ask help against Syracuse.
	72	Megara	Conquest of Minoa by Nikias.
		Athens	Second outbreak of plague in the summer.

SIXTH YEAR.

426	73	Melos	Unsuccessful expedition of Nikias to the Spartan colonies of Melos and Thera.
		Trachis . . .	Foundation of the Spartan colony of Herakleia.
		Akarnania . .	Demosthenes resolves on a campaign in Aitolia, with the view of advancing into Boiotia and there restoring the supremacy of Athens. His defeat and return to Naupaktos.
	74		Defeat of the Ambrakiots at Idomenê.

PELOPONNESIAN WAR. SEVENTH YEAR.

B.C.	PAGE		
425	74	*Pylos*	Demosthenes occupies Pylos, from which Brasidas tries in vain to dislodge him.
			Defeat of the Spartan fleet in the harbour of Sphakteria.
	78		Blockade of the Spartan hoplites in the island.
			Terms of truce arranged on the surrender of the Spartan fleet to the Athenian generals.
	79	*Athens*	Spartan envoys appear at Athens with proposals for peace. Kleon brings about their ignominious dismissal.
	80	*Pylos*	On the ending of the truce the Athenians refuse to restore the Spartan fleet.
	81		Distress of the besieging force.
		Athens	The news from Pylos causes great dissatisfaction at Athens. Nikias treacherously abandons his command to Kleon, who promises to return victorious in twenty days.
	82		
	83	*Pylos*	Kleon leaves the arrangement of the plan of assault to Demosthenes.
			Attack on Sphakteria. Capture of 292 hoplites, who are conveyed to Athens.
			Establishment of a permanent Athenian garrison.

EIGHTH YEAR.

424	84	*Peloponnesos*	The Athenians occupy Kythera, and take Thyrea by storm. The Aiginetans captured within it are taken to Athens and put to death.
	85		Alleged massacre of 2000 Helots by the Spartans, who receive overtures from Perdikkas and the Chalkidic towns for combined operations against the Athenian empire.
	86		Mission of Brasidas to Thrace.

PELOPONNESIAN WAR. EIGHTH YEAR (*continued*).

B.C.	PAGE		
424	87	*Peloponnesos* . .	The Athenians take Nisaia, but retreat from Megara when Brasidas offers battle. The Megarians demolish their Long Walls.
	114	*Sicily*	In the congress of Sicilian Greeks at Gela, Hermokrates inveighs against the aggressiveness of the Athenians. General peace between the Sikeliot cities.
	87	*Boiotia* . . .	Failure of the plan concerted between Demosthenes and Hippokrates for the subjugation of Boiotia.
	88		The Athenians fortify Delion. BATTLE OF DELION. Victory of the Thebans, who refuse to yield up the Athenian dead.
	89		Assault and capture of Delion.
	90	*Thrace* . . .	Brasidas appears before Akanthos, where the people are averse to the idea of revolt from Athens.
	91		The REVOLT OF AKANTHOS is brought about by the eloquence and threats of Brasidas, supported by the oligarchic faction. Surrender of AMPHIPOLIS to Brasidas.
	92		Thucydides arrives on the same day at Eïon.
	93		For his remissness in failing to save Amphipolis, Thucydides is banished or goes into voluntary exile.
	94		Brasidas takes TORÔNÊ, and discourses to the people on the blessings of Spartan freedom.

NINTH YEAR.

423	95	*Sparta* . . .	The Spartans draw up terms for a year's truce, which is accepted by the Athenians, the basis being generally the maintenance of the *status quo*.

PELOPONNESIAN WAR. NINTH YEAR (*continued*).

B.C.	PAGE		
		Thrace	Brasidas is received into Skiônê against the wishes of the party favourable to Athens, and by his eloquence wins for himself an enthusiastic welcome.
423	95		The commissioners arrive to announce the truce. Brasidas insists that Skiônê revolted before it began.
	96		Revolt of Mendê from Athens. Perdikkas resolves to ally himself again with the Athenians. Recovery of Mendê by the Athenians.

TENTH YEAR.

422	97	*Athens*	Kleon is placed in command of an army for operations in Thrace.
	98	*Thrace*	Recovery of Torônê by Kleon.
	100		BATTLE OF AMPHIPOLIS. Death of Brasidas and of Kleon.

ELEVENTH YEAR.

421	101	*Athens*	Ratification of the peace of Nikias.
	102		The peace is not accepted by the Corinthians, Boiotians, and Megarians; and the Chalkidians refuse to give up Amphipolis.
		Amphipolis	Klearidas withdraws the Peloponnesian garrison.
		Athens	Separate treaty between Athens and Sparta. The Athenians surrender the prisoners taken at Sphakteria.
	103	*Peloponnesos*	The Argives, urged by the Corinthians, invite adhesions to their confederacy, which is joined by the Mantineians, the Eleians, and the Chalkidians of Thrace. The Tegeans refuse to join it. The Athenians are induced to withdraw the Messenians and Helots from Pylos.

Chronological Table.

PELOPONNESIAN WAR. TWELFTH YEAR.

B.C.	PAGE		
420	104	*Peloponnesos* . .	The Spartans make a separate treaty with the Boiotians in violation of the terms of their agreement with the Athenians.
		Athens . . .	The Athenians refuse to give up Pylos in exchange for the site of the demolished fort of Panakton.
	105		ALKIBIADES stirs up their feelings of displeasure against the Spartans, and, having induced the Argives, Mantineians, and Eleians to send envoys to Athens, cheats the Spartan ambassadors into a denial of the powers with which they had been entrusted.
	106		Defensive alliance between Athens, Argos, Elis, and Mantineia.

THIRTEENTH YEAR.

419	107	*Peloponnesos* . .	Alkibiades makes a progress through Achaia.
			His plans at Patrai and Rhion are foiled by the Corinthians.
			The Athenians bring back to Pylos the Helots and Messenians whom they had placed in Kephallenia.

FOURTEENTH YEAR.

418			Invasion of Argos by the Spartans under Agis.
	108		Desperate danger of the Argive army, from which they are rescued by two of their generals, who obtain a truce for four months.
			Indignation on both sides.
			The people of Tegea ask help from Sparta. Agis advances into the territory of Mantineia.
			BATTLE OF MANTINEIA. Complete victory of the Spartans, who thus regain their old position.
	109		Oligarchical conspiracy at Argos by the Thousand and others.
			Mantineia joins the confederacy of Sparta.

Chronological Table.

PELOPONNESIAN WAR. FIFTEENTH YEAR.

B.C.	PAGE		
417	110	*Peloponnesos* . .	Rising of the Argive demos against the oligarchs.
			Building of the Long Walls of Argos, which in the following winter are destroyed by Agis.
		Thrace . . .	Failure of an Athenian expedition for the recovery of Amphipolis.

SIXTEENTH YEAR.

416		*Melos*	Expedition of the Athenians to coerce Melos into their confederacy.
	111		The massacre of Melos.
	115	*Athens* . . .	Arrival of envoys from Egesta in Sicily to ask help against the people of Selinous. The Egestaians promise to bear the costs of the war.

SEVENTEENTH YEAR.

415			The envoys sent to Egesta return with a glowing account of its wealth.
	116		The Athenians appoint Nikias, Alkibiades, and Lamachos generals of an expedition to maintain the cause of Egesta, and to further Athenian interests generally in Sicily.
			The expedition is opposed by Nikias, and vehemently urged on by Alkibiades.
	118		The scale of the enterprise is increased owing to the requirements of Nikias.
	120		Mutilation of the Hermai.
	121		Accusation of Alkibiades for profanation of the mysteries; his trial posponed until after his recall from Sicily.
	122		Departure of the fleet from Athens.
		Syracuse . . .	Hermokrates warns the Syracusans of the coming invasion. His statements are contradicted by Athenagoras.

PELOPONNESIAN WAR. SEVENTEENTH YEAR
(continued).

B.C.	PAGE		
415	123	*Italy*	The Athenian fleet reaches Rhegion. The wealth of Egesta is discovered to be a cheat.
	124	*Sicily*	Alkibiades fails in an attempt to gain the alliance of Messênê.
			The Athenian fleet sails to Syracuse.
	125		The Athenians occupy Katanê.
			Recall of Alkibiades, who escapes from Thourioi and is sentenced to death by the people in his absence.
	126		By a stratagem Nikias draws off the Syracusan force to Katanê, while the Athenian fleet lands the army in the Great Harbour.
			The Athenians win a victory, which is turned to no account. Nikias loses the opportunity for investing Syracuse while yet imperfectly fortified.
			The fleet takes up its winter quarters at Naxos.
	127		The Kamarinaians, after hearing the Syracusan Hermokrates and the Athenian Euphemos, resolve to remain neutral.
	129	*Sparta*	Alkibiades urges the active resumption of the war against Athens, the mission of a Spartan general to Syracuse, and the establishment of a permanent garrison in Attica.

EIGHTEENTH YEAR.

414	132	*Syracuse* . . .	Surprise of Epipolai by the Athenians, who build a fort on Labdalon.
			The Syracusans raise their first counter-work, which is taken by the Athenians.
	134		Capture of the second Syracusan counter-work. Lamachos is killed.
			The Athenian fleet enters the Great Harbour.

PELOPONNESIAN WAR. EIGHTEENTH YEAR
(continued).

B.C.	PAGE		
414	134	*Syracuse* . . .	The Athenians again have everything in their favour. Nikias loses the golden opportunity. Gylippos reaches Italy. Neglect of Nikias to intercept him.
	135		Gylippos enters Syracuse. He takes the fort on Labdalon.
	136		Nikias fortifies Plemmyrion. The Syracusans, being first beaten, defeat the Athenians.
	138		Nikias writes for further help from Athens.

NINETEENTH YEAR.

413	139	*Attica*	The Peloponnesians ravage Attica, and by fortifying Dekeleia begin the so-called

DEKELEIAN WAR.

	140	*Syracuse* . . .	A naval victory of the Athenians is made worthless by the loss of Plemmyrion, which is taken by Gylippos.
	141		Some reinforcements for Syracuse are cut off by the Sikel chiefs in the interior.
	142		The destruction of the fleet of Nikias is prevented by the arrival of Demosthenes with seventy-three triremes.
	143		Failure of the attempt of Demosthenes to break the Syracusan counter-wall by a night attack on Epipolai.
	144		Nikias refuses to retreat, or even to withdraw the fleet to Katanè or Naxos.
	145		Finally, after resolving on retreat, he retracts his consent owing to an eclipse of the moon, and refuses to move for twenty-seven days.
	146		Defeat of the Athenian fleet, and death of Eurymedon.

PELOPONNESIAN (DEKELEIAN) WAR. NINETEENTH YEAR (*continued*).

B.C.	PAGE		
413	147	*Syracuse* . . .	The Syracusans close up the mouth of the Great Harbour.
	148		Ruin of the Athenian fleet in the battle fought to break through the barrier.
	150		The Athenian retreat delayed by a stratagem of Hermokrates.
	152		After a retreat of terrible suffering, extended over seven days, the division of Demosthenes surrenders on a promise that the lives of all shall be safe.
	153		Destruction of the force of Nikias on the banks of the Assinaros. Nikias surrenders himself to Gylippos. The prisoners are thrown into the quarries of Epipolai. In defiance of the compact made with him, Demosthenes is put to death along with Nikias.
	154		
	156	*Attica*	The Athenian slaves desert in large bodies to the Spartans at Dekeleia.
	157	*The Egean and Asia Minor.*	The Euboians and Lesbians ask help from Sparta in their meditated revolt against Athens.
			The Persian king claims the tribute assessed on the Asiatic Greeks.
			Pharnabazos seeks to induce the Spartans to transfer the war to the Hellespont.
	158		By the influence of Alkibiades, the Spartans determine to aid the Chians first.

TWENTIETH YEAR.

412			The Athenians demand a squadron of ships from the Chians, according to the terms of the alliance.
	159		Alkibiades sails with Chalkideus for Chios, and brings about the revolt of that island, which is

PELOPONNESIAN (DEKELEIAN OR IONIAN) WAR.
TWENTIETH YEAR (*continued*).

B.C.	PAGE		
	160		followed by that of Lebedos and Erai. On hearing of these revolts, the Athenians resolve to make use of the reserve funds in the Akropolis (p. 53).
412		The Egean and Asia Minor	Revolt of Miletos. *First treaty between the Spartans and the Persians.*
	161		Insurrection of THE PEOPLE OF SAMOS against the oligarchical government: 200 of the oligarchic party killed, 400 banished, and their property confiscated.
	162		REVOLT IN LESBOS. The Athenians storm Mytilene and reduce the whole island.
			The Athenians ravage Chios.
	162		The Athenians fortify Delphinion and again ravage Chios.
	165		*Second treaty between the Spartans and Tissaphernes.*
	166		Lichas repudiates the two treaties made by the Spartans with the Persians.
			The revolt of Rhodes from Athens brought about by the oligarchic faction.
	167		The Spartans send an order for the assassination of Alkibiades, who takes refuge with Tissaphernes, and makes overtures to the oligarchs serving among the Athenians at Samos, promising them the help of the Persian king, if the Athenian democracy is put down.
	168		
	169		The envoys sent from Samos to Alkibiades return with assurances which make the oligarchs eager to carry out their schemes.
	171		PROTEST OF PHRYNICHOS, who out-manœuvres Alkibiades.

PELOPONNESIAN (DEKELEIAN OR IONIAN) WAR.
TWENTIETH YEAR (continued).

B.C.	PAGE		
412	171	Athens	Peisandros comes as an envoy from Samos, saying that the Persian king will supply them with money, if the Athenians will receive Alkibiades and change their constitution.
	173		The Athenians appoint ten commissioners to settle matters with Alkibiades and Tissaphernes.
			Peisandros organises the conspiracy in which Antiphon eagerly takes part, aided by Theramenes and afterwards by Phrynichos.
	174	The Egean	Alkibiades baffles the Athenian commissioners, by demanding that the Persian king shall maintain a fleet in the Egean.
	175		*Third treaty between Tissaphernes and the Spartans.*

TWENTY-FIRST YEAR.

411		Asia Minor	Revolt of Abydos and Lampsakos from Athens.
			Lampsakos is retaken by the Athenians.
	176	Thasos	An oligarchy set up in Thasos, which soon after revolts from Athens.
	177	Athens	By a series of assassinations, the oligarchical conspirators set up a reign of terror.
	178		The Demos is made to vote for the government of the FOUR HUNDRED and the Five Thousand.
			Expulsion of the Kleisthenean council of the Five Hundred.
	179		The first overtures of the Four Hundred are rejected by Agis, who, failing in an attempt to surprise Athens, allows a second set of envoys to go to Sparta.
		Samos	The Athenian army resolve to maintain the Kleisthenean constitution, and send Chaireas to

PELOPONNESIAN (DEKELEIAN OR IONIAN) WAR.
TWENTY-FIRST YEAR (*continued*).

B.C.	PAGE		
	180		Athens, where he is seized by the Four Hundred. Making his escape, he returns to Samos.
411	181	Samos	The Athenians and Samians join in solemn oaths to maintain the old laws of Athens, and declare Athens in revolt from the people. Thrasyboulos brings Alkibiades to Samos, where he is elected Strategos by the citizens.
	183		The envoys from the conspirators at Athens are sent back with the answer that the Four Hundred must be put down.
		Athens . . .	Theramenes insists that the Five Thousand shall be made a reality. The Four Hundred send envoys to Sparta, offering unconditional submission, and fortify Eetionia for the purpose of consummating their treason.
	185		Destruction of Eetionia. The Four Hundred propose a compromise.
	186	Euboia . . .	Total defeat of the Athenian fleet under Thymochares. Revolt of Euboia from Athens.
		Athens . . .	The Four Hundred are suppressed. Practical restoration of the Periklean polity.
	188		Trial and condemnation of Antiphon.
	189	Asia Minor .	Revolt of Byzantion from Athens. The Spartans send Mindaros to supersede Astyochos.
	190		Tissaphernes sends back the Phenician fleet from Aspendos.
	191		Victory of the Athenians under Thrasyboulos and Thrasylos off KYNOSSEMA.
	194		Defeat of Dorieus and Mindaros in the bay of Dardanos.

PELOPONNESIAN (DEKELEIAN OR IONIAN) WAR.
TWENTY-SECOND YEAR.

B.C.	PAGE		
410	195	Asia Minor . .	Theramenes sails to the Athenian naval station at Kardia, where he is joined by Alkibiades after his escape from prison at Sardeis.
			Battle of KYZIKOS. Death of Mindaros; destruction of the Peloponnesian fleet.
			By seizing Chrysopolis, the port of Chalkedon, the Athenians again become masters of the highway of the Hellespont.

TWENTY-THIRD YEAR.

| 409 | 196 | Pylos . . . . . | Attack of the Spartans on Pylos. The Athenian Anytos fails to succour the besieged Messenians, who are compelled to surrender. |
| | 197 | Megara . . . | The Megarians recover the fort of Nisaia. |

TWENTY-FOURTH YEAR.

| 408 | | Asia Minor . . | The Athenians reduce Chalkedon and Byzantion. |
| | | | The Athenian envoys on their way to Sousa are stopped by Cyrus, who is sent down as the Persian commander-in-chief in Asia Minor. |

TWENTY-FIFTH YEAR.

407	198		Lysandros organizes the oligarchical clubs.
		Athens . . .	Return of Alkibiades as general to Athens, where he conducts the Eleusinian procession along the Sacred Road.
	199		
	200	The Egean . .	Antiochos, the sailing-master of Alkibiades, disobeys orders, challenges Lysandros, and is defeated off Notion.

PELOPONNESIAN (DEKELEIAN OR IONIAN) WAR.
TWENTY-FIFTH YEAR (*continued*).

B.C.	PAGE		
407	200	*The Egean*	Alkibiades, having attacked and plundered Kymē, a town of the Athenian confederacy, is deposed from his command by the people.

TWENTY-SIXTH YEAR.

406	201		Kallikratidas, having succeeded Lysandros, blockades Konon in Mytilene.
	202		An Athenian trireme conveys the news to Athens, whence a fleet of 110 ships is sent to his aid. BATTLE OF ARGENNOUSSAI. Complete victory of the Athenians. Death of Kallikratidas.
	203		The Athenian generals commission Theramenes and Thrasyboulos to rescue the crews of the disabled vessels. A storm prevents the execution of the order.
	204	*Athens*	A despatch from the generals makes known these facts: and Theramenes resolves to destroy the generals, six of whom, returning to Athens, are charged with neglecting to save the crews.
	206		Theramenes avails himself of the festival of Apatouria to increase the feeling against them.
	207		The proposal of Kallixenos that the people shall proceed at once to pronounce judgement on all the six together, is submitted to the people.
	208		Protest of Sokrates. Euryptolemos vainly tries to secure for them a legal trial.
	209		Murder of the six generals.
	210	*Sparta*	Appointment of Lysandros as secretary to Arakos.

PELOPONNESIAN (DEKELEIAN OR IONIAN) WAR.
TWENTY-SEVENTH YEAR.

B C.	PAGE		
405	210	*The Egean* .	Lysandros takes Lampsakos.
	212		The Athenian fleet of 180 triremes, posted at AIGOSPOTAMOI, is betrayed into the hands of Lysandros, who orders all the Athenian prisoners to be put to death.
			Escape of Konon to Kypros (Cyprus).
	216	*Athens* .	Blockade of Peiraieus by Lysandros.
	218		Surrender of the city, followed by the dismantling of the Long Walls.

INDEX.

ABY

ABYDOS, 175
Acharnai, ravaging of, 52
Achradina, 127
Adeimantos, 210, 213
Admetos the Molossian, 17
Ægina, Æginetans [Aigina, Aiginetans]
Ægospotami [Aigospotamoi]
Ætolia [Aitolia]
Agathon, 188
Agis, king of Sparta, 74; grants a truce to the Argives, 108; wins the battle of Mantineia, 109; attacks Athens unsuccessfully, 179
Aigina, siege of, 30; fall of, 31
Aiginetans expelled by the Athenians, 53, 85
Aigospotamoi, 210
Aitolia, 73
Akanthos, 90
Akarnanians, 73, 74
Alkibiades, early career of, 104; deceives the Spartan envoys, 105, interference of, in Peloponnesos, 106; appointed to command in Sicily, 116; innocent of all share in the plot of the Hermokopidai, 120; accused of profanation, 121; recall and flight of, 125; at Sparta urges the renewal of the war and the fortification of Dekeleia, 129; brings about the revolt of the Chians and other allies of Athens, 159; makes his escape to Tissaphernes, 167; writes to the Athenian oligarchs at Samos, 168; and Phrynichos, 171; breaks with the oligarchic plotters, 174; at Samos, 182; at Aspendos, 190; victory of, in the bay of Dardanos, 194; at Kyzikos, 195; return of, to Athens, 199; plunders Kymê, and is de-

ATH

prived of his command, 200; warns the Athenian generals at Aigospotamoi, 211
Alkidas, 66
Allies of Athens, temper of the, 193
Ambrakiots, 73, 74
Amphipolis, foundation of, 28, 39; occupied by Brasidas, 92
Anaxagoras, 48
Antiochos, 200
Antiphon, 173, 184, 188
Anytos, 196
Apatouria, 206
Arakos, 210
Archidamos, 46, 52, 56, 68
Archonship at Athens, 37
Areiopagos, 37
Argennoussai, 202
Arginusæ [Argennoussai]
Argos, formation of a new confederacy under, 103; invasion of, by Spartans and Corinthians, 107; revolutions at, 109, 110
Aristeides, 6, 16; assessment of, 28
Aristokrates, 158
Arrhibaios, 96
Artaxerxes, 17, 19
Aspasia, 48
Assassinations, political, at Athens, 177
Astyochos, 165, 188
Athenagoras, 123
Athenian character, question of the deterioration of the, during the Peloponnesian war, 192; causes of the deterioration of the, 192, 207
Athenian constitution, 37
Athenian dislike of responsibility, 156, 200
Athenian empire, rise of the, 25 *et seq.*; character of the, 219

R 2

ATH

Athenian fleet, destroyed at Memphis, 31; snared at Aigospotamoi, 212
Athenian seamen, reputation of, 6; naval tactics, 43
Athenians, victorious at Oinophyta, 31; defeated at Koroneia, evacuate Boiotia, 34; make a defensive alliance with the Korkyraians, 43; not chargeable with the outbreak of the Peloponnesian war, 49; place a reserve fund in the Akropolis, 53; decree the massacre of the people of Mytilene, 67; withdraw the decree, 69; slaughter the Mytilenaian prisoners, 69; occupy Kythera, 84; defeated at Delion, 88; surrender the hoplites taken at Sphakteria, 102; make a defensive alliance with Argos, 106; try, unsuccessfully, to recover Amphipolis, 110; massacre the Melians, 111; decree an expedition to Sicily, 116; win a victory in the harbour of Syracuse, and lose Plemmyrion, 140; their fleet defeated by Gylippos, 142; fail utterly in the Sicilian expedition, 153; make use of the reserve fund in the Akropolis, 160; fortify Delphinion, and ravage Chios, 162; at Samos resolve to treat Athens as a revolted city, 180; lose Euboia, 186; suppress the Four Hundred, 187; victorious at Kynossema, 191; in the bay of Dardanos, 194; at Kyzikos, 195; lose Pylos, 196; and Nisaia, 197; make a convention with Pharnabazos, 197; victorious at Argennoussai, 202; murder the six generals, 209; lose their fleet at Aigospotamoi, 212
Athens, relation of, to her allies, 27, 65; and Sparta, two distinct political centres, 7; fortification of, 9; empire of, 28; Long Walls of, 30; land-empire of, 33; plague at, 55; oligarchical revolution at, 177 Long Walls of, pulled down, 218

BOIOTIA, movement in, in favour of Athens, 87
Boiotians reject the peace of Nikias, 102
Boudoron, 64
Brasidas relieves Methone, 53; sent to the fleet of Knemos, 62; proposes a night-attack on Peiraieus, 63; at

EKK

Pylos, 77; at Megara, 87; in Thessaly, 90; at Akanthos, 90; at Amphipolis, 91; at Torone, 94; at Skione, 95; killed in the battle of Amphipolis, 100
Byzantion revolts against Athens, 40 second revolt of, 195, 197

CHAIREAS, 180
Chalkedon, 197
Chalkideus, 158
Chios revolts from Athens, 159 ravaged, 162
Corcyra [Korkyra]
Corinthians, 9; quarrel with their colony of Korkyra, 41; defeated by Phormion, 61, 63; reject the peace of Nikias, 102; join the Argive confederacy, 103; demand the destruction of Athens, 217
Cyrus, the younger, 197

DASKON, 126
Dekeleia, 129
Delian confederacy, 4, 5
Delion, 87
Delos, synod of, 26, 27
Delphinion, 162
Demos at Mytilene, 66
Demosthenes, failure of, in Aitolia, 73; his successes against the Ambrakiots, 74; occupies Pylos, 75; at Nisaia, 86; at Siphai, 87; brings reinforcements to Syracuse, 142; fails in the night-attack on Epipolai, 143; his resolution to retreat opposed by Nikias, 144; abandons the lines along Epipolai, 147; surrender of, 152; murder of, 154
Diitrephes, 176
Diodotos and Kleon, 68
Diomedon, 180, 202; murder of, 209
Dorieus, 189, 194
Doriskos, 24
Dorkis, 24

EETIONIA, 183
Egesta, 114, 123
Egypt, revolt of against Artaxerxes, 30
Eion, 94
Ekklesia, 57

Index. 245

EPH

Ephialtes, 36 ; murdered, 38
Epidamnos, 40
Epidauros, 107
Epipolai, 132
Epitadas, 77, 81
Erai, 161
Erasinides, murder of, 209
Eresos, 190
Erythrai, 159
Eteonikos, 202, 203, 210
Euagoras, 212
Euboia, revolt of, against Athens, 34 ; second revolt of, 185
Eukles, 92
Euphemos, 127
Euryelos, 135
Eurylochos, 74
Eurymedon, the river, 28
Eurymedon, the Athenian general, 113, 145
Euryptolemos, 207
Euthydemos. 139

FIVE HUNDRED, 177
Five Thousand, 178
Forged letters of Pausanias and Themistokles, 12
Four Hundred, 178
Funeral oration of Perikles, 54

GELA, Congress of, 114
Geomoroi, 161
Gongylos, the Eretrian, 12
Gorgias, 113
Graphē Paranomōn, 178, 207
Gylippos sent to Syracuse, 130 ; enters the city, 135

HAGNON, 39
Heliaia, 37
Helots, revolt of the, 29 ; placed at Naupaktos, 32 ; massacre of, 85
Herakleia in Trachis, 73, 197
Hermai, mutilation of the, 120
Hermokopidai, 125
Hermokrates at congress of Gela, 114 ; deprived of his command, 134 ; delays the retreat of the Athenians by a stratagem, 150 ; at Miletos, 164, 189
Hetairiai, 173
Hippokrates, 86 ; killed at Delion, 88
— the Spartan, 195

LES

IDOMÊNÊ, 74
Imbros, 39
Ionians, 4

KALLIAS, convention of, 32
Kallikratidas, 200, 202
Kallixenos, 207
Kamarina, 125, 127
Katanê, 124
Kephisodotos, 210, 214
Kimon, victory of, at the Eurymedon, 28 ; at Ithome, 29 ; ostracism of, 38 ; death of 32
Kition, 32
Klazomenai, 159
Klearchos, 188
Kleisthenes, 2
Kleisthenean constitution, 3 ; restoration of the, after the tyranny of the Four Hundred, 187
Kleon, urges the massacre of the Mytilenaians, 67 ; terms demanded by, as conditions of peace with Sparta, 79 ; brings about the dismissal of the Spartan envoys, 80 ; and Nikias, 82 ; at Pylos, 83 ; and Thucydides, 93 ; sent to Thrace, 97 ; killed in the battle of Amphipolis, 100 : general policy of, 101
Klerouchoi, 39
Knemos, 61
Konon, 200 : blockaded at Mytilene, 202 ; escapes from Aigospotamoi, 212, 214
Korkyra, quarrel of, with Corinth, 40
Korkyraians ask aid of Athens, 42
Koroneia, battle of, 34
Koryphasion [Pylos]
Kritias, 206
Kymê, 200
Kynossêma, 191
Kythera, 84
Kyzikos, battle of, 195

LABDALON, 132
Lamachos appointed to command in Sicily, 116 ; his plan of operations, 124 ; his death, 133
Lampsakos, 18, 175, 21
Laureion, 129
Lebedos, 161
Lemnos, 39
Leon, 179
Leontinoi, 113
Lesbians ask aid of Sparta, 65

LES

Lesbos, revolt of, from Athens, 64; envoys from, heard at Olympia, 65; second revolt of, 162
Lichas, 166, 189
Long Walls of Megara, 30, 30, 87
— — of Athens, 30, 218
— — of Argos, 110
Lynkestai, 96
Lysandros, 198, 210, 216, 218

MAGNESIA, 18
Mandane, 19
Mantineia, battle of, 109
Maskames, 25
Megara, allies herself with Athens, 29; revolts, 34, 80; refuses to recognise the peace of Nikias, 104
Melos, 73; massacre of, 111
Menandros, 139, 210, 213
Mende, 96
Methônê, 52
Metoikoi, 7
Miletos, 160
Mindaros, 189, 195
Minoa taken by Nikias, 72
Mounychia, 11, 39
Myronides, 31
Mytilene, invested by Paches, 65; surrenders, 66; punishment of, 69

NAVARINO, 75
Naupaktos, 62
Nikias, takes Minoa, 72; and Kleon, 82; peace of, 101; appointed to command in Sicily, 116; opposes the expedition, 117; caught in his own trap, 109; asks for reinforcements at Syracuse, 136; fails to prevent the entry of Gylippos into Syracuse, 135; letter of, to the Athenians, 138; refuses to retreat, 145; surrender of, 153; death of, 154
Nisaia, 29, 79, 197

OINOPHYTA, battle of, 31
Oligarchs, intrigues of, 24; at Athens 177 *et seq.*
Olpai, 73
Oration, funeral, of Perikles, 54
Ortygia, 126

PACHES, 65
Pagondas, 88

SIL2

Panakton, 102, 103
Paralos, 58
Paranomôn Graphê, 178, 207
Parthenon, 39
Patrai, 107
Pausanias, 11, 19, 21
Pegai, 29, 79
Peiraieus, fortification of, 11; proposal of Brasidas to attack, 64
Peisandros, 171, 172, 178
Peloponnesian war, the Athenians not chargeable with the outbreak of the, 49
Perdikkas, 64, 90, 96
Perikles, builds the Long Walls of Athens, 30; and Kimon, 32; character of, 36; intrigues of the Spartans against, 47; funeral oration of, 54; later years of, 58
Perikles, son of Aspasia, 48, 58; murder of, 209
Phaleron 11
Pharnabazos, 157, 196
Pheidias, 48
Philokles, 210, 212
Phormion, victories of, in the Corinthian Gulf, 61, 63
Phrynichos, 165; protests against the proposed oligarchical revolution at Athens, 170; superseded, 180; murdered, 185
Plague at Athens, 55
Plataia, surprised by the Thebans, 50; attacked by the Spartans, 59; siege of, 60; destruction of, 70
Plemmyrion, 136
Potidaia revolts against Athens, 44
Probouleutic senate, 37
Propylaia, 39
Prytaneis, 208
Pylos occupied by Demosthenes, 75; recovered by the Spartans, 196

RHION, 107
Rhodes revolts from Athens, 166

SALAITHOS, 66, 67
Samians, revolt of the, 40; revolt of the demos in favour of Athens, 161; hold out against Lysandros, 216
Selinous, 114
Seuthes, 64
Sicily, first interference of the Athenians in the affairs of, 113; failure of the Athenians in, 154

Index.

SIN

Sinope, 39
Sitalkes, 64
Skiône, 95
Skyros, 39
Sokrates, 208
Solon, imprecation of, 2
Spartans withdraw from further interference in the struggle with Persia, 25; ask Athenian aid against the Helots, 29; summon a council of their allies, 44; in a secret debate decide that the Athenians have broken the Thirty Years' Truce, 47; promise to aid the allies of Athens, 28, 40, 44, 49, 64; send embassy to Athens for peace, 79; accept peace of Nikias, 101; first treaty of, with the Persians, 160; second treaty, 165; third treaty, 175; dictate terms of peace to Athens, 217
Sphakteria, geography of, 75; Spartan hoplites in, 78, 83
Stageiros, 91
Sthenelaïdas, 47
Stratonikê, 64
Stratos, 61
Strombichides. 160
Syracuse, 126

TANAGRA, battle of, 31
Thasians, revolt of the, 28; second revolt, 176

XEN

Thebans, the, surprise Plataia, 50, bring about the destruction of the city, 71; demand the destruction of Athens, 217
Themistokles, policy of, 4; mission of, to Sparta, 10; ostracism of, 17; alleged treason of, 20 *et seq.*
Thera, 73
Theramenes, son of Hagnon, 174, 183; accuses the generals, 204; sent to Sparta, 217
Thirty Years' Truce, 35
Thoukydides, son of Melesias, 39
Thousand Regiment at Argos, 109
Thrasyboulos, 181
Thrasylos, 181, 191
Thucydides fails to defend Amphipolis, 92; saves Eion, 92; banished, 93
Thymochares, 186
Thyrea, the Aiginetans at, 53, 85
Tissaphernes, 157, 189
Torônê, 94, 98
Tribes of Kleisthenes, 178
Tribute of the Asiatic Greeks, 18
Troizen, 35, 79
Tydeus, 210, 213

XANTHIPPOS, 58
Xenelasiai, 48

www.ingramcontent.com/pod-product-compliance
Lightning Source LLC
Chambersburg PA
CBHW031352230426
43670CB00006B/513